Democracy and Capitalism

DEMOCRACY AND CAPITALISM

Property, Community, and
the Contradictions of
Modern Social Thought

WITH A NEW INTRODUCTION BY THE AUTHORS:

The Politics of Capitalism and
the Economics of Democracy

SAMUEL BOWLES
HERBERT GINTIS

BasicBooks
A Division of HarperCollinsPublishers

Library of Congress Cataloging-in-Publication Data

Bowles, Samuel.
    Democracy and capitalism.

    Bibliographic references: p. 214.
    Includes index.
    1. Democracy. 2. Capitalism. 3. Economic
development. 4. Marxian economics. I. Gintis,
Herbert. II. Title.
JC423.B76 1986   321.8   85-47991
ISBN 0-465-06052-8 (cloth)
ISBN 0-465-01601-4 (paper)

For Aylette and Marci

CONTENTS

The Politics of Capitalism and

the Economics of Democracy

ACCORDING TO GENESIS 11, there was a time when the people of "the whole earth had one language" and had begun to build a city and a tower extending past Heaven's very door. But to curb their arrogance, the Lord descended to earth to "confuse their language that they may not understand one another's speech." Scattered abroad, they abandoned building the tower.

The Biblical story seems curiously inverted in the late twentieth century: the voices of the powerful around the world are a cacaphonous babel, asserting here the claims of private property or scientific truth, and elsewhere of religious purity, patriarchal privilege, or racial supremacy. By contrast, the voices of protest against domination, whether raised in French, Zulu, Polish, English, Russian, Tagalog, Spanish, or Chinese increasingly draw upon a single language: the lexicon of rights.

There is an irony here. The lingua franca of the students of Soweto, of the shipyard workers in Gdansk, of the alternatives and greens in Germany, of radical workers in Europe and North America, of feminists the world over, or of the 1987 constitution of Nicaragua cannot be traced to the *Communist Manifesto* or the discourse of revolutionary Marxism, but rather to the French *Declaration of the Rights of Man* and the American *Bill of Rights,* both products of the liberal tradition whose roots lie in the eighteenth century's revolt against state absolutism.

A year has passed since *Democracy and Capitalism* first appeared. The liberal lexicon continues to be deployed against bastions of privilege in situations where, in a previous era, the language of socialist revolution might have provided the discourse of rebellion. It is perhaps not surprising that liberal ideology has attracted dissidents in the Soviet Union, Eastern Europe, China, and Afghanistan. But the environmental, peace, labor, and egalitarian youth movements of Europe, the human rights protests in Latin America and South Africa, no less than the continuing struggle for democracy in the Philippines, also draw more from Mill than from Marx, more from Paine than from Plekhanov.

Yet while the voices of protest bear a liberal accent, the content of these initiatives is by no means foreign to the aspirations of the nineteenth-century socialist and anarchist visionaries. The emancipatory spirit which these new movements exhibit bear the unmistakable traits of their socialist ancestors.

The radicalized discourse of rights is the unwanted (albeit predictable) child of a liberal tradition which, by the late nineteenth century in the English-speaking countries, had come to focus almost exclusively on the rights of property and on a concept of freedom based on property. This version of the liberal tradition attains its epogee in Milton Friedman's virtually axiomatic identification of property and liberty in *Capitalism and Freedom*. But the doctrines of free trade, free contract, and the sanctity of property are part of a discourse that had once focused more on the freedom of religion and the inviolability of personal conscience, and that included a universal political idiom that quite as readily promotes political equality as class privilege. As labor activists, national liberation advocates, feminists, and opponents of racial privilege throughout the world have demonstrated, the language of liberalism can readily be transformed, and then deployed towards radical ends.

The quintessentially individualistic conception of rights promoted by liberal political philosophy might be thought to present an insurmountable barrier to this radical use of liberal discourse. But it does not. In practice, as we will show, the rights of citizens (or of persons generally), far from being God-given, as the U.S. Declaration of Independence asserts, have been won through the collective struggles of the dispossessed, women, racial minorities, and others. And the assertion of personal rights—of people of color to be treated with dignity, of homosexuals to choose their forms of sexuality, or of workers to vote or to attain the right of association in labor unions—has represented one of the major forms of expressing and building the solidarity which renders radical democratic action effective.[1]

The expansion of the discourse of rights challenges the coherence of liberal discourse itself. For while embracing a form of political equality, liberalism protects the disproportionate power of the wealthy from its critics with a rhetorical zeal unsurpassed in the annals of political discourse. Yet wealth, as Marx stressed, is not simply a claim on income. Wealth is a form of domination of the dispossessed. The political structure of the capitalist economy, by any reasonable account, lodges vast power in the hands of a relatively small number of individuals and organizations. Wealth, as all economists recognize, commands goods through the exercise of purchasing power. But it commands people as well through the undemocratic structure of the modern business enterprise. This class relationship in production—central to Marx's view of capitalism but invisible in the liberal account—is, to announce a theme extensively explored in this book, a form of social power which under capitalism escapes democratic accountability. Capitalism, more than a system of resource allocation and income distribution, is a system of governance.

It is difficult to imagine that the language which so effectively pierced the pretentions of Louis XVI, George III, and Nicolas II, would not eventually be turned against the absolutism of Imperial Chemicals, IBM, and Fiat. The liberal political tradition provides no coherent response to the obvious question: Why should the rights of ownership prevail over the rights of democratic citizenry in determining who is to manage the affairs of a business enterprise whose policies might directly affect as many as half a million employees, and whose choice of product, location, and technology touches entire communities and beyond?

The political critique of capitalism has until recently focused on the intimate relationship between wealth and political influence, and on the resulting capacity of the wealthy to circumscribe the choices of a democratic citizenry. Our focus in the pages that follow is less upon the state and more upon the structure of the capitalist economy itself: on its workplaces and its markets, as well as on its relationship to families and communities. Our assessment of these arenas adds a political dimension

---

1. Critiques of the intrinsically individualistic nature of liberal democratic discourse and hence its shortcomings as a tool towards socialist or radical democratic ends generally fail to distinguish between a political philosophy as a set of ideas and a political discourse as a form of social action and solidarity.

to the long established critique of capitalism's pyramidal distribution of economic reward and social status.

Such a political critique of capitalism renders obsolete many of the traditional debates on political economy. Consider, for instance, the age-worn debate pitting the advocates of the market against those of planning. The socialist side of the debate, represented in the 1930s by the Polish (and University of Chicago) economist Oskar Lange, apparently won the day by showing that in principle an ideal planned economy could allocate resources in a more nearly optimal manner than a perfectly competitive capitalist economy. But the rebuttal by conservative economist Friedrich von Hayek, and more recently by public choice theorists such as Gordon Tullock and James Buchanan, is well taken: market failure in capitalism is matched by a tendency towards bureaucratic sclerosis and lack of accountability in central planning. Further, the information processing costs of any actual planning exercise, they observed, would be prohibitive when compared to the market's imperfect but nonetheless decentralized and operable manner of informing buyers and sellers of the state of scarcities and wants. The disenchantment with the economic systems of state socialism, a mood that today spans the ideological spectrum, suggests that the conservative retort cannot be dismissed.

Even those who accept our assessment of capitalism as an undemocratic social order may thus rightly ask whether a democratic economy could attain levels of productivity and growth sufficient to allow an acceptable level of material welfare and free time, or even to secure society's long-term reproduction, in a world of continuing scarcity and interstate rivalry. Discussion of this subject has been marred by the tendency to view a democratic political structure of the economy as using centralized planning rather than the market to govern allocation, as employing moral incentives and cooperation rather than material incentives and competition to motivate performance, and as relying on an informal participatory democracy rather than on a hierarchical system of administrative decision making.

It should be clear, upon reflection, that there is no such simple connection between political democracy and organizational structure. Indeed, this confusion is reminiscent of the common eighteenth-century critique of democratic government on the grounds that democracy entails rule by the town meeting or the Greek city-state—a view belied by the highly complex character of modern representative democratic government. In point of fact, in a democratic economy, the citizenry may decide to rely heavily on the use of markets both to empower individuals and groups as economic actors, and as an effective device for implementing social objectives. Moreover, while there is every indication that political democracy builds the sort of loyalty and commitment upon which moral incentives thrive, this hardly entails the notion that material incentives are either unnecessary or ethically undesirable. Moreover, the view that there is an ineluctable conflict between moral and material incentives, between cooperation and competition, or that one of these modes can operate effectively in the absence of the other, is a quaint and anachronistic aspect of our intellectual heritage. It is belied by casual observation, historical experience, and a considerable body of social theory.

As Tocqueville long ago recognized, democracy has its own distinctive costs. These costs flow from the possibly excessive zeal and disarray generated when people manage their own affairs. It is little appreciated, however, that unaccountable authority has its own characteristic costs. There are enforcement costs, flowing from the need to induce people to obey laws and rules which they have not created or endorsed, and which may not be in their interests. *Democracy and Capitalism* explains why such costs are extensive and increasing in the present era.

Enforcement costs include the surveillance and supervision of workers who have no reason to care about their bosses' concerns, the labor disciplining functions of the unemployed, and the erection of sophisticated security systems to protect the wealthy from the destitute. Indeed, the sum total of the labor involved in enforcing the rules of the game—guard labor in our terminology—is a significant portion of the total labor force: in 1984, about one in four workers in the United States (up from one in five twenty years earlier), or considerably more than are involved in producing capital goods for investment of all types.[2] The economic promise of a democratic system of production and distribution is to significantly reduce the enforcement costs of the social order, transferring guard labor to productive work or towards the enhancement of free time for all.

Of course, democratic accountability in the economy generates distinctive problems of its own. Chief among these is perhaps the tendency toward technological conservatism and fear of innovation. Curiously, one of the most appealing aspects of the capitalist economy is least stressed

2. These estimates are contained in Center for Popular Economics, *The Economic Report of the People* (Boston: South End Press, 1986).

by its defenders among economists: the impressive ability of capitalist economic institutions to promote innovation.[3]

In principle there is no reason why a democratically organized economy could not be considerably more innovative than its capitalist rival. Indeed, capitalist societies would seem to be in many ways hostile to innovation: credit, essential to innovation, is generally available in large amounts only to the wealthy; highly selective educational systems further limit the potential number of innovators; widespread unemployment fosters worker resistance to new methods of production; profit seekers often avoid research the benefits of which cannot be appropriated and sold. The challenge to a democratic economy will be to maintain existing (or design new) systems of economic competition, entrepreneurial reward, and credit availability, fostering innovation and protecting economically creative individuals and groups against the rule of the majority.

The promise of the extension of personal rights over property rights is not merely feasible and abstractly desirable. Indeed, the shift in the terms of debate on economic organization is more than matched by the vast change in economic and political conditions facing democratic social movements in the advanced capitalist countries. Three underlying trends seem particularly germane to this development.

First, the costs of producing, storing, and processing information have fallen drastically in the past two decades and will continue to fall. The information revolution now vastly enhances the power of citizens and workers to control production and resource allocation in a decentralized manner. Yet at the same time it augments the capacity of states, businesses, and other hierarchical organizations to monitor the activities and invade the privacy of citizens. Democratization may be the only effective means of protecting privacy and directing the information revolution in socially benevolent directions.

Second, production is increasingly carried out on a global scale. The assembly in one country of parts produced elsewhere to fabricate a commodity to be sold in yet another corner of the globe is still the exception. But in many industries it is already much more than a gleam in a corporate planner's eye. The information revolution and the associated reduction in transportation costs have contributed strongly to this trend. In the ab-

---

3. Having virtually no theory of entrepreneurship, neoclassical economics has stressed the timeless static allocational virtues of capitalism. Others, Joseph Schumpeter and Karl Marx for example, have been more attentive to the progressive dynamic properties of capitalism.

sence of social control over investment, the globalization of production challenges the sovereignty of the nation state. In effect, it forces democrats to choose between the private control of investment, entailing ineffectual economic policy and a democratic impotence, on the one hand, and the development of democratic institutions for the social accountability of investment on the other.

Finally, the twentieth century has rightly been called the epoch of revolution. But the Chinese, Russian, and other upheavals are matched by a silent revolution in the advanced capitalist countries: the disappearance of the peasant and the housewife as the principal occupations in society. At the turn of the century in most of Europe and North America, well over half the adult working population were either farmers or homemakers (or both). These two occupations constituted a vast labor reserve for capitalist expansion, allowing the accumulation process to proceed through boom and depression without encountering the labor scarcity that would enhance the aspirations and the bargaining power of workers.

These two great labor pools—the home and the farm—are now substantially depleted. The prospect then is for a weakening of capitalist power at the center and perhaps another retreat of profit-seekers into the labor-abundant capitalist periphery reminiscent of Europe's fifteenth- and sixteenth-century expansion into Africa, Asia, and Latin America following the labor shortage resulting from the decimation of the European population in the later Middle Ages.

If a depletion of internal labor reserves makes the stick of unemployment increasingly costly for employers to wield, their control of work processes in Europe, North America, and Japan will depend more on the carrot of commitment and participation or perhaps on the development of new sources of labor supply or forms of domination less dependent on labor abundance.

All three of these trends—the globalization of production, the information revolution, and the demise of the home and the farm as labor reserves for capitalist employment—will shape not only the debate on economic democracy, but the evolution of the ongoing clash between citizen rights and property rights.

Samuel bowles
Herbert gintis
April 1987

PREFACE

OUR THINKING about democracy and domination represents a fusion of three quite distinct strands of thought. One is the radical democratic tradition and its expression in the social movements of the 1960s and later decades. The second is liberal social theory and social science. The third is Marxism. Or perhaps more correctly put, our thinking has evolved through a sustained encounter between the hope and rage of the radical democratic movements of our time and the two now-dominant intellectual traditions.

The outcome of this encounter has been two convictions: a recognition of the multifaceted character of power in modern societies, and an appreciation of the centrality of learning and human development in the analysis of power and the rectification of its abuses. These may be considered novel concerns for those trained academically as economists, but this impression would be only partly accurate. The intimate relationship between political theory and economics dates back at least to Thomas Hobbes and the origins of liberal social theory in the seventeenth century. It is today expressed in the almost wholesale adoption of neoclassical economic thinking as the model, if not the actual analytical framework, of much political theory.

Not surprisingly, our critique of contemporary Marxian and liberal political theory is in important measure based on the shortcomings of the often implicit economic theory that underlies both. In the themes raised, if not in the content, our analysis of the predicament of contemporary democratic thought echoes the concerns of earlier writers on economics such as Adam Smith, Karl Marx, and John Stuart Mill.

If there is anything novel about our integration of economics and politics it is that, unlike the dominant tendency for the past two centuries, which has seen the infusion of political thinking with economic metaphor, we propose the converse: a political critique of economic thinking and the importation of genuinely political concepts concerning power and human development into the analysis of economic systems.

Neither the complexity of the subject matter encountered in our studies nor the political defeats and disappointments of democratic political movements in recent years has diminished our conviction that the linkages between power, human development, and economic life are both understandable and—partly because they are understandable—susceptible to improvement. It is this conviction that has provided the impetus and the unifying principle in our own eighteen-year collaboration and for our publication of this modest contribution to the development of democratic thought.

Those who have taught us, criticized us, goaded us, infuriated us, and otherwise stimulated our research are too numerous to record here. But, even if inadequately, we would like to thank those whose criticism, advice, and assistance is reflected in the pages that follow: Robert Ackerman, Peter Alexander, Tariq Banuri, Harold Benenson, Charles Bright, Barry Clark, Joshua Cohen, Jean Elshtain, Ann Ferguson, Nancy Folbre, Gerald Friedman, David Gordon, Ian Gough, Philip Green, Jeanne Hahn, Susan Harding, Dolores Hayden, Ernesto Laclau, C. E. Lindblom, Elaine McCrate, Stephen Marglin, Chantal Mouffe, Bertell Ollman, Carla Pasquinelli, Nora Randall, Hannah Roditi, Richard Sack, Christine Di Stefano, Kathleen Stewart, Susan Tracy, Thomas Wartenberg, Thomas Weisskopf, Robert Paul Wolff, and Meg Worcester, as well as our students at the University of Massachusetts.

For financial support and hospitality we would also like to thank the John S. Guggenheim Foundation, the Institute for Advanced Study, the German Marshall Fund of the United States, the University of Massachusetts Faculty Fellowship, the University of Siena, and the Institute for the Advanced Study of the Humanities at the University of Massachusetts.

We would also like to thank Martin Kessler, Sandra Dhols, and David Graf of Basic Books for their insight and care.

Democracy and Capitalism

1

Present: Politics,
Economics, and Democracy

THIS WORK is animated by a commitment to the progressive extension of people's capacity to govern their personal lives and social histories. Making good this commitment, we will argue, requires establishing a democratic social order and eliminating the central institutions of the capitalist economy. So stark an opposition between "capitalism" and "democracy," terms widely held jointly to characterize our society, may appear unwarranted. But we will maintain that no capitalist society today may reasonably be called democratic in the straightforward sense of securing personal liberty and rendering the exercise of power socially accountable.

"Democratic capitalism" suggests a set of harmonious and mutually supportive institutions, each promoting a kind of freedom in distinct realms of social life. Yet we will show that capitalism and democracy are not complementary systems. Rather they are sharply contrasting rules regulating both the process of human development and the historical evolution of whole societies: the one is characterized by the preeminence of economic privilege based on property rights, the other insists on the priority of liberty and democratic accountability based on the exercise of personal rights.

Our commitment to democracy is thus an affirmation of a vision of a society in which liberty and popular sovereignty govern both learning and history. Democracy, not the interplay of property rights, should provide the fundamental principle ordering the processes by which we become who we

3

are and by which the rules regulating our lives are continually renewed and transformed.

Except to argue that they are feasible and attainable, we will not seek to justify these commitments. Instead we will explore their implications for the way we think about the individual, about society, and about history. Although justification may be unnecessary, clarification of terms is surely in order. In practice we identify democracy with liberty and popular sovereignty. Liberty involves an extensive range of social life over which individuals have the freedom, and where appropriate the resources, to act, and to seek to persuade others to act, as they see fit, without social impediment. Ronald Dworkin has expressed this well:

> Individual rights are political trumps held by individuals. Individuals have rights when, for some reason, a collective goal is not a sufficient justification for denying them what they wish, as individuals, to have or to do, or not a sufficient justification for imposing some loss or injury upon them.[1]

Liberty thus entails freedom of thought and association, freedom of political, cultural, and religious expression, and the right to control one's body and express one's preferred spiritual, aesthetic, and sexual style of life.

By popular sovereignty we mean that power is accountable, and in some sense equally accountable, to those affected by its exercise. But popular sovereignty cannot be unitary. We shall argue that there are multiple centers of power in liberal democratic capitalism and indeed in most social orders, and that this pluralism of powers captures an essential aspect of the conception of a democratic society. We thus reject the concept of a unifying "popular will," and we take sovereignty as ultimately and irreducibly heterogeneous. In effect, democracy requires that both individuals and groups have trumps to play.

We will identify several modifications of social theory implied by a commitment to a democratic society. Our interests, however, are not exclusively contemplative. Our recasting of democratic theory as well as our reading of the tumultuous trajectories of democracy and capitalism over the past two centuries will commit us not to a democratic utopia, but to a broad historical project of making good the long-standing radical but thwarted promise of democracy.

Democratic institutions have often been mere ornaments in the social life of the advanced capitalist nations: proudly displayed to visitors, and admired by all, but used sparingly. The places where things really get done—in such core institutions as families, armies, factories, and offices—have been anything but democratic. Representative government, civil liberties, and due process have, at best, curbed the more glaring excesses of these realms of unaccountable power while often obscuring and strengthening underlying forms of privilege and domination.

But democracy does not stand still. Where democratic institutions have taken root, they have often expanded and deepened. Where a democratic idiom has become the lingua franca of politics, it has often come to encompass unwonted meanings. In the course of its development, democracy thus may challenge, indiscriminately and irreverently, all forms of privilege. The road from the eighteenth-century Rights of Man, which excluded not only women but most people of color as well, to the late twentieth-century civil rights movements, feminism, and the right to a job has been a tortuous one, but the route was amply prefigured even in the discourse of eighteenth-century liberalism.

When democratic sentiments begin to so encroach upon a fundamental social institution as to threaten its ability to function, democratic institutions will find themselves obliged to supplant it or to retreat. This situation precisely captures the present predicament of the liberal democratic capitalist societies of Europe and North America. The beleagured realm is the capitalist economy itself.*

The post–World War II development of the welfare state and Keynesian economic policy gave notice that profit-making business activities would be monitored and that the capitalist corporation, while permitted a considerable expansion, would be subject to social scrutiny. The striking economic success of the liberal democratic capitalist societies in the postwar era attests to the advantages of this mutual accord of economic elites and citizenry. But the expanding claims of democracy proved to be the accord's undoing. By giving citizens the power to encroach upon the capacity of capital to invest profitably and to discipline its labor force, democratic institutions challenged the basic operations of the capitalist economy and sapped its dynamism.

Yet the welfare state and Keynesian economic policies had been carefully circumscribed; they did not give citizens the power to assume these critical

---

* By liberal democratic capitalist societies we mean those two dozen or so nations whose social life is structured by a limited state that extends civil liberties and suffrage to most adults and an economy characterized by production for the market using wage labor and privately owned means of production. We will return to this characterization in later chapters.

economic functions, nor did they provide the public arena within which citizens could develop their capacities to render economic decision making democratically accountable. Equally important, the postwar system in most liberal democratic capitalist countries gave capital a decisive upper hand in dictating the pattern of organizational innovation and structural change. The result has been an economic and political standoff in which business elites and the citizenry alike have veto power over economic change but share no viable common vision of an economic future.

The political and ideological consequences of this stalemate radically altered political discourse during the 1970s. The Keynesian focus on the state management of total demand for goods and services in the interest of full employment as the key to capitalist prosperity was increasingly seen to be contradictory. The attenuation of economic insecurity brought about by Keynesian policies and the welfare state, it became clear, had compromised an essential basis of capital's power over labor: the threat of unemployment.

Though the architects of the welfare state had not stressed the point, economic stagnation and instability may occur not only because the capitalist class is "too strong" but also because it is "too weak." When the capitalist class is "too strong" it shifts the income distribution in its favor, reducing the ratio of working-class consumption to national income and rendering the economy prone to a failure of total demand. By contrast, when the capitalist class is "too weak" the working class or other claimants on income squeeze the rate of profit and reduce the level of investment (perhaps by inducing investors to seek greener pastures elsewhere).

Capitalist economies regularly experience difficulties of both types. There is much evidence that the Great Depression of the 1930s was a crisis of total demand, brought about in part by the political and economic defeats of the European and North American working classes in the post–World War I era. But the faltering profits in the advanced capitalist economies of the late 1960s and 1970s could hardly be attributed to inadequate demand: the decline in profits coincided with exceptionally high levels of capacity utilization and demand expansion in most countries.[2]

The nature of the crisis of the Great Depression—the deficiency of working-class buying power based on capital's overarching economic power—offered a ready program for labor, social democracy, and progressive groups: the egalitarian redistribution of income would both ameliorate the material situation of labor and end the economic crisis. No such happy coincidence of particular and universal interests is obtained when the crisis has resulted from the capitalist class being "too weak." The economic difficulties experienced by the advanced capitalist liberal democracies in the 1970s and 1980s are not the symptom of inadequate consumption demand; they may be traced more accurately to a collision of capitalist and democratic social relationships. Thus if the immediate economic project of labor and the Left during the last great crisis was first and foremost to redistribute purchasing power so as to alleviate material distress and support a higher level of demand, the task today must be to redistribute power itself in order to provide a new democratic model of production and distribution.

The project of the Right, correspondingly, is to reassert its hegemony in the economy, either through the time-honored methods of using the market to discipline labor and other claimants on income, or through the development of more effective institutions of control.

In this situation, democratic initiatives may either move forward toward rendering investment and production decisions democratically accountable, or they may recede. Should they recede, a strategic withdrawal could easily turn into a massive rout of liberal democratic institutions and a renaissance of authoritarianism.

Understanding the complex issues raised by these conflicting tendencies and elucidating what might be meant by a democratic economy requires a reconsideration of contemporary political and economic philosophy. We will begin by assessing social theory according to its capacity to provide principles that allow a reasonable application of the norms of liberty and popular sovereignty to the areas of production and investment.

This volume may recall the debates on socialist planning and the economic rationality of the market a generation ago, which engaged economists of various stripes in discussions of economic theory. Our contribution to the theory of a democratic economy, however, may blur some of the familiar battle lines, for we will not propose the superiority of planning or of the market, of Marxian economic categories or of the neoclassical calculus. Rather we will point to the poverty of virtually all strands of economic theory as a basis for thinking about democracy, illustrate the unfortunate consequences of the dominance of economic metaphor in our political and moral thinking, and demonstrate the need for integrating genuinely political concepts—concerning power and human development—with economic reasoning.[3]

Democratic Theory in Disarray

The inspiration for this integration of politics and economics is the radical democratic tradition—the seventeenth-century levellers and the eighteenth-century *sans culottes*, the nineteenth-century chartists and agrarian populists, and the twentieth-century feminists and advocates of worker councils. Our debt to these movements is more than sentimental; they have suggested two essential themes of what we take to be an adequate democratic theory. The first is that oppression takes many forms, and that the economy and the family in particular are no less arenas of domination and political contest than is the state. The second is that politics is not simply about the manner in which power adjudicates competing claims for resources. It is also a contest over who we are to become, a contest in which identity, interests, and solidarity are as much the outcome as the starting point of political activity.

The rise and fall of English chartism in the 1830s and 1840s dramatically illustrates the importance of our first theme, the political nature of the economy. The chartists—advocates of a people's charter of rights—represented the most successful radical mass movement in the first half of the nineteenth century. British historian Gareth Stedman Jones's masterful "Rethinking Chartism" stresses an enduring thread in the radical democratic tradition:

> The central tenet of radicalism—the attribution of evil and misery to a political source—clearly differentiated it from both a Malthusian-based popular political economy which placed the source of dissonance in nature itself, and from Owenite socialism which located evil in false ideas which dominated state and civil society alike.[4]

Like the radical democratic tradition generally, the chartists embraced political solutions to problems seen as political in origin. But again "political" to them meant "state":

> In radical discourse the dividing line between classes was not that between employer and employed, but that between the represented and the unrepresented ... it was through a corrupt and unrepresentative political system that the producers of wealth were conceived to be deprived of the fruits of their labor.[5]

The radical chartist Bronterre O'Brien summed up this faith:

> Universal suffrage is . . . a grand test of Radicalism. . . . Knaves will tell you that it is because you have no property that you are unrepresented. I tell you, on the contrary, that it is because you are unrepresented that you have no property. . . . Thus your poverty is the result not the cause of your being unrepresented.[6]

The chartists were not mistaken in thinking that their plight could be traced to political sources, nor were they wrong in seeing the undemocratic state as a source of their oppression; they erred in underestimating both the political nature of the relationship between the employer and employee and the unaccountable social power wielded by the owner of capital. As a result they thought that the achievement of a democratic state through universal suffrage would usher in a democratic society, believing that "civil society and the relations between masters and men would function harmoniously, but for the parasitic plundering of the state and its beneficiaries."[7]

The demands of chartism were not class demands per se but rather political demands around which unrepresented groups of diverse economic stations rallied. The universal appeal of the radical message was more than balanced by its vulnerability. According to Stedman Jones,

> the program of Chartism remained believable so long as unemployment, low wages, economic insecurity and other material afflictions could convincingly be assigned political causes.[8]

The increasingly liberal state, marked both by the gradual extension of the suffrage and by the emergence of laissez-faire as an economic ideology and framework for state policy, would erode both the credibility of this analysis and the urgency of the chartist prescriptions.

In the decade of chartism's demise, Karl Marx sketched a theory of capitalist exploitation that would displace the radical analysis and language.* This theory focused on the power of capital over labor rather than on the predations of an unrepresentative state. Our insistence on the political nature of the economy thus may be considered to be a reaffirmation of both the radical democratic belief in the centrality of politics and the Marxian con-

---

* The radical democratic tradition was not so much eliminated as it was deprived of its integral connections with working-class movements. Nineteenth-century feminism and anarchism retained much of the radical democratic vision and language.

ception of the capitalist economy as an arena of oppression and contest rather than harmony.

Our second theme—that politics produces people—is a lesson derived from more recent experience. Since World War II, the political lives of the advanced industrial societies, capitalist and state socialist alike, have increasingly been shaped by popular movements whose concerns strain the conceptual framework of traditional political philosophies. These movements embrace novel visions of social justice. Their concerns move beyond the question of who gets what, to identify with such social needs as sexual and racial equality, environmental protection, nuclear disarmament, and world peace. The contemporary political temper, moreover, is increasingly uncomfortable with traditional authority and shows a proclivity to embrace procedural demands not only for a democratic community and workplace but for an extended conception of civil rights—the right to control one's body, the right to know the chemical properties of the materials one handles on the job, the right of equal and secure access to a job, the right to exercise one's own sexual preference.

Although in important respects these political movements conform to familiar patterns of mobilization and express standard objectives, they share a novel aspect: their dissatisfactions and aspirations are not only distributional, they are moral and cultural as well. Their aims include the creation and transformation of community and the establishment of individual and collective identities.

These movements seek to redefine as much as to pursue interests. "Black is beautiful!" and "Women unite, take back the night!" are not claims on resources. They are brush strokes in a new political landscape—one in which meaning and metaphor are at once the tools and the stakes of the contest. Movements of the Right—the political turn of religious fundamentalism, nationalism, the "right to life" movement, and others—exhibit an equal focus on the cultural aspects of politics. What resources are being claimed, for example, by the American Right's favored bumper stickers: "Better dead than red!" and "America: love it or leave it!"?

The emergence and appeal of these cultural–political movements will remain opaque to those who conceive of politics primarily as a struggle over the distribution of goods and services—a contest, as Harold Lasswell defined it, over who gets what, when, and how.[9] These new movements do not so much reject the importance of control over resources and distributive justice as they do deny the separability of economic, moral, and cultural concerns, and assert the primacy of moral and cultural ends and the general status of economic concerns as means. These new political actors have supplemented the politics of *getting* with the politics of *becoming*.

The conservative onslaught of the 1980s has been more successful in containing democratic and populist movements than in restoring the shattered boundaries between private and public spaces and erasing the new vocabulary of the hitherto nameless politics of family and workplace. The student and worker uprisings of May 1968 in France, and of the "hot Autumn" of 1969 in Italy made offices and factories terrains of struggle. In both cases workers could hardly claim victory, but in defeat they helped lay to rest the notion that "politics" is something that happens only in the state. Similarly, the resonant feminist phrase "The personal is political" challenged both the liberal boundary between private and public and the Marxian conception of politics as class struggle.

The radical democratic tradition, no less today than during earlier centuries, thus prompts a rethinking of fundamental categories of political philosophy. The intellectual agenda before democrats today may be readily inferred from the democratic commitment itself: if a viable integration of popular sovereignty and personal liberty is to be attained, democrats must develop a conception of social constraint and individual action that respects the autonomy and power both of our intentions and of the sometimes obscure ways in which social structures limit our actions. Equally, if the project of democracy is to make history rather than to spin out utopias, democrats need a theory of how individuals bond together as collective social actors, and how social structures are renewed or overturned through the political actions of contending groups. These tasks are on the agenda of democratic theory simply because none is adequately accomplished within the liberal or Marxian political traditions.

Both liberalism and Marxism have inspired influential movements of human liberation. Yet their timeworn claims ring hollow to many modern ears. Still the champion of a kind of freedom, liberalism increasingly appears as an apologia for economic privilege and the concentration of political power in the advanced nations, and for superexploitation and dictatorship in the Third World. A leading liberal economist, Friedrich von Hayek, recently stated:

> It is possible for a dictator to govern in a liberal way. And it is also possible that a democracy governs with a total lack of liberalism. My personal preference is

for a liberal dictator and not for a democratic government lacking in liberalism.[10]

And while Marxism proudly retains its historical vision of social equality and internationalism, it also evokes the actuality of despotism and imperialism in the nations that claim to wear its mantle.

In practice, the traditional doctrines often appear to be little more than pawns in a world struggle of competing economic and military empires. The war of position between capitalism and state socialism, moreover, has provided an inhospitable climate for self-criticism, inviting supporters of each doctrine to gloss over its own weaknesses in the overarching quest for ideological advantage. As a result, political philosophy—and political economy—have been called to serve as rearguard defenses of one intellectual status quo or the other.

Predictably, radical democrats today often regard liberalism as hostile, or at best inadequate, to their causes. Similarly, even the socialist portions of most democratic political movements now treat Marxism with a respect due to its past achievements, while remaining mindful of its limited relevance to the concerns of feminists, environmentalists, national minorities, or even rank-and-file workers. Just as frequently, these movements regard Marxism with hostile indifference. The notion that either capitalism or state socialism holds the key to the future of social emancipation is the illusion of an era now happily behind us.

Nor can the tarnished reputations of both liberalism and Marxism be attributed entirely to the company they have kept. For both traditions, as we shall see, will be found theoretically wanting. Neither has fostered an adequate understanding of the distinct forms of oppression characteristic of the nations in which they have been adopted as conventional wisdom. Neither has offered a view of history capable of understanding and informing the democratic movements that seek to overcome these forms of oppression.

The sparse intellectual heritage available to radical democratic political movements today is thus not to be found among the masterworks of political philosophy and political economy. Their inspiration is more likely to spring from able works like *Adieu au Proletariat* (Andre Gorz), *L'Apres Socialisme* (Alain Tourraine), "The Unhappy Marriage of Marxism and Feminism" (Heidi Hartmann), or *Quale Socialismo?* (Norberto Bobbio), than from *The Wealth of Nations, On Liberty, Capital,* or *State and Revolution.* Just as the radical democratic movements of the nineteenth century generally eschewed classical philosophy, liberal political economy, and Marxism alike, the new democratic politics has bypassed traditional terms of political debate, sometimes regarding such venerable concerns as the delegation of authority and the claims of economic necessity as little more than veils of reaction.

But this "plague on both your houses" stance toward liberal and Marxian social theory is misplaced. Only at its peril can a democratic politics ignore the classical philosophical debates concerning representation, accountability, privacy, property, exploitation, and scarcity. It may be true that the two great classical political and economic traditions are part of the problem; but they are surely part of the solution as well. Both were conceived not to legitimate but rather to understand and to overcome prevalent forms of social oppression. Indeed, while remaining deliberately agnostic or vague on the nature of the good life, both liberalism and Marxism maintain that the elimination of traditional forms of oppression is a precondition for its attainment.

Liberalism, moreover, has justly enshrined the democratic tenet that choice and agency are the keystones of freedom, whereas Marxism has shown us that individual choice and agency are but false freedoms in the absence of collective action: people make their history and forge their freedoms not one by one, but in solidarity with others.

For liberalism, the nemesis of agency is domination through physical coercion—the use of force to compel individuals to do what they otherwise would not do. The liberal ideal is a world of perfect liberty, in which individuals are free to do as they please, limited only by the equal liberty of others. Indeed, liberalism arose precisely as a progressive response to the perceived threat of the consolidation of the absolute state—progressive in the sense of accepting the inevitability and desirability of national sovereignty, yet seeking to neutralize its potentially despotic power. Liberalism is in principle the inveterate enemy of the despot.

Marxism is preoccupied with domination through unequal property ownership—privileged access to the means of production in economic life. The Marxian ideal is a world free of class domination. Indeed, Marxism arose in the nineteenth century as a response to the concentration of wealth and economic power that resulted from the consolidation of European industrial capitalism. Marxism is in principle the inveterate enemy of class privilege.

The respective concerns of liberalism and Marxism—the despotic ruler and the despotism of want—are hardly less germane today than they were during the times that gave birth to these two great traditions. Physical coercion has grown in the modern era through scientific advances in the tools of violence, surveillance, and the administration of coercion. These were merged in the modern authoritarian state that had been envisioned in the seventeenth century, but only achieved technical feasibility in the current era.

Correspondingly, the dominion of property has grown in modern times through the development of world markets, modern financial institutions, and the limited-liability business corporation. Its most dramatic incarnation is the multinational firm, controlling the lives of millions, keeping a dispassionate eye on profits alone, and navigating a sea of nation-states that increasingly are sovereign in name alone.

Our commitment to the development of political theory within the common Enlightenment framework of liberalism and Marxism stems from our appreciation of the enormity of the forms of social oppression to which they are addressed, and from our conviction that a good society in a peaceful world is inconceivable in the absence of solutions to the problems to which liberalism and Marxism have been the historical responses.

Commitments of Traditional Political Doctrines

We would be mistaken to treat such complex traditions as liberalism and Marxism as if they exhibited more or less obvious distinctive characteristics. True, each is often depicted as a unified set of ideas or as a social movement with a definite set of objectives. Yet on closer inspection, both liberalism and Marxism appear as an incoherent tangle of divergent and often inconsistent strands of thought and as the inspiration for movements of bewildering variety.

Liberal social theorists have included utilitarians, for whom the notion of natural rights is either unnecessary or positively incoherent (Jeremy Bentham once branded the French Declaration of the Rights of Man as "nonsense on stilts"), as well as natural rights advocates, for whom a calculus of pleasure represents a potentially totalitarian compromise of principles. Methodologically, liberalism includes individualists such as John Locke and Robert Nozick, who deduce the just society from the principles of personal and voluntary choice, as well as system-theorists such as Emile Durkheim,

Talcott Parsons, and John Rawls, for whom institutions are judged in large measure by the social effects that they foster and sustain.[11] The social commitments of liberals are no less diverse: they have both favored and opposed monarchy, popular democracy, free trade, rights of worker association, government intervention in economic affairs, and the welfare state.[12]

If Marxism is less variegated, this is only due to its youth. In less than a century and a half, its ranks have embraced democrats and autocrats, exponents of revolutionary free will and revolutionary inevitability, those who espouse the labor theory of value and those who prefer the marginalist calculus, and advocates of market socialism and of centralized planning.

The positions and arguments of both liberalism and Marxism have varied so widely over space and time as to render it fatuous to include consistency among their virtues, or to seek in the intellectual content of these doctrines their coherence and specificity.

The distinctiveness and unity of liberalism and of Marxism are to be found not so much in *what* they say about the world, but in *how* they say it. Whatever internal coherence these traditions possess derives more from their status as systems of communication than from their substantive propositions about how the world works or ought to work. Their particular characteristics lie not in their specific theoretical assertions but in the way each, considered as a system of communication, establishes rules as to how social reality will be represented in terms of its vocabulary. In short, both traditions are discourses whose most fundamental orientation concerning structure and action in social life are revealed by the customary usage of key terms.[13] Each system is better viewed as what Ludwig Wittgenstein has called a "form of life" rather than as either a coherent theoretical system or a unified philosophical doctrine.*

The fundamental commitments of liberal theory are reflected in two aspects of its discursive structure. First is its silence on the issues of exploitation and community.

The liberal lexicon lacks fundamental terms representing the conditions of material exploitation. True, liberal usage draws on a well-appointed store of terms of economic abuse: a person may be unjustly deprived of property,

---

* Particular writings of some major thinkers customarily called "liberal" lie outside of liberal discourse as we will define it; the younger Mill's treatment of liberty and learning and his advocacy of economic democracy are examples. Similarly, some of Marx's own writings and more of what might be called neo-Marxist scholarship today only dubiously is included as part of the Marxian discourse. However, our representation of both discourses is far from arbitrary and, we believe, quite defensible.

or discriminated against on the basis of race, or cheated in exchange, but one may not be exploited in the simple sense that one is deprived of the fruits of one's own labor. This lack is not altogether surprising, nor is it an entirely innocent oversight; the liberal right to claim income associated with the ownership of property would be empty if nonproperty-owning workers were paid an amount equal to the average product of their labor. This assertion is a matter of arithmetic, not of conviction: income from property is simply a residual claim equal to the net product minus the amount paid to nonproperty owners; were the wage to equal the average product of labor, there would be no residual income, and hence no return would flow to the owners of property.

The liberal lexicon is no less impoverished when it comes to community. The two privileged terms that might represent community—family and state—fall far short of the rich repertoire of the forms of identification and solidarity that make up the warp of social life. Even family and state only appear to represent community. The family is rendered in most liberal theory as an indivisible organic whole barely distinguishable from the individual. Correspondingly, in liberal theory the state appears primarily as a decision-making structure regulating some mixture of self-regarding and altruistic instrumental action, rather than as the repository of loyalty, learning, identity, and solace.[14] Moreover, the most powerful form of collective organization in contemporary capitalism—the modern business corporation—is stripped of its communal status in liberal theory. It is ignored in neoclassical economics, treated as a quasi individual in law, and considered "private" in political discourse. Its status as a form of social power is thereby obscured and its reality as the terrain of class conflict is systematically slighted.

Liberalism incorporates basic political commitments into its discursive rules, not only by its silence, but in a second way as well: arbitrarily limiting the admissible range of application of its basic terms relating to freedom, equality, and democracy. These liberal partitions of social space precede any particular theoretical representation of social life. Michael Walzer expresses this view well.

> I suggest that we think of liberalism as a certain way of drawing the map of the social and political world. The old, preliberal map showed a largely undifferentiated land mass, with rivers and mountains, cities and towns, but no borders. . . . Society was conceived as an organic and integrated whole. . . . Confronting this world, liberal theorists preached and practiced the art of separation. They drew lines, marked off different realms, and created the sociopolitical map with which

we are still familiar. . . . Liberalism is a world of walls, and each one creates a new liberty.[15]

Two fundamental partitions are central to liberalism. Social space is divided into a private and a public realm. The public realm of social space is considered to be the state, whereas the private realm houses the family and the capitalist economy.[16] In similar fashion, individuals are partitioned into two groups: rational agents whose intentions and choices are the subject of the explicit political and economic theory of liberalism, and those who for reasons of age, incapacity, or citizenship are excluded from this privileged category. The logic of the liberal discourse may be underlined if we term the first *choosers*, and the second *learners*.

Our critique of the dichotomies of liberal thought is readily summarized. The walls that liberalism erects do more than create liberties; they also obscure and shelter the citadels of domination. According to its usages, liberty is held to apply to rational agents (choosers) but not to others (learners), and the norms of democracy are held to apply to the actions of choosers in the public realm alone. As a result, democratic institutions are held to be merely instrumental to the exercise of choice: democracy facilitates the satisfaction of perceived needs.

We will show that both limits on democracy in liberal thought cannot be coherently defended even within liberal theory. The liberal partitions of social space arbitrarily exempt such basic social spheres as the economy and the family from scrutiny according to democratic norms. Further, the treatment of democratic institutions as simply means rather than also as ends ignores the substantial impact of democracy on the formation of individual wills and minimizes the contribution of participatory institutions to the viability of a democratic community. The liberal interpretation would seem to render democracy safe for elites—democracy is confined to a realm (the state) relatively unlikely to interfere with the wielding of economic power and limited to forms (representative government) insufficient for the consolidation of popular power. But as we shall see, the walls erected by liberalism have been breached, and their ability to restrain the radical potential of democracy is tenuous.

Marxian theory does not share these particular shortcomings. Indeed Marx's work provides a starting point for two essential aspects of our study of democratic theory, for he focused on the social construction of people through their own practices and the practices of others, and stressed that realms of society deemed private in liberal discourse—the patriarchal family and the capitalist economy—are in fact spheres of domination. Yet, these essential insights notwithstanding, the fundamental commitments of Marxian theory are hardly more auspicious than the liberal.

Marxian political theory, unlike liberalism, is not hampered by incoherent partitions. "The art of separation," writes Walzer, "has never been highly regarded on the left, especially the Marxist left."[17] Rather, Marxism is weakened by unsustainable attempts to treat distinct spheres of social life as passive reflections of others. Its critique of the liberal private–public division, for example, fails to provide a coherent alternative concept of the private. It accords no status to the private at all. Similarly, Marxism exposes the false ghettoization of learning (more broadly, human development) in the liberal discourse. But it does not solve the problem thereby raised: how and to what extent can people effectively and legitimately come to regulate their own learning? Instead it denies the relevance of the learning–choosing distinction by denigrating the importance of the autonomy of choice. These commitments are directly embodied in Marxian discourse.

First, Marxism's discursive structure lacks the fundamental theoretical vocabulary to represent the conditions of choice, individual liberty, and dignity, and hence cannot fully address the problem of despotism. Second, the terms *domination, exploitation,* and *class* are virtually interchangeable in the Marxian lexicon, each entailing the other. The effect is to hide nonclass and noneconomic forms of domination—whether of the state, of white over black, of nation over nation, or of men over women—as surely as liberal discourse serves as protective cover for the power of capital.

Clearly, in neither case can the Marxian resolution to the liberal problem be accepted, because it fails to provide an adequate foundation for liberty and democracy. This failure, moreover, is systemic. The denial of a private realm and the denigration of individual choice flow from the first of two major fusions—the identification of the individual with the class of which he or she is a member. According to Marxian theory, individuals are merely representatives of the social groups to which they belong by virtue of their social (or more accurately, their specifically economic) relationships. Marx notes this in the preface to the first edition of *Capital*, vol. 1:

> To prevent possible misunderstandings, let me say this . . . individuals are dealt with here only insofar as they are the personifications of economic categories, the bearers of particular class relations and interests. My standpoint, from which

the development of the economic formation of society is viewed as a process of natural history, can less than any other make the individual responsible for relations whose creature he remains.[18]

In effect, this stance, which we term the *expressive conception of action*, cannot lay the basis for democratic thought, for it divorces social outcomes from individual wills. Whereas liberalism reduces social action to a means toward an end, Marxism denies the relevance of instrumentality—and hence of choice itself.

The Marxian tendency to treat distinct aspects of social life as theoretically indistinguishable is also manifested in its collapse of the terms domination, exploitation, and class to a single usage. The result is to force the most diverse forms of domination—imperialism, violence against women, state despotism, racism, religious intolerance, oppression of homosexuals, and more—either into obscurity or into the mold of class analysis. The collapse of terms in Marxian discourse bids us either to disregard forms of exploitation based on such mechanisms as the spoils of war, patriarchal control over the labor of women and children, state control of economic activity, and forced taxation, or to simply regard these forms of exploitation as the result of class relationships or perhaps as the conditions necessary for their perpetuation. Consequently, the bureaucrat and the patriarch alike are shielded from criticism.

Although the Marxian analysis of exploitation and other forms of domination has immeasurably advanced democratic understandings, we remain deeply skeptical of the proposition that exploitation, particularly class exploitation, provides a sufficient conceptual foundation for a rigorous and critical treatment of the variety of forms of political domination and cultural supremacy commonly observed in social life.

Not surprisingly, then, the Marxian theoretical lexicon does not include such terms as freedom, personal rights, liberty, choice, or even democracy. The Marxian historian Eric Hobsbawm comments that "Marx was not only indifferent to 'rights of man' but strongly opposed to them, since they are essentially individualistic." As a result, continues Hobsbawm, the main difference between pre-Marxian and post-Marxian working-class movements is that the former "saw the achievement of political democracy as an end rather than as a means," whereas the latter "saw political democracy chiefly as a way of creating the conditions for achieving [their economic and social program]."[19]

The Marxian commitment to democracy even where it is most heartfelt, as in the writings of Rosa Luxemburg and Nicos Poulantzas, is thus without firm theoretical roots.[20] This commitment can disappear as quickly as it has appeared in the post-Stalin era, and nothing in Marxian discourse per se will remain to mourn its passing. Classical Marxism is theoretically anti-democratic in the same sense that any political philosophy that fails to conceptualize the threat of state authoritarianism, and the centrality of privacy and individual liberty to human emancipation, provides a haven for despots and fanatics.[21]

Toward a Reconstruction of Democratic Theory

The absence of an adequate democratic theory in both liberal and Marxian traditions may be attributed more to the priorities of those doctrines than to the daunting difficulty of the task. Neither has made democracy its primary objective; the former focuses on liberty and the latter on classlessness. Our brief review of liberalism and Marxism has suggested some steps toward a more coherent theory. Though it would be folly to attempt to summarize our argument in a few terse paragraphs, figure 1.1 exhibits some major concerns that will inform the analysis in the following chapters.

We shall argue that Marxism and liberalism share two basic commitments, one on the level of interpreting individual action (top row of the figure) and the other on the level of understanding social structure (second row of the figure).

The first shared premise is the notion of exogenous interests, according to which individual action is held to be a means toward the realization of the goals of which are given prior to action itself. In the liberal system, the goals are determined by individual preferences (whether selfish or altruistic), and thus action is instrumental to the satisfaction of pregiven wants. In the Marxian case, the goals are determined by the objective interests of the social class to which the individual belongs. In effect, Marxism considers group practices as historically specific collective embodiments of the objective interests of the group, and individual action as a token of the group practice.

The problem with the liberal treatment of action lies in its inability to

FIGURE 1.1

Commitments of the Traditional Doctrines

Concerns	Shared Commitment	Liberal Form	Marxist Form
Individual Action	Exogenous Individual Interests	Instrumental Conception of Action	Expressive Conception of Action
Social Structure	Unitary Treatment of Power	State Conception of Politics	Economistic Conception of Power

deal with the link between action and the formation of preferences. We shall argue, in particular, that the individual is socially constituted in such a way that preferences and action are mutually determining, and hence that preferences are formed through choice.

The Marxian treatment of action suffers from similar problems, but on the level of group action. Marx's theory of group action is inextricably linked to his theory of domination. A mode of production defines a direct relationship between producers and the exploiters who appropriate the fruits of their labor. This relationship of superior to subordinate or exploiter to exploited may be termed *vertical*. This vertical relationship in turn defines a *horizontal* relationship among the exploited—a type of communality among producers that may allow them to face their exploiters from a position of class solidarity.

But though Marxian theory correctly stresses the centrality of classes as historical actors, it provides only the barest outline of how such horizontal structural relationships come to be important to people's identities and political projects. This means that some of the most pressing issues of solidarity, division, and collective action—why a worker chooses to honor a picket line or to join a union—cannot be addressed. It is simply assumed that individual action is either an expression of class interest or of "false consciousness," and the problem of choice disappears. This theory thus betrays a misplaced objectivity of class interests, which become divorced from social practice, only to be repositioned among the "iron laws" of history.

Marx did not simply overlook the problem of choice, of course. He believed that interests are related to social structure in a relatively straightforward manner: the structure of exploitation gives rise to a corresponding structure of objective interests. These common interests of the working class thus provide a relatively unproblematic basis for the formation of the horizontal bonds leading to working-class unity and ultimately to revolutionary political action. The development of a revolutionary working-class consciousness paradoxically was given only the most minimal and declaratory attention by Marx. By contrast, we find the notion of objectively given interests either vacuous or incoherent, and hence the process of "discovery of objective interests" meaningless. With the benefit of historical hindsight, moreover, we may add that the process of creating a set of interests capable of supporting unified political action among those sharing a common form of oppression is far from unproblematic. We shall claim that interests—as the term is generally used—not only motivate practices, they are also formed through practices.[22]

The premise of exogenous interests—in both the liberal and the Marxian versions—renders a balanced defense of liberty and democratic sovereignty impossible. In both, institutions are seen as conduits for social action rather than powerful influences on the formation of individual wills and group solidarity. Institutions—whether they be democratic elections or trade unions—therefore are evaluated primarily on the basis of their ability to record, aggregate, enforce, or satisfy preexisting interests. The manner in which institutions engender preferences and interests is thereby obscured.

In rejecting the premise of exogenous interests, we argue that an adequate conception of action must be based upon the notion that people produce themselves and others through their actions. According to this conception, action is neither instrumental toward the satisfaction of given wants nor expressive of objective interests, but it is an aspect of the very generation of wants and specification of objective interests. Individuals and groups, accordingly, act not merely to *get* but to *become*. The politics of becoming, we believe, provides a central corrective to both the normative and the explanatory dimensions of traditional political theory.

A second pervasive (and we believe mistaken) premise common to liberalism and Marxism concerns what we call the vertical relationships that make up the social structure: their characteristic patterns of domination and subordination. Each theory expresses a view of power as unitary; in liberalism power emanates from the state and in Marxism it emanates from the class structure.

Liberal theory—in adopting and extending the theory of unitary sovereignty of Jean Bodin and other sixteenth-century theorists of the nascent absolute state—sees the state as the unique locus of power in society, other realms being both formally and substantively subsumed under its authority. Marxian theory tends to represent the apparent power of the state and of the male family head as unimportant or epiphenomenal—directly or indirectly expressive of the class structure.

In opposition to the unitary conception of power we propose what we term the *heterogeneity of power*. Power is multifaceted and not reducible to a single source or structure. For this reason, we insist on distinct usages of the three terms collapsed in the Marxian discourse: domination, exploitation, and class. In our proposed alternative usage domination is a systematic relationship of unequal power, exploitation is a particular economic form of domination, and class is a form of exploitation based on the ownership of property. All class relationships are characterized by exploitation, but not all exploitative relationships are class relationships; all exploitative relationships are characterized by domination, but not all forms of domination are exploitative; and all relationships of domination are social, but not all social relations are characterized by domination.

Insisting on the heterogeneity of power might seem to foster a conception of politics so general as to be vacuous. If politics, like "labor," takes place everywhere and adopts a limitless variety of forms, what possible insight can the concept have other than to signal the narrowness of conventional renderings of the word? We believe, however, that this danger is more apparent than real. By a common but unfortunate usage in contemporary political theory, the word *politics* refers to both an activity and a structure. Political *activity* is conventionally understood as a contest for power to determine the distribution of economic resources or status, or to make, defend, and change the rules of the game; whereas the political *arena* is the state. Politics, or political activity, is one of many distinct practices, distinguished by its object: power. The political arena, or the state, by contrast, is one of many distinct rules of the game governing social activity, or more precisely, imparting regularity to practices.

It might seem that the dual usage of the word politics is but a semantic awkwardness, reflecting nothing more serious than intellectual indolence on the part of social theorists. That we regularly use the word *football* or *chess* to denote both a set of rules and an activity seems inconsequential enough. For politics this is not the case. If politics is both a structure and an activity, which of these is the object of political theory? If both conceptions are relevant to political theory, why do we not have a political theory of the family and the economy, both of which are undoubtedly terrains of contest in the previously discussed sense? This critical question is conveniently elided by an unwarranted collapse of conceptual categories reflected in what we term the *state conception of politics*. The state conception of politics limits the object of political theory to practices in the state arena: politics is what goes on in the state.

The state conception of politics is a defining characteristic of liberal political theory, but it is not entirely absent from Marxian theory. In fact, the difference between the two traditions in this respect is to be found not in the rejection of the state conception of politics in the Marxian tradition, but in the refusal to give the state the attention or the central role afforded it in the liberal tradition.

The state conception of politics is but one expression of the common tendency of liberal and Marxian social theory to identify specific sites of social action with distinctive human practices—such as the economy with production, educational systems with learning, the family with sexuality and reproduction, and so on. It is because of this tendency, for example, that both liberal and Marxian paradigms have succeeded in ignoring the fundamentally political nature of economic life. Because it denies the variety of types of social practices in the various realms of society, the presumed one-to-one correspondence between structures and activities is also implicated in the liberal learning versus choosing partition; it buttresses the liberal penchant for exempting educational institutions from norms of democratic choice, and economic institutions from norms of personal growth and development.

We suggest, as an alternative, that all spheres of social life, at least in principle, give structure to a wide variety of human practices. The economy is the site not only of political practices, but of cultural practices as well. The family is not only a political terrain but a locus of production. All social arenas, then, are susceptible to a common set of normative principles and can be analyzed in terms of the differential manner in which they organize the range of human practices.

Conclusion: Making Sense of Making History

Both liberalism and Marxism have had immense appeal not only to the contemplative but also to the practical-minded. Both theories have been deployed in the guidance and justification of governing elites and of mass movements. As a rationale for rule or for popular mobilization the attractions of each are clear enough. But as a guide to radical democratic action the partial nature of the focus of each constitutes a serious shortcoming.

Partly as a result, neither liberalism nor Marxism has ever fully understood the logic of social action and the resulting dynamic of social change in liberal capitalist societies. In ironically complementary ways, both fail to comprehend the basic emancipatory thrust of advanced capitalist societies. This movement results neither from the advance of the productive forces of society and the resulting elevation of working-class consciousness, as the Marxian view might have it, nor from the liberal vision of moral and intellectual enlightenment of the population and the resulting flowering of respect for individual rights. Rather, as we seek to show in the pages that follow, progressive social change in the liberal democratic capitalist societies has followed the logic of collective opposition to oppression suggested by Marxian theory, while adopting the liberal language of rights and the goal of democratic empowerment.[23]

In short, liberalism gives us the discourse of social change, whereas Marxism gives us the theory of social change. Social change itself, however, is opaque to both liberalism, which does not recognize that its discourse developed through class and other collective struggles, and Marxism, which misconstrues what these struggles were for.

Though often turned effectively against popular movements, the discourse of rights has framed the hopes and rage of ordinary people for three centuries; in the process, bonds of popular solidarity have been formed, broken, and formed again, and the discourse of rights itself has been transformed into an effective weapon of social emancipation. Marxism has trivialized the egalitarian potential of personal rights and even of democracy itself, and thus has treated the fact that popular demands have been couched in the liberal language of rights not as a sign of power but of false consciousness and defeat.

By contrast, we believe that a *visionary-historical* approach to democratic political action can be forged—one that deploys the radical potential of the deeply rooted but contradictory language of rights toward the goal of making people more nearly the authors of their personal and collective histories. Such an approach is *visionary* in that it takes as its project the construction of a social order and a way of life that is at best prefigured only in the interstices of liberal democratic capitalist societies today. It is *historical* in that it sees the fruition of this vision as the outcome of the concrete dynamic of already well-established social forces. Among the forces propelling a visionary conception of democracy to the stage of history, none is more important than the collision of property rights and citizen rights, to which we now turn.

2

Past: Citizens, Property,
and the Clash of Rights

IN FEBRUARY 1960, four black students refused to leave a Greensboro, North Carolina, lunch counter after being denied the cups of coffee they wished to purchase. At the time, they were assaulted and vilified as "outside agitators." In fact they were quite the reverse. The students' undoubtedly radical protest was a simple affirmation of quintessentially *liberal* rights. The spreading wave of sit-ins, though unsettling to the racial status quo, was not antiliberal: rather it proclaimed the priority of one aspect of liberalism, personal rights, over another, rights of property.

Less obviously, the civil rights movement in effect sought to enforce one aspect of the capitalist economy against another: the students deployed the commodity against property. Their protest insisted that the ideology of the capitalist market be taken at its word—if you pay the price you get the goods, no matter who you are. The students could have done no better than to quote Milton Friedman: "No one who buys bread knows whether the wheat from which it is made was grown by a Communist or a Republican, by a Constitutionalist or a Fascist, or, for that matter, by a Negro or a white."[1] Ironically, this staple of the liberal identification of capitalism and freedom—the anonymity of exchange and the irrelevance of the identities of the parties to a contract—was thus taken up in opposition to the right of exclusion generally conferred by the ownership of property.

The result of this pitting of right against right, after a decade of intense conflict, was a profound change in the system of racial domination in the United States. No less profound was the manner in which this change challenged the private–public boundary separating the sphere of personal rights and that of property rights.

The U.S. civil rights movement is perhaps the most dramatic testimony to the contradictory nature of the rights conferred by the structure of liberal democratic capitalism. But it is far from unique. In Europe and North America, workers, feminists, the elderly, peace activists, and others have regularly resorted to the discourse of rights, regarding the liberal democratic lexicon as their arsenal if not always their inspiration. Predictably arrayed against the advocates of a broad usage of personal rights have been the defenders of rights of property, bureaucratic privilege, white supremacy, and male domination.

Nor is the recognition of the contradictory character of rights of recent historical vintage. The tension between property rights and personal rights has been felt from the very birth of liberal republicanism. Oliver Cromwell in the seventeenth century had to contend with the leveller movement, which upheld a then radical conception of equal legal rights.[2] In the Putney Debates of 1647, the leveller general Thomas Rainsborough proclaimed:

> I think that the poorest he that is in England hath a life to live as the greatest he; and therefore . . . every man that is to live under a government ought first by his own consent to put himself under that government.

Cromwell's general Henry Ireton confronted Rainsborough with a Lockean logic to be repeated incessantly throughout the next three centuries:

> I think that no person hath a right to an interest or share in the disposing of the affairs of the kingdom . . . that have not a permanent fixed interest in this kingdom.

The radical potential of the leveller conception of rights did not escape Ireton:

> By that same right of nature . . . by which you can say, a man hath an equal right with another to the choosing of him that shall govern him, by the same right of nature, he hath the same right in any goods he sees.

For if such an extended concept of rights is recognized, continues Ireton, "I would fin have any man show me their bounds, where you will end, and take away all property?" The less philosophical Colonel Rich more directly expressed the qualms of the propertied: "if the master and servant shall be equal electors, then there may be a law enacted, that there shall be an equality of goods and estate."[3]

The historical importance of this clash of rights has been facilitated by the fact that, as the lunch-counter sit-ins suggest, it is never perfectly obvious which rights ought to prevail in any given case. Were it possible to identify one sphere of social life as "economic" and another as "political," this ambiguity might be attenuated (though not eliminated, for as we have just seen, even rights customarily considered to be economic may conflict). But this convenient division of social space, favored by liberal social theory and academic convention, appears arbitrary given the evidently political nature of corporations, markets, and other institutions commonly termed "economic," and in light of the transparently economic activities of the state. The resulting indeterminacy concerning the range of application of particular rights has allowed conflicting parties to adapt contrasting conceptions of rights to their diverse political ends.

The resulting clash of rights is elevated to a central dynamic of liberal democratic capitalist societies by two fundamental historical tendencies. The first is the expansionary logic of personal rights, progressively bringing ever-wider spheres of society—the management of the economy and the internal relationships of the family, for example—under at least the formal if not the substantive rubric of liberal democracy. The second tendency concerns the expansionary logic of capitalist production, according to which the capitalist firm's ongoing search for profits progressively encroaches upon all spheres of social activity, leaving few realms of life untouched by the imperatives of accumulation and the market. If we are correct, the present and future trajectories of liberal democratic capitalism will be etched in large measure by the collision of these two expansionary tendencies.

Our view of liberal democratic capitalism as an intrinsically conflictual social system may be contrasted with its traditional conception as, at least in pure form, a harmonious ensemble of rights. In this more widely held view, dynamic pressures for conflict and change either are absent or they are external, lying perhaps in an unexplained pattern of technical change or reorientation of values, in foreign incursions, or in the uneven process of overcoming the anachronistic residues of earlier social orders. Typical of this view is Milton Friedman's classic defense of capitalism, *Capitalism and Freedom*. Writing at the time of the first lunch-counter sit-ins, Friedman saw property rights and citizen rights as barely distinguishable, and in any case as symbiotic:

> Freedom in economic arrangements is itself a component of freedom broadly understood, so economic freedom is an end in itself. . . . economic freedom is also an indispensable means towards the achievement of political freedom.[4]

Friedman's confidence in the unity of rights in liberal democratic capitalism was not complete, however; he feared that citizen rights might come to encroach on what he termed economic freedom.

No such doubts cloud the writings of Louis Hartz, who argues in *The Liberal Tradition in America* that the history of class antagonism in liberal capitalism is due not to inherent properties of the system itself but rather to its emergence from a system of feudal privilege, remnants of which persisted long after the consolidation of liberal states. Hartz's thesis was perhaps the most durable product of the "End of Ideology" period in America's intellectual history. With its feudal past an ocean away and with its precocious republican tradition deeply rooted in the soil of the new continent, America is the purest case of liberal capitalism, wrote Hartz. America is the archetype of which conflict-ridden Europe is but an imperfect realization. Hartz thus erected a challenging affirmation of the intrinsically harmonious character of liberal capitalism.[5]

Hartz held that America alone, undistorted by an aristocratic parentage, exhibits the true harmony to which liberal capitalist societies can everywhere aspire. If in Europe the idea of individual rights bore radical overtones, in America, he asserted, it served as the common coin of political debate. Echoing Alexis de Tocqueville, Hartz took the harmony of personal and property rights as assured:

> In a society evolving along the American pattern . . . where virtually everyone, including the nascent industrial worker, had the mentality of an independent entrepreneur, two national impulses are bound to make themselves felt: the impulse toward democracy and the impulse toward capitalism. The mass of the people, in other words, are bound to be capitalistic, and capitalism, with its spirit disseminated widely, is bound to be democratic.[6]

For this reason, and in direct contrast to the European experience, the propertied classes in the United States have not had to face the threat of revolutionary socialism. A nonfeudal society, wrote Hartz, lacks a genuine revolutionary tradition, the tradition which in Europe has been linked with the Puritan and French revolutions; that is it is "born equal," as Tocqueville said. And this being the case, it lacks also a tradition of reaction: lacking Robespierre, it lacks Maistre, lacking Sydney it lacks Charles II . . . [S]ocialism is largely an ideological phenomenon, arising out of the principles of class and the revolutionary liberal revolt against them which the old European order inspired.[7]

Socialism, far from being the wave of the future, will exist in liberal societies only to the extent that, and only so long as, the old order refuses to cede its place to the new. America is the harbinger of Europe's future: no feudalism, no socialism.

If the structural harmony of liberal capitalism is assured, its history must march not to the drum of its own internal conflicts but to external oppositions: liberalism versus fascism, capitalism versus communism, individualism versus collectivism, gemeinschaft versus gesellschaft. The Hartzian position implies that once history has abolished the vestiges of the old order, and has contained the Soviet Union and other challengers of the world hegemony of liberal capitalism, the full harmony of the liberal system will be assured. The end of ideology is no less than the end of history.

The notion that history, having worked out its quirky past, would be laid to rest in capitalist America no doubt fell on ready ears in complacent mid-century America. Hartz regretted only that it seemed to have taken Americans so long to figure this out. With no basis for grave conflict, early American political leaders should have developed

some sort of theory of democratic capitalism which fit the Tocquevillian facts of American life. But this, as we know, is precisely what Whiggery failed to do until it saw the light in . . . the post–Civil War days of Horatio Alger and Andrew Carnegie.

The opponents of democracy may be exonerated on the grounds of ignorance, however. "Their crime," says Hartz, "was not villainy but stupidity."[8]

There is merit in Hartz's position. The absence of a feudal past in America has left an unmistakable imprint on the political history of the nation. But the resulting social order has been no less prone to systemic social conflict of a sort that might one day prove to be its undoing. Nor does the progressive elimination of the remnants of precapitalist economic systems in Europe seem likely to inaugurate a harmonious Hartzian social universe with an Old World flavor.

Our differences with Hartz stem from his presumption of structural harmony in liberal democratic capitalism. According to this presumption, although individuals and groups in liberal society may have conflicting needs and interests, all are served by, and hence act to maintain and secure, the mutually reinforcing rules of liberal capitalism. We take an alternative view. Liberal democratic capitalism is a contradictory ensemble of institutions in which distinct rights are as often conflicting as they are mutually reinforcing. Major forms of social change in this contradictory system, however far-reaching and substantive, have been internal transformations of the dominant organization of rights. Not socialism, but the full extension of personal rights has been the fundamental threat facing the capitalist order in the liberal context.

Our emphasis on conflict as the engine of social change suggests our affinity with Marx's historical materialism. But the dynamic etched by the clash of rights cannot be reduced to economic issues or to class conflict. Social change in liberal capitalism is better understood as the product of the interaction of the two systemwide expansionary logics of personal and property rights, rather than as a result of the internal contractions of the system of capitalist accumulation. Further, we take issue with the notion that social power reduces ultimately to one source (that of a dominant class structure) and with its corollary, the view of social conflict as fundamentally bipolar. We shall argue instead that social power is irreducibly heterogeneous, and that it gives rise to a multiplicity of distinct structures of dominance and subordinacy in social life. Correspondingly, resistance to oppression gives rise to a multiplicity of historically important forms of solidarity and lines of battle. Finally, we see little merit in the view that the radical opposition to oppression requires that a group reject dominant forms of political discourse in favor of a novel or alien consciousness unintelligible to traditional culture. The voices arising from the plural terrains of social action in liberal democratic capitalist society are not harmonious, but we contend that they are generally mutually intelligible, expressing not the babel of exotic or oppositional discourses, but the counterpoint of a common tongue. This lingua franca of politics is the discourse of rights.

But if personal and property rights do not form a harmonious unity, and if each follows an expansionary logic in the course of liberal capitalist development, why do not conflicting forces simply cause the system to fly apart? Why, indeed, as Colonel Rich worried, do not the many deploy their personal rights against the privileges of property? And equally, why do not the propertied deploy the formidable weapons that wealth may command to overturn the system of personal rights altogether?

We suggest that social stability in the face of the contradictory nature of rights has depended upon a series of historically specific institutional accommodations. In Europe and North America, these accommodations have deployed such diverse mechanisms as what might be termed the Lockean practice of limiting political participation to the propertied, the Jeffersonian vision of distributing property widely among the citizenry, the Madisonian strategy of fostering a sufficient heterogeneity of interests among citizens so as to prevent the emergence of a common political program of the nonpropertied, and the Keynesian model of economic growth through redistribution of income with the resulting communality of interests between the dispossessed and the wealthy.

Each of these accommodations—Lockean, Jeffersonian, Madisonian, and Keynesian—constituted a definition of the range of application of personal rights and property rights capable of muting the explosive potential of the clash of these rights. At the same time, each promoted, or at least was powerless to prevent, the evolution of new tensions. In each case the result was the erosion of the dominant form of accommodation in favor of a novel form or combination of forms.

The period extending from World War II to the 1970s exemplifies the most recent of these accommodations, which we call "Keynesian" in recognition of the role played by egalitarian state redistribution and macroeconomic management in spurring both capital accumulation and social harmony. The faltering of this accommodation, we shall argue, is both cause and effect of the period of economic stagnation and instability experienced by the the advanced capitalist countries during the 1970s and 1980s.

If a common underlying logic of each of these accommodations and their demise may be discerned it is this. On the one hand, even in a society characterized by a scrupulously liberal democratic state, wealth (particularly the ownership of the productive apparatus) confers powers that are relatively resilient in the face of populist assault. On the other hand, the discourse of personal rights is far from an ephemeral ideological flourish with which elites may choose to ornament their rule or which they may readily cast aside when the going gets rough. The discourse of personal rights fosters the formation of powerful ties of solidarity among the dispossessed and less well-to-do, and imposes heavy bureaucratic, military, and other costs on those who would seek to override them. Each of the four accommodations

.we have identified has incorporated both the power of capital and the discourse of personal rights in ways that, at least for a time, simultaneously promoted the process of economic growth and contained the explosive potential of coexistence of economic privilege and representative political institutions.

The Collision of Rights

The past two centuries have not witnessed the eclipse of one complex of rights by another, they have seen the simultaneous expansion of the realms of social life governed by liberal democratic institutions and by the institutions of the capitalist economy. The expansion of liberal democratic rights has attracted the acute attention of historians and political commentators; the universalization of suffrage and the extending reach of state power in the liberal democratic countries have provided the material for a century-long ideological and theoretical debate. Capitalist accumulation has produced its share of political drama as well, particularly where world-scale economic expansion has sparked nationalist rebellions, international rivalry, and world war. But in contrast to the penetration of capital to the far reaches of the world, the domestic expansion of the realm of property rights has been for the most part invisible, as the logic of the market has quietly encroached upon the intimate relations of the family; insinuated itself into the domains of sentiment, life-style, and psyche; and bound the state with subtle threads of economic dependency.

Perhaps for this reason liberal historians have generally represented the past century of "government-business relations" as one of gradual democratic ascendancy extending at least through the 1970s. But, curiously, the ascendancy of capital has also apparently grown, for who could doubt that the imperatives of profit have a more far-reaching effect upon the everyday lives of most citizens today than they did two centuries ago?

The expansionary logics of personal rights and property rights have operated to some extent at the expense of other logics—those of patriarchal privilege and precapitalist civic culture, for example—and to some extent they have operated symbiotically, as in the frequent support by capitalists of expanded state power. When these two logics have collided, the result has been intense social conflict. Nowhere is the endemic ambiguity concerning the appropriate range of application of a right more evident than where it has begun to encroach upon another right's traditional, and doubtlessly well-defended, turf.

The expanding reaches of personal rights and property rights are structurally determined historical tendencies of liberal democratic capitalist social orders. For this reason we refer to them as "logics" rather than simply empirical historical regularities. The basis of each, we shall see, is the manner in which the characteristic structures of liberal democratic societies favor and empower certain practices and projects and inhibit others.

The expansionary logic of capitalist production is one of the great dramas of modern history. The capitalist class is the first dominant class in human history whose individual members' statuses depend upon their ability to command the ever-greater production of ever-cheaper products. Resting on one's laurels is a sure way to become an ex-capitalist. Equally important, through the political activities of its members and subgroupings the capitalist class has effectively secured an array of economic and political institutions that make low-cost production a decisive element in the long-term survival of alternative organizational forms, rendering the family farm, the liberal professions, and artisanship alike peripheral and endangered economic species. The low-cost production imperative has thus provided both a discipline for the individual members of the capitalist class and something akin to Darwin's natural selection for the evolution of social organization, systematically favoring some forms of production, some social innovations, and some family structures, while consigning others to extinction or marginality.

Thus the global mobility of capital, the marketability of land, the market in labor, and other institutions of capitalism have limited the autonomy of the state, usurped many economic activities of the family, and impinged upon local communities. The logic of capitalist production is often explicitly employed even when it is apparently superseded, as in the design of state policy. For instance, market measures are explicitly invoked in such unlikely areas as the legal valuation of a human life and evaluation of projects likely to impinge upon the preservation of the natural habitat of unborn generations.

Although the expansionary nature of the logic of property rights may be traced quite directly to the rules of capitalist competition, the structural basis for the expansionary tendency of personal rights in liberal capitalism

35

is somewhat more difficult to explain. Why, in the course of liberal capitalist development, have successive groups taken up the discourse of rights, and despite the variety of alternatives available to them, why have they chosen to transform and broaden a project begun by others with very different social stations, life chances, and goals? Why has social conflict in liberal capitalist societies been so regularly channeled into the ostensibly "reformist" direction of extending rights rather than in the more straightforward direction of overturning social institutions and constructing an entirely new social order?

The liberal may respond that no better institutions are feasible, so that reformism is the only sensible approach, even for those least advantaged by the present order of things. This traditional liberal response takes personal and property rights as fundamentally harmonious and ultimately compatible. In this view, the full extension of rights is that ideal and universally desirable point toward which liberal capitalist development moves. That highly diverse groups have found it in their common interest to contribute to this movement hardly occasions surprise within liberal theory.

Marxists, by contrast, have held no such illusions about the benign nature of liberal democratic capitalist institutions or the harmonious nature of the struggle for rights. Indeed, they have traditionally argued that the struggle for personal rights is a necessary way station on the road to socialist revolution. They have also clearly understood that liberal society itself induces oppressed groups to express their emancipatory concerns by demanding the extension of personal rights. This much was explained with great clarity by Karl Marx, who in the *Eighteenth of Brumaire* analyzed popular democratic movements in mid-nineteenth-century France in the following terms:

If the parliamentary regime lives by discussion, how can it forbid discussion? . . . The struggle of the parliamentary orators calls forth the struggle of the scribblers of the press; the parliamentary debating club is necessarily supplemented by debating clubs in the salons and the alehouses.

Moreover, Marx recognized, the problem spilled beyond the realm of ideology into that of the real struggle for power:

The parliamentary regime leaves everything to the decisions of majorities, why then should the great majority outside parliament not want to make the decisions? When you play the fiddle at the summit of the state, what else is there to expect than that those down below dance?[9]

Marx, however, viewed the situation of "those down below" mimicking the ways of their "social superiors" as temporary, provisional, and derivative. In the long run, the growth of class consciousness would impel the oppressed to reject the entire liberal capitalist edifice.

This they have not done; the struggle for the extension of rights has in fact displaced rather than preceded more ambitious strategies of the oppressed.

Why? First, oppressed groups had a relatively limited menu from which to choose a political strategy. The consolidation of national states in early modern Europe involved the destruction of precapitalist forms of popular solidarity and rendered access to state power through political representation a critical element in enhancing the social position of all social groups. The control of the state thus became a prime object of social conflict. (Even laissez-faire capitalists required access to state power, if only to neutralize it.) With the rise of capitalism, rights-based political power emerged as the only serious contender to the power of capital as an instrument of social change. Second, the discourse of rights was well developed and universally understood, making the transformation of its terms a more auspicious strategy of cultural struggle than aiming toward its wholesale replacement by un- familiar political discourses. Third, without minimizing the residual powers of the well-to-do, the demand for personal rights spoke to the real needs of oppressed groups, as couching political debate in terms of universal rights enhanced popular majorities' power in opposition to traditional political and economic elites. And finally, the fact that the emergent working class could expect either to become a numerical majority or to enter into comfortable alliances with other oppressed groups (farmers, for instance), appeared to render unnecessary the need to move beyond electoral and trade union demands. Under these conditions—conditions obtaining in early liberal capitalism—an alternative to the extension of rights must have appeared an extraneous detour.*

Why, however, did elites in liberal capitalism accede—however slowly and reluctantly—to popular demands for the extension of rights? Of course in many countries they simply did not; especially in the period after World War I, initiatives toward extending voting rights were viewed as dangerous by many of the well-to-do, and there was a widespread retreat from de-

---

* A similar analysis would explain the adherence of the women's movement to the discourse of rights. To understand the position of ethnic, racial, and religious minorities in liberal capitalism requires a more complex analysis, in which coalition formation must be taken into account.

mocracy throughout Europe. World War II was, among other things, a battle between two responses of an emergent capitalist order to deal with the popular demand for democracy.*

But this answer is too facile. The capitulation of well-ensconced centers of economic and social privilege as England, France, and Sweden to popular demands is totally without historical precedent. The elites of these nations perceived themselves more threatened by both novel and traditional forms of despotism than by republican government. They sensed that as soon as liberals resort to mass coercion, they are displaced by nonliberals for whom such strategies form normal parts of their social repertoire. Yet given their commitment to republican government, liberals found themselves incapable of curbing the expansion of personal rights. Why?

For the same reason that the expansion of personal rights served the needs of the emerging working class, their denial drove working-class movements into the arms of revolutionaries. But in addition, the costs of enforcing political and military obligations and eliciting popular loyalty were considerably reduced by the extension of personal rights.

A patriotic citizenry was a central aspect of the liberal capitalist process of nation building. As both markets and secular ideology weakened traditional habits of deference, the more forward-looking sought to find new forms of social cement. Universal suffrage, according to Alexis de Tocqueville, was one form.

> In a country with universal suffrage . . . the moral strength of the government . . . is greatly increased. . . . Whereas the . . . man in Europe would be prejudiced against all authority, even the highest, the American uncomplainingly obeys the lowest of his officials.[10]

Citizenship became a key force in the stabilization and legitimization of the nineteenth-century nation-state. Securing national identity involved providing universal education, inventing public ceremonies, and mass-producing public monuments. But more important, as Eric Hobsbawm has noted of nineteenth-century Europe, because liberalism abhors traditional

---

* The governments of Hungary (1921), Albania (1924), Poland (1926), and Yugoslavia (1929) all abandoned parliamentary methods during the first decade after World War I. Bulgaria (1934) and Rumania (1938), in addition to the fascist states, instituted authoritarian forms under the stress of the Great Depression. In eastern Europe, only Czechoslovakia and Finland conserved representative government until World War II.

forms of community, and hence offers no substitute for the active participation of the citizenry in national political life,

> an alternative "civic religion" had to be constructed. . . . What made it particularly
> urgent was the dominance both of liberal constitutional institutions and of liberal
> ideology. The former provided no theoretical, but only at best empirical, barriers
> against electoral democracy. . . . The latter . . . systematically failed to provide
> for those social bonds and ties of authority taken for granted in earlier societies,
> and had indeed set out to and succeeded in weakening them.[11]

Perhaps the most decisive impulse for the expansion of personal rights
arose because military realities of the nineteenth century required a strongly
loyal citizenry. The development of the rifled percussion musket, breech-
loaded artillery, and the machine gun made light infantry cost-effective.[12]
These changes in the design and manufacture of firearms, as well as the
development of better methods of commanding large numbers of men on
the battlefield and lower military training costs, rendered war a highly labor-
intensive undertaking.[13]

Both the potency of mass armies and the intimate connection between
loyalty and fighting effectiveness were vividly illustrated by the French revolutionary government at the turn of the century. Samuel Finer has observed,

> Napoleon succeeded with hitherto unheard-of vast numbers of soldiers, which,
> while untrained, were brave and loyal. . . . The Prussian failures led [Prussian
> ministers] Stein, Hardenburg, and [general] Scharnost to realize that citizen
> participation was necessary if the Prussian army was to work.[14]

Of course, other states did not adopt this new form of military organization
unless and until it was absolutely necessary. But it often did become absolutely necessary. Reinhard Bendix has noted,

> In a number of countries the demands for universal manhood suffrage became
> intimately tied in with the need for universal *conscription*. . . . In the Swedish
> suffrage debates, the slogan "one man, one vote, one gun" reflects this tie up
> between franchise and military recruitment.[15]

It would be stretching a point to claim that the extension of liberal democratic government is the only source of widespread national loyalty and
patriotism. Hitler, Stalin, and many others have given the lie to any such
notion. But where the rules of the game link political power to electoral

success, and where the contest of politics is governed by the language of general personal rights, democracy and patriotism become inexorably related. Ironically, perhaps, "One man, one vote, one gun" becomes the slogan of the expansion of personal rights.

The claim that personal rights of the citizenry were wrested from the well-to-do is scarcely one of serious historical dispute, as our review of the historical record will demonstrate. The same cannot be said of our interpretation of this evidence. Our clash of rights perspective stresses the conflict *among* parties to the new industrial and commercial order, and thus breaks sharply with the standard account of the growth of rights as a contest *between* the new commitment to democracy and the old faith in robe, sword, and crown. There is no question that once liberal democracy was forced upon a resistant liberalism and a reluctant capitalism it was touted by exponents of both as their bountiful contribution to social emancipation. Indeed, liberal historians in the post–World War II period have sometimes gone further than Hartz by assigning a fundamentally harmonious structure to liberal democratic capitalism in Europe as well as America. Though the support for this position is often (like Milton Friedman's) axiomatic, historians have contributed to the view that democratic rights and property rights are not fundamentally at odds. In this view the struggle for democratic rights and inalienable private property alike pitted a new enlightened individualism against an archaic hierarchical and collectivist tradition.

This misconception is no doubt fostered by the illusion—perpetuated at least as much by Marxist as by liberal historians—that feudal institutions survived throughout Europe well into the eighteenth century. But by far the most important source of this dubious reading of the historical record is simply the common proclivity to project meanings from one historical period onto the movements of another. Joyce Appleby noted such an error in her analysis of the changing content of republicanism in the Jeffersonian era.

> Voltaire once described history as a pack of tricks that the present plays on the past. He failed to mention that the people of the past have their own dissembling pranks. The most troublesome for historians is the tendency to change without notice the meaning of words. Whole new concepts can take shape behind an unvarying set of terms.[16]

Often, however, the confusion operates in the other direction, with modern usages being impressed upon the past. In particular, there is an almost irresistible temptation to confuse democratic and personal rights, which were the product of bitter conflict in the nineteenth and twentieth centuries, with "republicanism," "constitutional rule," and other aspects of modern government which were promoted by liberals, and accepted by all parties to industrial capitalism in an earlier period.

The historian is as susceptible as the next person to this confusion. Typical, for instance, is R. R. Palmer, whose valuable *The Age of Democratic Revolution* covers a period in which, in fact, there was virtually *no* movement toward democratic institutions! This feat of intellectual legerdemain is accomplished by equating democracy with "a new feeling for a kind of equality." Here are Palmer's exact words:

> It is held that this forty-year movement [1760–1800] was essentially "democratic" and that these years are in fact the Age of Democratic Revolution. "Democratic" is here to be understood . . . not primarily in the sense of a later day in which universality of the suffrage became a chief criterion of democracy . . . it signified a new feeling for a kind of equality, or at least a discomfort with older forms of social stratification and formal rank.[17]

The error in this type of reasoning is to project into a "feeling" and a "discomfort" a nexus of political commitments that were historically totally absent, and were in no way derivable from the actual commitments of the historical actors. Is it not inevitable that, should the democratic control of production and investment be added to our fundamental liberties at some future date, consensus historians will come forth to interpret William of Occam, Marsiglio of Padua, and John Locke as incorporating their essential spirit?

Claims of Citizenship and the Demise of the Lockean Accommodation

Most nineteenth-century liberals saw little harmony in the joint expansion of personal and property rights and understood that a society dedicated to civil equality and economic inequality faced novel problems of social stability. Alexis de Tocqueville expressed the problem with great clarity.

Equality makes new men of servant and of master, and establishes new connections between them. . . . Why then has the latter the right to command and the former obey? . . . Within the terms of the contract, one is servant and the other master; beyond that, they are two citizens . . . [The servants] are inclined to consider the man who gives them orders an unjust usurper of their rights.[18]

The first attempt at an institutional modus vivendi of these two forces was what we shall call the *Lockean accommodation*. According to the Lockean accommodation, social harmony was to be ensured by limiting political participation to the propertied and their natural allies among the upper classes.[19]

Nineteenth-century liberals generally recognized three sorts of franchise restrictions of a Lockean nature: the *regime censitaire*, basing suffrage on the possession of wealth or the payment of taxes; the *regime capacitaire*, restricting suffrage on the basis of literacy and formal education; and *household responsibility* criteria, which limited political participation to heads of households occupying dwellings of a minimum size or rent. Among these franchise criteria, property restrictions were favored, according to the reasoning that the affairs of the national community are best left to those who are independent and who have "real stakes" in society in the form of property and investments.

The Lockean accommodation reconciled representative government with capitalism by disfranchising that group most likely to contest the hegemony of wealth—the working class itself. It was, as might be expected, a stopgap measure, as political representation became a central project of the popular movements emanating from the Industrial Revolution—a project that could be resisted only by the resort to preliberal forms of despotism. Nevertheless, the liberal thinkers and capitalist employers nurturing the new industrial order resisted the challenge to the Lockean accommodation in a holding action that did not collapse until World War I. It is a historical irony that in the nineteenth century the popular demand for extended suffrage was abetted by such conservatives as Bismarck and Disraeli, who expected the enfranchisement of the dependent peasantry and the pitting of worker against employer to strengthen the hand of traditional landed interests.[20] The conservative landed interests' support for an extended suffrage was contingent upon their possessing sufficient power over a dependent peasantry, of course. Thus the first Reform Bill in England strengthened the aristocracy and gentry, and manhood suffrage later consolidated the position of the *notables* of rural France and the *Gutsbesitzer* of rural Prussia.

Where the loyalty of the agricultural producers to their social betters was in question, no such symbiosis occurred. In the U.S. South, late nineteenth-century planters and northern capitalists concurred in the systematic disfranchisement of black farmers. By contrast, the powerful freehold peasantry in the Scandinavian countries pushed for democratic reform and parliamentary rule along with the working classes, quite against the wishes and efforts of the rural elites.[21]

Throughout Europe the progress toward an extended suffrage was slow. The extent of property restrictions on the vote in England during the 1800s is frequently underestimated. In England and Wales at the turn of the nineteenth century, about 3 percent of the adult male population could vote. Just before the Reform Act of 1832, this figure had fallen to about 2 percent.[22] The threat of working-class upheaval was exploited by the middle-class elements agitating for the franchise in 1831.[23] Even the so-called Philosophical Radical supporters of extended suffrage, such as Jeremy Bentham, felt the need to reassure their readers: shortly after advocating universal manhood suffrage Bentham published a pamphlet entitled *Radicalism Not Dangerous*.[24] The effect of the supposedly democratic Reform Act of 1832 on working people was disastrous. Not only did it drive a wedge between workers and "the middling sorts," it is probable that fewer working men possessed the vote after 1832 than before.

Eventually liberal England was drawn, kicking and screaming, to democracy. About 4 percent of the adult population possessed the vote in 1832; this figure increased to only about 8 percent after the reforms of 1867. The Reform Act of 1884 instituted political democracy in name only. Even in 1911 less than 30 percent of the total adult population of the United Kingdom was able to vote.[25] Genuine manhood suffrage was delayed until 1918. And universal suffrage had still longer to wait.

For different reasons, extended suffrage fared no better on the continent. In liberal Europe the Lockean accommodation remained intact through the Paris Commune and the Franco-Prussian War. After a century of bitter antagonisms between monarchy and nobility in Europe (of which the French Revolution was the outcome most costly to traditional elites), the first half of the nineteenth century saw the crown and aristocracy draw together in the face of a common threat from new industrial elites. The new propertied classes found themselves outside looking in on the political power centers of the day. As William Langer notes, "Even Louis Philippe's supposedly 'bourgeois revolution' of 1830 in France was controlled not by bankers and business men, but by the progressive elements of the nobility. . . . Elected officials were mostly landowners."[26]

There was thus a strong temptation for liberals to ally with the increasingly organized working classes. In this period, many businessmen advocated constitutional, representative government; equality before the law; and freedom of thought, speech, association, and contract. But according to Langer they "feared the growing numbers of the dark, illiterate, unpropertied masses which, under a democratic system, might overthrow the existing social order and confiscate property of all kinds."[27] Not surprisingly, then, merchants, capitalist employers, and professionals often found themselves pressed between an exclusive aristocratic oligarchy and a dispossessed populace, whence their stress on property as the basis for political participation.[28]

The last third of the nineteenth century saw a qualitative change in this situation. Like the aristocracy before it, late-nineteenth-century liberals throughout Europe turned conservative—this time under the increasing pressure of working-class demands. The situation in Germany, carefully analyzed by Volker Rittberger, appears to typify these strains:

> Out of fear of the working class the greater part of the German bourgeoisie became reconciled to their "junior partner" status of the traditional ruling class. . . . The bourgeois intelligentsia, heretofore the chief carrier of the political aspirations of the bourgeoisie, split deeply. The greater part turned toward nationalism and imperialism.[29]

By 1880 the parliamentary tradition had been established in virtually all European countries, with the exception of Russia. In most cases, however, the power of the traditional elites remained secure if not unchallenged, for parliaments had only nominal powers against the executive, and hence were at best weak influences on state policy.[30] Theodor Scheider summarizes this situation in the following stark, but not overdrawn, terms:

> At the close of the [nineteenth] century Europe was still predominantly monarchical; and it was obvious . . . that the middle classes, at any rate for the time being, preferred monarchical to republican forms of government. . . . The industrial workers' associations and their political organizations, moreover, almost all supported the principle of a democratic republic; and it was mainly they who brought about the fall of the great monarchies at the end of the first World War.[31]

Indeed, the working classes in this period assumed the revolutionary role in the expansion of rights, and liberalism became the cautious defender of the *status quo ante*.[32]

Accepting democratic institutions was difficult for liberals, for whom the Lockean accommodation appeared as an increasingly elusive ideal. Reinhard Bendix observed,

> For decades elementary education and the franchise are debated in terms of whether an increase in literacy or of voting rights among the people would work as an antidote to revolutionary propaganda or as a dangerous incentive to insubordination.[33]

This fear was by no means unfounded, nor was the blocking of democratic demands without major political implications. In countries like Germany, which resisted working-class suffrage until the first part of the twentieth century, the thwarted drive for political representation produced a powerful if eventually unsuccessful revolutionary socialist movement. In words reminiscent of Hartz, Seymour Martin Lipset writes:

> Where the workers were denied both economic and political rights, their struggle for redistribution of income and status was superimposed on a revolutionary ideology. Where the economic and status struggle developed outside of this context, the ideology with which it was linked tended to be that of gradualist reform.

Germany, according to Lipset, provides a telling example:

> The workers of Prussia . . . were denied free and equal suffrage until the revolution of 1918, and thereby clung to revolutionary Marxism. In southern Germany, where full citizenship rights were granted in the late nineteenth century, reformist, democratic, and nonrevolutionary socialism was dominant.[34]

During the first two decades of the twentieth century, the unlikely Lockean marriage of democratic promise and elite prerogatives was gradually dissolved by the irresistible extension of the suffrage in some countries and the rise of fascism in others. It was, moreover, far from a universal European phenomenon. Whole regions and nations bypassed its logic, Russia and the Iberian Peninsula chief among them. The historical preconditions of such an accommodation had been the presence of a traditional aristocratic order with which the new middle classes could ally in containing the popular demand for general political representation, and the absence of a working class strong enough to require a retreat to despotic government—a retreat bound to be led by the traditional antirepublican elites. Such conditions, quite simply, nowhere survived the waning of the nineteenth century.[35] The Lockean accommodation was all but dead in Europe by the 1920s.

Those readers who believe, with Tocqueville, that America was "born free," might object that at least in the United States no Lockean accommodation existed. But as in Europe the conception of a property-based republic had formed a central part of early American political thinking and the general resistance to popular suffrage, though less dogged and effective than in Europe, was hardly absent.

The American colonists of ordinary means benefited from the anti-aristocratic fervor of seventeenth-century England, obtaining what their English counterparts did not—an extensive suffrage. But with the Stuart Restoration, and despite opposition from the many in the colonies, the standard Lockean freehold qualification became a common criterion for suffrage. During the eighteenth century stiffer qualifications were imposed, and a restricted suffrage was common in the American colonies to the very eve of independence from Britain.[36]

The American Revolution itself significantly strengthened the hand of opponents of property qualifications. By carrying the day, the radicals who opted for separation greatly enhanced the pressure for a relatively egalitarian constitution:

> As Cromwell's men had demanded the right to vote if they were deemed fit to fight for their country and its liberties, colonials of military age demanded the same right for the same reason. . . . With the approach of the Revolution, the demand for democratic election of militia officers became as important an issue as that of the future electoral privileges of civilians.[37]

Yet the story of the demise of the Lockean accommodation remains a complex battle against the delaying tactics of elites, which persisted down to the Civil War and beyond.

The Jacksonian era saw the emergence of a party system in America which, however elitist and antidemocratic, was forced by popular pressure to extend personal rights. Indeed, during the second quarter of the nineteenth century, dominant groups, liberal and conservative alike, fought a rearguard action against insurgent democratic, egalitarian, and social reform movements. Just as in Europe, then, liberal capitalism in America saw an elitist and antidemocratic party system foster, despite itself, an expansion of personal rights. The second party system, in effect, presided over a quantum leap in popular political participation.[38] Nor does the story of the Lockean accommodation end with the Civil War and the formation of the modern party system. We need only look to the women's suffrage and black civil rights movements in the twentieth century to recognize the long historical sweep involved in the logic of the expansion of voting rights in the United States.

American Exceptionalism and
the Jeffersonian Accommodation

Never did the Lockean accommodation assume in the New World the central position it held in Europe. America's late-nineteenth-century poets promised and her politicians affirmed that the Old World had long since been left behind. Unlike Europe, where land titles had been the focus of social strife for centuries, the prospect of virtually universal landownership in North America offered a vision of a new liberal order with little need to suffer the conflict of personal and property rights. The political promise of America was what we may call a *Jeffersonian accommodation*: the harmonization of private property and democracy through the generalization of property ownership at least to freeborn male household heads. American exceptionalism, then, consisted not so much in its lack of a feudal past or the vibrancy of its democratic culture, but in its abundance of land.

The roots of Jefferson's thought in Locke's theory of property right are of course well established.[39] His commitment to an extended suffrage is no less well known.[40]

The factors allowing for the uncommon integration of democracy and property in Jefferson's political philosophy were, first, the abundance of land in postcolonial America, and second, a notion that capitalist economic growth could be spearheaded by, and contained within, a nexus of small, progressive, commercial farmers and artisans. Jefferson thought that economic growth in a democratic setting would level the rich and raise up the poor, causing both to approach "that middle point, at which the love of order, of industry, of justice and reason naturally establish themselves."[41]

In effect, Jefferson synthesized Locke and the levellers, within a framework devoted to commercial and economic development. In Virginia, he suggested a 25-acre property qualification for voting, as part of a general proposal for enfranchising every adult male. In Section I of his third draft of the Virginia Constitution of 1776, he prescribed:

> All male persons of full age and sane mind having a freehold estate in [one-fourth of an acre] of land in any town, or in [25] acres of land in the country ... shall have the right to give their vote in the election of their respective representatives, and every person so qualified to elect shall be capable of being elected.[42]

But later in the same document, we find him advocating that "Every person of full age neither owning nor having owned [50] acres of land, shall be entitled to an appropriation of [50] acres."[43] Moreover, in attempting to abolish primogeniture, successfully opposing the speculative land companies, and steering the first land ordinance through the Continental Congress, Jefferson, writes Joyce Appleby, insisted that governments

> did not exist to protect property but rather to promote access to property or more broadly speaking, opportunity. It was in deference to this distinction that he changed Locke's "life, liberty, and property" to make the Declaration of Independence affirm the natural rights to "life, liberty, and the pursuit of happiness."[44]

The vision of a unified, democratic society of commercial farmers and artisans set Jefferson apart from much of the political elite of his time, yet accorded well with popular aspirations. Unlike the Federalists, Jefferson did not want merely to balance government, but also to limit government's interventions in personal and commercial life.[45] Unlike the nostalgic defenders of traditional civic virtue, and quite at odds with Anti-Federalist ideology, he affirmed the importance of a strong and unified if limited government, as well as the centrality of commercial capitalist economic relationships. Appleby has wisely stressed that Jefferson's support of Destutt de Tracy indicates a fundamental rejection, not only of the aristocratic system of multiple representation and the English form of balanced government, but of anticommercial agrarian localism as well:

> The composition of the Republican party also indicates that the choice was not between a Jeffersonian *Gemeinschaft* and a Hamiltonian *Gesellschaft*, as the Court and Country interpretation of early national politics would have it. Com-

mercial farmers, small planters, urban tradesmen, and aspiring professional men poured into Jefferson's party as soon as he sounded the alarm about Hamilton's program.[46]

Appleby concludes that Jefferson's philosophy represents a distinct pro-democratic and procommercial position in the political life of the United States. This is the Jeffersonian accommodation, which accounts for the distinct form taken in the United States by the clash of rights in the first half of the nineteenth century.

But the American exceptionalism that may be detected in this form proved to be ephemeral, for unlike the absence of feudal parentage, abundant land proved to be a temporary blessing. The vistas opened up by "free soil" were to be quickly shuttered, ironically by the very same vibrant commercial expansion that Jefferson had sought to promote.

The crisis of the Jeffersonian accommodation was prompted by several developments in the last third of the nineteenth century. First, the Jeffersonian accommodation since its inception had been based on a sleight of hand. America had never been without a propertyless working class; although perhaps only one in five freeborn male household heads did not own land or tools of their trade in the late eighteenth century, slaves constituted about a third of the total economically active population. Propertyless workers—slave and freeborn—thus constituted roughly half of the labor force, certainly a larger portion than in any European nation at the time except England.[47] The abolition of slavery and the subsequent impetus to extend the terms of liberal political discourse to former slaves resulted first in the historically unprecedented extension of the vote to a large propertyless working class, followed by their rapid disfranchisement after the Compromise of 1877 and the end of the Black Reconstruction in the South. The result was not so much the erosion of the Jeffersonian accommodation as the unmasking of its false premises.

Second, capitalist accumulation supplemented the abolition of slavery in swelling the ranks of the class of wage workers. In the century following Jefferson's authorship of the radical redistribution scheme embedded in the Virginia Constitution, the evolution of the U.S. class structure had reduced the number of owners of productive property to roughly a third of the population. Terrance Powderly, former grand master workman of the Knights of Labor, poignantly captured the implications of this change.

The village blacksmith shop was abandoned, the roadside shoe shop was deserted, the taylor left his bench, and all together these mechanics turned away from their country homes and wended their way to the cities, wherein the large factories had been erected. The gates were unlocked in the morning to allow them to enter, and after their daily task was done the gates were closed after them in the evening.

Powderly did not miss the ominous implications for a fading Jeffersonian tranquillity:

> Silently and thoughtfully, these men went to their homes. They no longer carried the keys of the workshop, for workshop, tools, and keys belonged not to them, but to their master. Thrown together in this way, in large hives of industry, men became acquainted with each other, and frequently discussed the question of labor's rights and wrongs.[48]

As the expansion of industry under capitalist auspices swelled the ranks of the propertyless, it thinned the ranks of the small property owner. The consequences for the viability of the Jeffersonian accommodation were disastrous, if not immediately obvious; the shift was at least as much ideological as numerical. Joseph Schumpeter writes:

> The political structure of a nation is profoundly affected by the elimination of a host of small and medium sized firms, the owner-managers of which, together with their dependents, henchmen and connections count quantitatively at the polls . . . the very foundation of private property and free contracting wears away in a nation in which its most vital, most concrete, most meaningful types disappear from the moral horizon of the people.[49]

The third element in the crisis of the Jeffersonian accommodation was an agrarian challenge to economic privilege in the late nineteenth century. The concentration of economic power mobilized the democratic sentiments and voting power of farmers to promote state intervention more favorable to the agrarian interests of lesser producers. The fact that most populists were themselves property owners perhaps immunized them to socialist appeals, but it made them no less radically opposed to the railroads and the banks.[50]

If the Lockean accommodation had crumbled before the expansionary logic of citizen rights, the Jeffersonian accommodation had succumbed to the expansionary logic of capitalist property.

Europeans, whether or not they approved of the Industrial Revolution, had from its inception understood capitalism as a crass, mean-spirited, and unsentimental system. Only in pristine and land-rich America could the benign Jeffersonian vision of the agrarian commercial order as a new age for ordinary folk serve as a credible accommodation of capitalism and democracy. In due course, Marx's prognosis for the capitalist disease came to appear as pertinent to the New World as to the Old.

The Waning of the Madisonian Accommodation

"The real difference between democracy and oligarchy is poverty and wealth," wrote Aristotle. "The rich are few and the poor are many . . . where the poor rule, that is a democracy."[51] The specter of popular power perhaps prompted the same concern among the well-to-do in fourth-century-B.C. Athens as it did in many late nineteenth-century liberal capitalist societies. With the failure of the Lockean and Jeffersonian accommodations in the late nineteenth century, democracy for the propertyless appeared the only alternative to the complete abrogation of liberal institutions.

The Lockean and Jeffersonian attempts to wed political participation and property ownership had eventually proved unsustainable, yet it must have seemed to many that any lesser scheme would be structurally doomed at the start by its own internal contradictions. Marx, writing about liberal republicanism in mid-nineteenth-century France, thought as much:

> The general contradiction . . . of this constitution consists in this: the classes whose social slavery it perpetuates—proletariat, farmers, the petty bourgeoisie— it places through universal suffrage in the seat of political power. And from the class whose very social power it sanctions—from the bourgeoisie, it withdraws the political guarantees of this power. It renders democratic the political rule of the bourgeoisie, which at every moment propels the underclasses to victory and jeopardizes the very foundations of bourgeois society.

The result, Marx thought, would be a precarious class stalemate:

> From the oppressed, this democratic constitution demands they not push from political to social emancipation; from the bourgeoisie, it requires that they not regress from social to political hegemony.[52]

How, in such a situation, was the conflict of rights to be accommodated? The answer, in both Europe and the United States, was to rely increasingly on what we call the *Madisonian accommodation*, which maintained that the few might be safe from the many even in a liberal democratic environment as long as society is marked by a large number of fundamental and cross-cutting cleavages, ensuring the lack of unity on the part of the majority save with respect to the preservation of liberal democracy itself. The Madisonian accommodation relied upon the heterogeneous economic and social situation of the major producing classes (farmers, wage workers, and artisans), upon the strategic exclusion of some groups (such as blacks and women), as well as upon racial, ethnic, religious, and regional antagonisms, to forestall the threat to the structure of privilege posed by the extension of the suffrage.

Though it did not become the dominant form of accommodation in any major nation until the late nineteenth century, we call it "Madisonian" because James Madison presented this argument perhaps for the first time in the context of arguments over the framing of the U.S. Constitution. Indeed, while Jefferson was laying the ground for his democratic society of freeholders, the more realistic Madison was setting up principles of government compatible both with an extended suffrage and with widespread inequality in property holding. Marx thought that those facing a common exploitation at the hands of capital would readily come to speak with a single voice; Madison had a more astute sense of the complex relationship between class position and political identity.

Madison stated the problem clearly in his famous contribution to *The Federalist* No. 10:

> Those who hold and those who are without property have ever formed distinct interests in society. . . . The regulation of these various and interfering interests forms the principal task of modern legislation.

Indeed, in his address to the Constitutional Convention he stressed that a failure to solve this problem must lead to the elimination of either property or liberty:

> In future times a great majority of the people will not only be without land, but any other sort of property. These will either combine under the influence of their common situation; in which case the rights of property and the public liberty will not be secure in their hands, or, which is more probable, they will

become the tools of opulence and ambition; in which case there will be equal danger on the other side.[53]

Yet unlike Locke, Madison does not propose the property franchise as the key to political stability. Unlike Jefferson, he does not envision the widespread enjoyment of property. And unlike Adams, he has no faith in hereditary privilege. The rule of the few might be secured, he thought, by the perpetual division of the many: "communication and concert result from the form of government itself," he reassured readers of his tenth *Federalist* paper, so that even under "popular government," a "majority . . . included in a faction" may "be rendered by their number and local situation unable to concert" or "to discover their strength and to act in unison."[54]

The Madisonian accommodation thus represented a form of democratic elitism that has formed a critical element of North American and European political life from colonial times to the present. Daniel Walker Howe, in a thoughtful review of recent political literature, stresses that

> Madison still believed in an elite of the wise and virtuous, whose government would be best. . . . Enlarging the commonwealth would . . . he hoped, so multiply selfish special interests and their political expression in "factions" that they would cancel each other out, leaving the wise and the virtuous to govern in the interest of the community as a whole. It was not so much a philosophy of free competition as one of divide and rule.[55]

Indeed, Madison's great fear was that the legislature, as the branch of government most closely associated with electoral politics, might eclipse the power of the other branches of government, tilting the balance of power dangerously toward popular whims. Leaders must carefully avoid promulgating a critical attitude toward government, Madison asserts in *Federalist* No. 49, which might deprive the government "of that veneration, which time bestows on everything, and without which perhaps the wisest and freest governments would not possess the requisite stability."

Robert Dahl once argued, in Hartzian fashion, that Madison's fears were unfounded, and that even in the absence of his proposed buffers between government and polity, the protection of property was virtually assured:

> The men at the Convention misunderstood the dynamics of their own society. . . . They did not really understand that in an agrarian society lacking feudal institutions and possessing an open and expanding frontier, radical democracy

was almost certain to become the dominant and conventional view, and almost certain to be conservative about property.[56]

But Madison's fears *were* justified, and although the material forces that Dahl outlines were indeed operative in the period of the Jeffersonian accommodation, they were effectively counteracted by the economic expansion that characterized the next century. If Jefferson better captured the American spirit, in the long run the Madisonian analysis better anticipated the clash of rights that evolved in the course of liberal democratic capitalist development.

Indeed it may be argued that even the first half of the nineteenth century represented at least as much a Madisonian as a Jeffersonian accommodation in view of the slavery-based racial division among workers. The enduring importance of racial division to this day suggests the continuing relevance of the Madisonian accommodation.

In most countries on the European continent, the period of greatest relevance of Madisonian accommodation was more circumscribed, lying between the economic downturn of the 1870s and World War II. To gauge the effectiveness of the divide-and-conquer accommodation, we might compare the urban–agrarian relations in Germany and Sweden during their periods of industrialization. In Sweden, strong linkages between the emerging working-class movement and the independent agrarian freeholders gave rise to universal suffrage, a strong legislature, and extensive social welfare provisions.[57]

In Germany, by contrast, the working class became socially isolated and unrealistically radicalized. The Great Depression of the Bismarckian period began a consolidation of all the upper classes—the celebrated marriage of iron and rye—which was to mark German politics until World War II. If the middle classes were not to be working-class allies, perhaps the peasantry could have taken this position. Alexander Gerschenkron posed the problem by stating that

> relations between democratic labor and the peasants became a paramount problem of democracy. If the leadership of the Junkers over the peasants could be broken and some alliance between labor and peasants could be established, then the period of dangers and uncertainties for the democratic system in the country would pass.[58]

Gerschenkron makes it clear that economic difference alone cannot explain the failure of such an alliance, as small farmers and workers alike were harmed by high grain prices. Rather, cultural differences were paramount; namely, the peasants' provincialism and antiurban sentiment, and the workers' attachment to a social vision, which, quoting Gerschenkron, "threatened socialization of the soil and transformation of the free peasants, working on the land of their fathers, into hired laborers of the socialist state."[59] However, in Germany, the success of the Madisonian vision of a divided electorate of have-nots unable to unite against the haves hardly spelled the effective accommodation of capitalism and democracy; rather it provided the necessary foundation for the triumph of fascism.

The ultimate failure of the Madisonian accommodation in the first third of the twentieth century resulted from the combined effects of the gradual disappearance of nonworking-class producers, the tendency toward a homogenization of the life conditions of workers, the growing numerical and potential electoral preponderance of the working class, and the increasingly apparent need for state regulation of economic instability and growth.[60] This failure of the divide and rule accommodation was, moreover, directly related to its previous success: the continued pace of accumulation and its correlates, the progressive elimination of artisans and small farmers, the growth of a wage-labor force, and the heightened impact of the business cycle on society as a whole. The cleavages marking the heterogeneous character of the laboring classes in the early stages of industrial capitalism were progressively eroded with the incursion of capitalist economic relations into agriculture, small business, and independent proprietorship. The post–World War I era thus witnessed a period of liberalism at the crossroads. The result was the crumbling of republican government in all but the most secure of European democracies, and the polarization of liberal and fascist forces leading up to that greatest of monuments to the failure of Madisonian accommodation, World War II.

Contingent Harmonies: The Keynesian Accommodation as History

In the closing days of World War II, few could have suspected that Europe and America were on the eve of an unprecedented era of political calm and economic boom. The tumult and stagnation of the years between the two world wars seemed a more likely trajectory. The precarious modus vivendi of liberal democracy and capitalism appeared if anything to have been weakened, for the interwar years had brought not only universal adult suffrage, but a growing commitment—even on the part of business—to an economically interventionist state. The collision of property rights and personal rights could no longer be averted by the liberal walls that separated a private economy from a quarantined public state.

But paradoxically, if a case may be made on historical grounds for the enduring compatibility of capitalism and liberal democracy, it would have to draw heavily on the experience of precisely this apparently ill-starred post–World War II period.

As we have seen in our discussion of the late extension of the suffrage in Europe and the disfranchisement of blacks in the United States, the universal suffrage and civil liberties generally associated with liberal democracy simply did not exist in any country before World War I. It was only distantly approximated in a handful of nations. Between the wars, the general record of economic depression and political turmoil hardly suggests a stable accommodation of property rights and personal rights. Ominously, where liberal democracy prevailed economic collapse was the rule; the only major capitalist nations escaping the ravages of the Great Depression were Japan and Germany.[61]

But after World War II a group of some two dozen liberal democratic states emerged, the number and internal stability of which were historically without precedent. Equally important, these countries enjoyed a period of unusually rapid and stable economic growth: even setting aside the disastrous economic record of the Great Depression and the war years, per capita product in Germany, France, the United Kingdom, and the United States grew well over twice as fast during the two decades after 1950 than during the sixty years before 1929.[62]

The pessimism of the immediate post–World War II years rapidly gave way to an optimistic conception of the enduring affinity of capitalist property and democratic citizenship. Hartz's *Liberal Tradition in America* was a prescient manifestation of this new optimism. Further, as the wave of decolonization swept first Asia and later Africa, it became possible to imagine a significant flowering of democratic states in the Third World as well, along with their rapid economic advance under capitalist institutions.

The optimism of the early 1960s could not be sustained, however. A handful of the less-developed nations did experience rapid and sustained capitalist development—all under authoritarian tutelage. It is equally depressing that of the perhaps hundred nation-states in Africa, Asia, and Latin America, those that might claim to conform to even moderately stringent standards of liberal democratic rule can be counted on the fingers of one hand.

More pointedly, economic performance in the advanced capitalist nations began to falter in the mid-1960s to early 1970s. The trajectory of two sure indicators of the health of the capitalist economy attests to the end of the post–World War II economic miracle. First, the business net rate of profit fell in virtually all of the major capitalist nations; the average profit rate in the seven leading nations fell from 18 percent in the mid-1960s to 11 percent in the early 1980s.[63] Second, and partly as a result, the accumulation process slowed: in most countries investment as a fraction of total output peaked during the late 1960s or early 1970s, and has declined since.

The coexistence of rapid economic development and democratic stability in the advanced nations during the two decades or so after World War II now appears to have been based more upon a particular set of favorable circumstances than on any structural symbiosis of the two systems. These circumstances gradually eroded, in part due to the very success of the economic and political arrangements that they had fostered. The impressive record of liberal democratic capitalism during this period is the expression not of an intrinsic harmony but rather of a novel, if short-lived, alliance of democracy and capitalism which we call the *Keynesian accommodation*.

Whereas the Lockean accommodation politically *excluded* nonpropertied producers, the Jeffersonian promised *property* to the producers, and the Madisonian *divided* them, the Keynesian accommodation *assimilated* the now-powerful class of wage and salary workers. Why do not the economically dispossessed use their civil powers to dispossess the propertied? Keynes's answer to the age-worn question was that egalitarian economic policy and the expansion of state economic activity serves the interest of both capital and labor.[64]

As in the case of the other accommodations, the Keynesian accommodations in Europe and North America differed considerably among countries. Some occurred only partially, others solidified quite late in the period. But all involved a series of mutual concessions. Capital agreed to accept the integration of trade unions into the political and economic process, as well as to the guarantee of minimum living standards, relatively full employment, and granting workers a share of productivity gains. Labor accepted capitalist control over production and investment, and acknowledged the criterion of profitability as the fundamental guide to resource allocation—and relatively unencumbered capital mobility and international trade.

The political economy shaped by these accords departed in four critical ways from its predecessors. First, Keynesian regulation involved the management of aggregate demand through a large and growing state sector. Partly as a result, unemployment levels were low and the business cycle considerably tamed compared to the pre–World War II years.

Second, the established political presence of the working class led to a vast extension of the welfare state, with a resultant considerable reduction in the dependence of the working people on the labor market for material security. Among the major capitalist nations, the average fraction of the total product devoted to publicly financed consumption doubled between the early 1950s and the early 1980s. An increasing share of workers' living standards took the form of what some have termed the social wage, referring to the workers' access to goods and services secured simply by dint of citizenship rather than through the sale of labor time. The growth of the social wage represented a major extension of personal rights and, as we shall see, an impingement on the hegemony of property rights in the economy.[65]

Third, workers in general ceased disputing the right of employers to control the workplace, which allowed the consolidation of property rights in the sphere of production. Finally, the general commitment to relatively unimpeded capital mobility and an open international economy strengthened capitalist control of investment and growth, bringing to new heights the capacity of the threat of capital flight to serve as a check upon state policy deemed unfavorable to capitalist profits.

Workers and citizens now had the formal power to impinge on capitalist prerogatives and the accumulation process by virtue of their increased presence in an increasingly interventionist state. On the other hand, capitalist control of production and investment and the mobility of capital posed an effective counterweight to this popular power. The Keynesian accommodation thus promoted a strong tendency for capitalist property relations to deepen and consolidate its control of production and investment within the economy, while democratic rights were deepened and consolidated in the spheres of political life and economic policy.

Regulating this tenuous balance in the conflict of rights during the Keynesian accommodation was a distinct structure of economic growth which muted distributional conflicts between capital and labor. Three aspects of this new structure are of critical importance. First, the Keynesian logic of *demand-constrained growth* led to a distributional symbiosis: working-class living standards and profits became complementary rather than competitive objectives. This counterintuitive logic resulted because egalitarian redistributions supported an expanding level of total demand for goods and services, and because high levels of demand contributed to the relatively full utilization of productive capacity. This in turn supported a high level of profits, giving rise to a positive relationship among wage growth, the egalitarian redistributions of the welfare state, and corporate profitability.

Second, the consequent rapid growth in the demand for labor brought about shortages of trained labor and increased social and private returns to education and other forms of human resource development. The expansion of educational opportunity thus afforded another reciprocal relationship between egalitarian social policy and profitability. In addition, the rapid development of nonmanual and service-related jobs in the postwar economy favored the substitution of upward individual social mobility for changes in the rules of the game as the focus of group conflict. With a rapidly expanding pie, it became less critical to dispute the inegalitarian character of its distribution.

Third, the openness of the world economy and the military and political weakness of the resource-rich nations further enhanced the growth of the advanced nations in two distinct ways. Until the late 1960s, the international terms of trade were increasingly favorable to the advanced countries, and the role of international demand buffered and attenuated the vicissitudes of the domestic business cycle. This stabilization of demand did not in itself temper distributional conflicts, but it provided (most effectively for the United States and Great Britain) a rationale for the closing of ranks (among capital, the working class, and others) around overseas expansion and the cold war.

One political consequence of the Keynesian accords was a narrowing of the political spectrum: the deradicalization of labor in Europe and North America alike, and the parallel defeat of right-wing capital. This development was no doubt favored by the rapid rate of growth of living standards. Those who favored alternatives of either the Right or the Left were up against the most sustained period of prosperity in living memory. A second and parallel consequence was the depoliticization of capital–labor conflict. The late 1940s and early 1950s had witnessed a series of state interventions against the labor movements of many countries, and particularly against its more leftist elements. Such conflict was not abolished, but business organizations had increasingly little need (or capacity) to resort to direct governmental intervention against workers to secure the conditions for profitable production and investment. Labor discipline was secured not through state intervention but by the force of macroeconomic conditions—the prospect of capital flight and unemployment being paramount.

The Keynesian accommodation, however, led cumulatively to serious economic difficulties, which came to a head in the period between 1965 and 1974. There is a lovely irony in economist Paul Samuelson's remark that Keynesian business cycle theorists would do themselves out of a job: he had in mind permanent full employment with macroeconomic management being run as routinely as if by the post office, rather than the monetarist rout of Keynesian macropolicy which was to take place in the 1970s and 1980s. But he was correct in this: it was at least in part the very success of the Keynesian model that spelled its demise. The effectiveness of the international and domestic aspects of the policies adopted under the Keynesian accommodation, we believe, are directly implicated in the extinction of both the distributional symbiosis and the favorable conditions of profitability, both of which had been essential to its ability to contain the explosive potential of the clash of rights.

Profits were squeezed by a pincer that was in part the creation of the postwar accommodation itself—namely, cost pressures from labor that could not be passed on to consumers because of the increasingly competitive and open world economy. The combined effect of the growth of the social wage and the generally low levels of unemployment greatly enhanced labor's bargaining power by taking some of the bite out of the employer's threat of job termination.[66] Labor's new bargaining power could not be easily accommodated, however, for price increases by employers were met with losses in market shares due in part to the burgeoning of international competition, especially in the years since the late 1960s. The profit squeeze was considerably tightened in the mid-1970s, because in most countries labor was strong enough to resist paying in full the cost of the increasingly adverse international terms of trade and the rising price of oil in particular. The result was a rise in labor's share of the national income in virtually every major capitalist country extending from the early 1950s through the mid-1970s.

The conditions of labor scarcity underlying the profit squeeze point to a second development tending to erode the Keynesian accommodation. As the economies of Europe and North America more nearly approached full capacity production in the 1960s and early 1970s, the Keynesian expansion of total demand through egalitarian redistribution no longer supported higher profits. Rather it tended to step up the demand for labor, thereby further strengthening labor's bargaining position. As the advanced capitalist economies moved from a demand-constrained growth logic into a situation of both demand- and supply-constrained economic growth, the fortuitous distributional symbiosis of the Keynesian accommodation evaporated. The capitalist economy increasingly resembled a zero-sum game.

This erosion of the conditions for both capitalist profitability and the hegemony of an egalitarian public ideology under the Keynesian accommodation is the background to the monetarist resurgence in the 1970s. But the monetarist strategy—of restoring the power of capital by escalating the scarcity of jobs and halting or reversing the growth of the social wage—has itself proved remarkably costly. In part as a result of the social policies of the Keynesian accommodation, the neutral rate of unemployment—the unemployment rate at which the share of labor wages as a claim on net output neither rises nor falls—has drifted upward. Ever more unemployment is needed to maintain a given level of power of capital over labor. The result has been a sharply rising cost of using labor market slack to control labor. And under these new conditions, only *very* high unemployment rates over prolonged periods appear to be able to shift the distributional advantage toward capital. And high levels of unemployment generally are associated with slack demand for output, resulting in high levels of unutilized capital stock and lagging rates of technological innovation—hardly a prescription for buoyant profits.[67]

The monetarist revival of the 1970s was an attempt to deploy the logic of the market against labor's rising power, to reverse labor's encroachments on capital without substantial direct state intervention. The sluggish economic growth of the 1970s, and the (even to monetarists) surprisingly long period of recession required to turn the tide against labor in Britain and the United States since 1979, testifies to the monumental costs (to capital as well as to labor) of this attempt at a market-based system of labor discipline.

The Keynesian accommodation, in the end, offered only a temporary respite in the clash of rights. Like the Lockean, Jeffersonian, and Madisonian visions before it, the Keynesian accommodation represented a structure defining the range of applicability of property rights and personal rights. For a time this modus operandi contained the expansionary logics of both. But it did nothing to abolish the underlying contradiction between economic privilege and democratic rights, which has constituted the warp of the rich tapestry of social conflict and solidarity extending over the past two centuries in the now-liberal democratic capitalist nations.

Conclusion: Liberalism, Socialism, and Democracy

If we are to affirm the notion that the political history of the advanced capitalist societies has been etched by the collision of personal rights and property rights, we cannot avoid the implication that socialism—as a language and a program, if not as a movement—has been largely irrelevant to this evolution. Where workers' movements have mobilized more than handfuls of isolated militants—as in England in the early nineteenth century, in Germany in the late nineteenth and early twentieth century, or in Italy or Spain in the twentieth century—their inspiration and their solidarity has been based more on the demand for democracy than for socialism. This is the case in Italy, Spain, and Germany, where many of the leaders of these movements were Marxists, and in England, where the pre-Marxist chartists took their lead from Thomas Paine and other radical democrats. Socialist movements are thus no exception to the rule: mass radical political forces in the liberal democratic capitalist societies have not introduced a new language of politics; they have exploited the ambiguities and contradictions of liberal democratic discourse.

One may bemoan the impressive hegemony of liberal discourse or one may celebrate it; but one need not dwell on it. It has simply been part of the discursive landscape that political actors inhabit. We use it as we will and fashion it to our own ends if we can, but we seek to escape it only at the cost of becoming historically irrelevant.

Not surprisingly, where workers' demands for democratic rule have been resisted or thwarted, the result was commonly a simultaneous popularization and radicalization of demands. Where progress toward universal suffrage and the extension of civil liberties was evident, by contrast, socialist parties languished. Lenin insightfully attributed the lack of broad-based radicalism in the U.S. working class to the "absence of any big, nation-wide democratic tasks facing the proletariat."[68] Paraphrasing the similar views of Lewis Corey (an early twentieth-century international secretary of the U.S. Communist party) concerning Europe as well as the United States, Harvey Klehr writes:

> Once democratic rights largely prevailed . . . and domestic politics became a struggle for the achievement of socialist goals, the single-minded emphasis on the interests of the working class prevented socialists from making successful appeals to other groups whose support was necessary for obtaining a majority.[69]

Engels, too, had earlier sketched the paradoxical interpretation that Louis Hartz would later popularize: no feudalism, no socialism.[70]

But Lewis Corey gave this position a novel twist:

> Organized socialism was essentially an expression of the democratic backwardness of Europe. . . . We must recognize and build upon the fact that the American working class rejected the older types of European reformist socialism not because it was backward but because it was ahead of the working classes of Europe.[71]

Though perhaps objecting to the apparent opposition between socialism and democracy, Corey might have applauded Peter Bachrach's assessment:

> If any lesson can be learned from the rich history of working-class struggle in America, it is that militancy and radicalism have been nurtured within the existing hegemonic order . . . within the context of American experience, democracy rather than socialism is subversive; our history shows that democracy, taken seriously, disrupts the existing distribution of power.[72]

Despite the impressive variety of the particular histories involved, we suspect that Bachrach's analysis may be extended to the other liberal democratic capitalist societies.

But how might democracy be a radical demand in those nations characterized by the "absence of any . . . democratic tasks facing the proletariat"? Our answer is that the conflict of democratic personal rights and capitalist property rights does not end with the extension of the suffrage and the granting of rights of trade union association. Lenin's overly generous characterization of the extent of democracy in early twentieth-century United States like the English chartist conviction that the tasks of democracy were reducible to representation in the state, exhibit a common flaw. Both overlook the authoritarian political structure of the capitalist economy.

3

Economy: The Political Foundations of Production and Exchange

THE CLASH of property rights and personal rights in liberal democratic capitalism is nowhere more evident than in current debate and social conflict concerning the economy. While Robert Dahl, one of the leading political theorists of our day, wonders pointedly why property rights should predominate over the democratic rights of workers in the modern corporation, a U.S. district court upholds a business that has barred a federally mandated safety inspection of its plant on the grounds that private property is nothing if not the right to exclude.[1] Both reflect the inherent ambiguity of the appropriate range of application of the fundamental rights structuring political discourse and shaping public policy and in the liberal democratic capitalist nations. The erosion of the post–World War II Keynesian accommodation seems likely to intensify the collision of rights and to make the economy a major terrain on which the competing claims of property and citizenship will clash. For the collapse of this accommodation has dramatized the conflictual nature of the capitalist economy not only as a system of income distribution but also as a structure of command. At the same time the stagnation of living standards and widening circles of economic instability have heightened the saliency of economic concerns in people's everyday lives.

Economic democracy is on the agenda today, in part because the insufficiency of the Keynesian focus on income redistribution has become increasingly apparent. However well attuned to the needs of the economic crisis of the 1930s, the expansion of the welfare state does not, by itself, provide a coherent response to the economic problems of the late twentieth century. Perhaps more important, the global mobility of capital has made it clear that further pursuit of egalitarian redistribution will be severely constrained by the threat of capital flight unless it is accompanied by an effective democratic accountability of investment. Equally, in the absence of a profound democratic restructuring of the social organization of work, greater economic security for workers is likely to be associated with an intensification of work resistance, mounting costs of supervision and surveillance, and an enduring crisis of productivity. If Keynes and the Great Depression politicized the distribution of income, the 1970s and 1980s have politicized the economy as a system of control.

Dahl's query concerning the priority of democratic rights over property rights in the modern corporation is motivated by his perception of the economy as an arena in which life and death powers are wielded by employers. To concur that wealth is indeed power risks belaboring the obvious. The statement that, say, the chief executive officers of the top hundred multinational firms in the world exercise a significant amount of power may evoke the same degree of astonishment as the observation that dogs bark. The distinguished modern jurist Abram Chayes writes:

All the instruments agree: the modern corporation wields economic and social power of the highest consequence for the condition of our polity. Let us resist this conclusion, or belabor it no further. Let us accept it as our first premise.[2]

However evident to the practical-minded and observant, this truism finds no place in liberal theory. Liberal political theory, which deals with power, does not deal with the economy, while liberal economic theory ignores politics. The respected economist Abba Lerner speaks for his profession in his proud observation: "An economic transaction is a solved political problem. Economics has gained the title of queen of the social sciences by choosing *solved* political problems as its domain."[3]

Liberal theory thus renders the power of capital invisible: democrats cannot assail economic power within liberal theory because they lack the tools for making such power visible. However, the disappearance of power when one moves from the practical world of economics to its theoretical models is based on an easily exposed liberal sleight of hand, for it is the private–public partition that makes power invisible in the economy, and this partition, we will show, is wholly arbitrary.

The liberal position may be summarized as follows. The principle of liberty holds that individuals have certain rights which a just society ought not violate. The principle of democracy holds that the just society must ensure popular sovereignty: people ought to have a voice—and in some sense an equal voice—in the substantive decisions that affect their lives. Liberal democratic theory generally supports the application of both liberal and democratic principles to the state, but only the principle of liberty to the economy. We contend that that liberal democratic theory supplies no coherent justification for this asymmetric treatment of the state and the capitalist economy.

In this chapter we shall seek the source of this bias in the economic principles implicit in liberal political theory, trace these principles to their origin in neoclassical economic theory, and suggest an alternative approach in which the political structure of the capitalist economy is highlighted. In our alternative model both liberty and democracy will apply in assessing economic institutions, and hence we will be capable of adjudicating in a balanced manner the conflicting demands of property rights and personal rights.

Let us begin by defining some terms. We shall call "public" those spheres of social life over which the twin norms of liberty and democracy may rightly be held to apply. Clearly liberal democratic theory considers the state in this sense a public institution. Let us call "private" those spheres over which only conditions of liberty may be rightly held to apply. Many modes of expression of individual rights clearly fit into this category—freedom of conscience, expression, association, and choice, among others. Let us also take as an indispensable assumption of democratic theory the proposition that a sphere of social life is to be considered public if its operation involves the socially consequential exercise of power.

"Socially consequential exercise of power" itself deserves some elucidation. By an "exercise of power" we mean an action that causes others to act in ways they otherwise would not, yet goes beyond the mere protection of one's negative liberties. Refusing to marry someone, for instance, is not an exercise of power. By a socially consequential action we mean one that both substantively affects the lives of others and the character of which reflects the will and interests of the actor.

Liberal social theory's arbitrarily asymmetric treatment of state and economy stems, we believe, from the untenable notion that the capitalist economy is a private sphere—in other words, that its operation does not involve the socially consequential exercise of power. Most liberals go on to argue that the economy, perhaps with suitable state regulation, should *remain* private. This, however, is beside the point, for if our argument is correct, the capitalist economy is not *now* a private sphere, and the basic issue concerns its proper organization as a *public* sphere. Recognizing this fact, we believe, renders political economy relevant to the historical concerns of groups who have struggled for the consistent extension of personal rights to the economy.

We shall argue that the capitalist economy confers three types of socially consequential power upon capital.* The first power that owners of firms exercise—often through managers and supervisory personnel—is *command over production*, according to which the organization of the work process and the ordering about of workers are tailored to the interests of capital. Second, owners exercise *command over investment*, imparting a systematic bias to the range of organizational forms of business enterprise permitted to flourish. Finally, owners exercise *influence over state economic policy*, through which substantive limits are placed upon the range of democratic control over economic life. These assertions may be sustained even for an economy and a state that meet the liberal ideal. Our argument in no way relies on monopolistic violations of perfectly competitive economic principles. Nor does it rest on any failure of ideal liberal democratic procedures.

Of course, to assert the public nature of the capitalist economy is to challenge the fundamental liberal distinction between private and public. It is curious that the theoretical specification of this critical boundary is not easily reconstructed from the standard texts. Nor is a defense of the boundary prominent among the familiar themes of political philosophy. A rather powerful argument for the notion that the capitalist economy is private may, however, be constructed on the basis of two central propositions from neo-

---

* The term *capital* is intentionally vague. We do not suggest where exactly this power comes to rest—upon owners, stockholders, managers, boards of directors, the wealthy, and so on—or even whether it is ultimately possessed by persons at all. This issue will become important, however, in our subsequent discussion of the business corporation as a "chartered freedom." In the meantime, we will simply speak of owners, bosses, managers, or whatever seems appropriate.

classical economics. The first asserts that the exchange between capitalist and worker has the same character as other and presumably "private" exchanges: the employer thus has no more power over the worker than the shopper has over the grocer, or any other buyer has over a seller. We shall call this the *labor commodity* proposition.

The second proposition asserts that the existence of competitive capital markets divorces the substantive control of economic activity in business and finance from the ownership of assets: any entrepreneur with a better mousetrap or a better way of doing business can readily find the necessary credit to set up in business. According to this view it is not owners of capital but the dictates of competitive survival that determine economic outcomes. We will call this the *asset neutrality* proposition.

These two propositions, if true, would indeed undercut the major ground for considering the economy public. They imply that economic outcomes—whether the level of income, the organization of work, the rate of unemployment, or the degree of environmental pollution—are actually determined by the initial distribution of wealth, available technologies, and the preferences of consumers and workers. Thus what appears to be substantive power (wielded by owners or their delegated managers) in commanding production and investment is appearance alone. The decision maker is merely implementing an allocation of resources the determinants of which in no way include the substantive power of capital, except, of course, insofar as capital exerts influence upon state economic policy.* The resulting invisibility of power in the competitive capitalist economy is celebrated by Joseph Schumpeter:

> The means of production and the productive process have in general no real leader, or rather the real leader is the consumer. The people who direct business firms only execute what is prescribed for them by wants. . . . Individuals have influence only in so far as they are consumers, only in so far as they express a demand. . . . In no other sense is there a personal direction of production.[4]

* Strictly speaking, the validity of the labor commodity and asset neutrality propositions would imply the absence of economic power only if market clearance entailed a *unique* configuration of prices and quantities. This highly untenable presumption of uniqueness is widely assumed in traditional economic reasoning. For instance, economists who should know better regularly recommend that markets ought to be allowed to "determine" prices. However, the notion that market clearance determines a unique configuration of prices and quantities in no way follows from the general models of traditional economic theory, and it is true only under quite implausible conditions. No doubt a theory of economic power could be built on this nonuniqueness of market competition, but we have not chosen to do so.

On the basis of this reasoning, Robert Nozick, in addressing the problem of worker alienation, completely divorces the problem from the distribution of power:

> How does and could capitalism respond to workers' desires for meaningful work? If the productivity of the workers in a factory *rises* when the work tasks are segmented so as to be more meaningful, then individual owners pursuing profits so will reorganize the productive process.... [If the alternative] is *less efficient* ... the workers in the factories themselves might desire meaningful work. ... and they [may be] willing to give up something (some wages) in order to work at meaningfully segmented jobs.[5]

The result, according to this view, is that the nature of work task segmentation is dictated by workers' own preferences, given a technologically determined trade off between desirable work and desired goals and services. A more perfect example of the application of the labor commodity proposition would be difficult indeed to discover.

But there are two characteristics of labor which set it apart from the general attributes of commodities in a neoclassical model, and which together invalidate the labor commodity proposition. In the first place the worker is inseparable from the labor service supplied. Labor is embodied in and inalienable from people. Furthermore, the general superiority of production techniques brings together in one location, and in direct interaction, the labors of distinct workers. Together these two characteristics imply that capitalist production is a social relationship among persons, a relationship that cannot be reduced to an exchange of property titles. The capitalist enterprise brings into social and physical interaction not only the labor services supplied to the employer but the very suppliers of these services. As we will see, it follows that major aspects of the contract between capitalist and worker—especially those concerning the quality and intensity of labor services delivered—are not guaranteed by the formal terms of contract; instead they are directly contingent upon the capitalist's control of the work process. From these premises it will be shown that the command of capital over labor represents a socially significant exercise of power.

The failure of the labor commodity proposition would be of slight importance, however, if the asset neutrality proposition were true. In that case, any democratically constituted group of workers could, given the soundness of their proposed enterprise, obtain the capital necessary to set themselves up for business in direct opposition to capitalist-controlled firms. The fact that few such firms exist would then imply either that democratically controlled production is technically or organizationally unsound, or that workers prefer an undemocratic to a democratic working environment. The unaccountable power of the employer might nonetheless be criticized on democratic grounds, of course, but the critic would need to explain why the workers' preferences for material reward over democracy should not dictate the most appropriate form of work organization as long as conditions of scarcity prevail.

Yet we shall argue that democratically controlled firms are, all else being equal, economically more efficient than their capitalist controlled counterparts in the straightforward sense that they are able to produce the same outputs with less inputs. In this context, it is the failure of the asset neutrality proposition coupled with the fact that workers are generally not independently wealthy that account for the fact that worker-controlled firms do not win out in the competitive marketplace.

Everyday facts should convince most observers of the dubious status of the asset neutrality proposition. Capital funds are *not* available to all comers on an equal basis. There is something ludicrous in the idea that a group of workers might borrow money to set up in competition with U.S. Steel or IBM.* The privileged access to funds enjoyed by those already well endowed may result from purposeful discrimination against the less well-to-do. But it can be shown to arise quite simply from the dictates of competitive profit maximization on the part of banks and other lenders.

The asset neutrality and labor commodity propositions share the following weakness: enforcing the contractual quid pro quo is conventionally taken as unproblematic, when in fact enforcement is a *central concern* of, in the one case, the purchaser of labor and, in the other, the lender of capital funds. The lender is particularly concerned with the possibility of default, and to avoid default, strives to establish conditions under which the *borrower* as well as the *lender* stands to lose from default, and hence will be properly motivated to avoid it. In the case of the lending of capital, the symmetrical position of buyer and seller is ensured normally by the requirement of *collateral*, itself represented by the possession of wealth by the borrower.

---

* It should be clear that the asset neutrality proposition is required in this strong form to justify the traditional liberal position on economic power. If a small group of democratically organized workers (for example, "partners") with a new idea or a new product do manage to attract capital funds, it is in their interest to shift to a corporate form in the process of expansion, in order to avoid sharing their gains with new workers. Indeed, this phenomenon is quite common in contemporary capitalism.

The power of capital, then, includes the power to lend, to borrow, and to invest. The capital market, rather than fostering a separation of asset ownership and economic power, virtually guarantees that the latter will serve the interests of the former.* Credit rationing according to prior ownership of assets is the only rational policy for profit-maximizing, competitive, noncollusive financial institutions—even when they are not prejudiced on general principles against firms organized in a noncapitalist manner.

The Economics of Unsolved Political Problems

Capitalism is not merely a system of private property and market exchange of goods and services. It is also a wage labor system in which individuals (workers) transfer, within certain contractual and legal limits, the disposition over their activities to others (capitalists), in return for a wage. The centrality of wage labor to capitalism is frequently overlooked. It is often presumed that general considerations of exchange and private property are sufficient to establish the justice of capitalism. Robert Nozick, in his sophisticated analysis of property and the state, considers the issue of wage labor only after having established his major propositions, and then only as an afterthought. Nozick affirms the general principle that "a person who acquires a holding in accordance with the principle of justice in transfer, from someone also entitled to the holding, is entitled to the holding," but he nowhere discusses whether the hiring of a worker is "in accordance with the principle of justice in transfer."[6] Similarly, John Rawls, in his incisive A Theory of Justice, while affording lexical priority to liberty, never inquires as to whether liberty is violated by the surrender of disposition over one's services in return for a wage.[7]

Yet capitalism is not even *in its most pure form* simply a system of exchange; it is always a system of employment as well. Capitalism, as opposed to simple commodity production or market economies in general, implies

* We are here simplifying considerably. State loan guarantees and the lender's direct participation in management decisions, among other mechanisms, can serve as complements or alternatives to collateral requirements for lenders. Direct control over production and investment may be delegated by owners to managerial and other groups for whom the threat of dismissal replaces collateral as the means of contract enforcement. Corporate behavior need not merely reflect the preferences of investors.

the existence of enterprises in which production takes place according to the wage-labor relationship. On this basis, capitalism consistently confers upon a specific minority (the owners of capital and their representatives) a form of effective command to be used for the satisfaction of their private ends. Or more bluntly, as Thomas Hobbes put it, "To have servants is to have power." His archaic language reminds us that the generic term *employee* itself had to await the full flowering of the capitalist system in the nineteenth century.[8]

Legal doctrine in the United States for the past century has wavered between the poles of contradiction entailed by its penchant for dealing with labor as simply another commodity, and its commonsense awareness that labor is quite unlike the textbook commodity. In 1898 the U.S. Supreme Court noted that

> proprietors . . . and their operatives do not stand upon an equality. . . . The former naturally desire to obtain as much labor as possible from their employees, while the latter are often induced by the fear of discharge to conform to regulations which their judgement, fairly exercised, would pronounce to be detrimental.[9]

On this point there is little fire to be exchanged across the no-man's-land between Marxian and liberal economists. The capitalist enterprise exists *precisely* as a system of authority within a system of markets. We shall see presently that the sharply contrasting conclusions of Marxists and liberals concerning the authority of those who command the firm derive from more subtle differences. The liberal asserts the insubstantial scope of action of the putative powers of the owners of the firm, while the Marxist affirms its status as socially consequential power.

The existence of a structure of command within the firm is not at issue. The neoclassical economist D. H. Robertson, contrasting the structure of command in the enterprise with the invisible hand of the market, notes that firms are "islands of conscious power in this ocean of unconscious cooperation."[10] Moreover, "If a workman moves from department Y to department X," writes R. H. Coase, whose work represents the locus classicus of the modern neoclassical theory of the firm, "he does not go because of a change in relative prices, but because he is ordered to do so. . . . The distinguishing mark of the firm is the supersession of the price mechanism."[11] The existence of the firm in a capitalist economy, Coase goes on to suggest, demonstrates the inferior profitability and inefficiency of conducting all economic transactions on the basis of the contractual exchange of goods and services.

We conclude that the capitalist economy cannot be judged to be private simply by virtue of the prominent role played by markets. A no less important role is played by firms, institutions that liberal thinkers are more than ready to deem authoritarian.

Nonetheless, the liberal may still argue that the labor exchange, as a voluntary relationship among uncoerced individuals, deserves the status of what Nozick calls "justice in transfer." The critic might ask whether the exchange is indeed voluntary, given that workers, who must work in order to live and do not own the means of production, have no choice but to enter into an exchange with at least one capitalist: the unequal distribution of property may be such as to render "free choice" purely formal. But this criticism of the liberal position is not persuasive, even granting the generally unequal power of the exchanging parties. We would not say, for example, that one's choice of a doctor to cure an illness is "purely formal," and hence involuntary, because one must choose *at least one* doctor.[12] Nor is this argument adequate to our task here, as it in no way challenges the notion of the capitalist economy as an essentially private sphere. At most it suggests a *redistribution* of property or income—or a substitution of public for private property.

Our argument, therefore, does not challenge the voluntary nature of the labor exchange. Rather, we shall suggest that even within liberal democratic theory not all voluntary exchanges are considered just; hence it might not be inconsistent for a liberal to consider the labor exchange as one of these voluntary but unjust transfers. Let us accept the proposition that if individuals have just title to their holdings, and if they voluntarily exchange some of these holdings, the result of the exchange must satisfy liberal criteria of justice. But must the result satisfy *democratic* criteria of justice as well? If no public institution has been created or transformed in the process of exchange, the answer would seem to be affirmative. But do social relations arrived at through private acts of voluntary accord thereby acquire the status themselves as private? Although this assumption is often taken as a presumption of liberalism (as in Nozick's notion of procedural justice), it cannot be sustained.

First, liberal political philosophy generally holds that a state itself may be justly created under certain conditions through the mutual and voluntary accord of free and independent individuals. Yet the state is surely a "public" institution, and is to be judged according to its conformity with the principles of democracy as much as those of liberty, however private and voluntary the compact leading to its creation.

Second, to the liberal, the injustice of slavery does not lie in its representing a state of servitude entered into involuntarily. Indeed, one could easily imagine conditions motivating an individual's *voluntarily* to assume the status of slave (for example, personal comfort, reverence for the master, or the benefit of loved ones). Slavery may be deemed unjust either because it involves a violation of personal rights, however entered, or because it represents a public, undemocratic, and hence unjust relation of domination. Thus in liberal society slavery becomes a status into which individuals are *forbidden* to enter. After all, if we accept the liberal principle that the effects of voluntary contracts based upon just holdings cannot violate the principle of liberty, the prohibition of slavery would be difficult to justify save on its being a "public" institution and hence accountable on the additional grounds of conformity with democratic norms.*

These examples demonstrate that liberal democratic theory recognizes that public institutions may be created through voluntary agreement, and hence may be appropriate areas for the application of democratic political norms. The point of the foregoing examples is simply that institutional arrangements resulting from freely contracted exchanges may subvert the very conditions of their legitimacy; that is, the equality and reciprocity of participating individuals. We submit, then, that the refusal to assess economic institutions according to the joint norms of liberty and democracy cannot be justified by recourse to the voluntary nature of the contracts thereby generated.

Accordingly, in order to uphold the notion of the capitalist economy as private, liberal democratic theory must sustain the claim that the command of capital over labor *in fact* represents no socially consequential exercise of power.

Liberal economic theory in general holds that this is the case. According to the neoclassical theory of the firm, although some individual or group actually commands, who really commands is theoretically indeterminate

---

* It might be argued that the traditional liberal treatment, rather than being arbitrary, merely involves the unstated assumption that private agreements generate public institutions only when they sanction the use of force among its participants. It seems clear, however, that (at least contemporary) liberals would remain dissatisfied with slavery even were the master required to enforce his claims against his slaves only by recourse to the judicial and penal institutions of the slavery-sanctioning state.

and without social consequence. It is theoretically indeterminate because in a competitive market system, workers are just as capable of hiring capital (that is, obtaining loans and renting productive equipment) as capitalists are capable of hiring workers. In Paul Samuelson's words, "in a perfectly competitive market it really doesn't matter who hires whom: so let labor hire 'capital.' "[13] Furthermore, the locus of command is without social consequence because the rational allocation of resources within the enterprise will produce the same organization of production whatever the locus of control, and market competition will ensure that enterprises that do not rationally allocate resources will be eliminated.

This reasoning is clearly the underpinning of Nozick's affirmation of the labor commodity proposition. It is a strong argument indeed; if correct, it might justify the treatment of the apparent power relations in the firm as socially inconsequential. The reasoning implicitly assumes, however, the labor commodity proposition: that the contract between "management" and worker arising from the exchange of labor for a wage is not essentially distinct from the textbook rendition of a market exchange of goods or services among their owners, an exchange in which the costs of contract enforcement are so small as to be negligible. But this is not the case.

The Specificity of Labor

Why *does* it matter who hires whom? It matters because the labor contract does not enforce itself, nor is it enforced primarily by the state; it is enforced by the employer, and the costs of enforcement depend on the social organization of production, or more prosaically, on who hires whom.

Neoclassical economic theory has generally ignored the costs of contract enforcement. When the terms of a market exchange or contracted agreement are violated, the injured party simply seeks restitution by recourse to the courts. By contrast, the special nature of the problem of enforcement of the contract between employer and employee was a central concern of Karl Marx, who referred to it as the problem of extracting "labor" from "labor-power." The capitalist purchases the *capacity* of the worker to produce (labor-power), and is then faced with the problem of actually *eliciting* an adequate level of work (labor).[14]

We may illustrate this point by noting the substantive difference between an employee and an independent supplier of services to the enterprise. In hiring a worker, the employer becomes bound to supply a wage or salary, as well as to comply with other jointly contracted terms. But the employee does *not*, in return, generally agree to supply any specific service to any specified standard. Where such specifics are fully described in the contract, the supplier is not an employee but rather an independent contractor, as in the case of an electrical, plumbing, or refuse removal service supplied to the enterprise by an independent agent.[15] By contrast, the worker agrees formally only to participate in the enterprise and conform to its rules and regulations, for the duration of the contract. The independent contractor is paid for a job done, irrespective of the time it takes to do it; the worker is paid by the amount of time on the job irrespective of the amount of work that is done.

In hiring workers, then, the capitalist enterprise does not enforce a previously agreed upon exchange, but rather determines the content of the exchange itself. In this sense the amount and quality of labor performed by employees is not what Abba Lerner termed a "solved political problem," and the locus of command must be considered socially consequential.[16]

In recent years the general issue of contract enforcement has been taken up by some neoclassical economists, who have argued its centrality to the very logic of market behavior.[17] The grounds for this position include the following four points. Contracts rarely (if ever) make provisions for all eventualities, and a buyer may consider carefully the "reputation" of a seller for resolving disputed issues in a fair and equitable manner.[18] Contracts require interpretation, and the aggrieved buyer is not guaranteed success in a legal suit. Some of the consequences of contract violation may be so severe that the violator does not have the financial means of compensation. Finally, the very monitoring of the contract's provisions may require costs of supervision and information gathering which are not recoverable even in the case of contract violation.

Clearly the labor contract involves all of these problems in severe form. By agreeing to work for a capitalist, the worker makes no commitment as to exactly *what* will be done, with what degree of intensity, or how well. Also, the employer has no recourse to civil law for the recovery of damages in case the amount or quality of work is deemed unacceptable. The worker does not usually have the financial means to reimburse the employer for sloth, negligence, or willful destruction. Finally, costs of surveillance, supervision, and information gathering are normally much greater for monitoring work than for monitoring the delivery of general goods and services for which the capitalist has contracted.

But the labor exchange is not merely a severe case of the more general problem of contract enforcement. Two special characteristics set it apart.[19] First, the service delivered by the worker cannot be separated from the person of the worker. Thus the conventional model of commodity exchange, in which buyer and seller meet, exchange, and then part with their new holdings, does not obtain in the case of the labor exchange, in which the seller both maintains continual control over the service supplied and is in constant contact with the forms of surveillance instituted by the buyer to ensure contract enforcement. Second, by gathering workers together under one roof, the process of production establishes a network of direct social relations among the sellers of labor. In contrast to the competitive commodity market situation, where each supplier to the enterprise is unrelated to and indeed in general unknown to each other supplier, the social nature of production continuously brings sellers of labor services into face-to-face contact. This means they are capable of at least partially coordinating their behavior vis-à-vis the buyer of their services (the capitalist), thus raising or lowering the level of services provided as well as the degree and cost of surveillance required to elicit this level of services.

The special nature of the labor exchange may be illustrated by a simple model of a capitalist firm that purchases labor and other inputs, and sells the commodity produced in perfectly competitive markets.[20] We may assume, for simplicity, that labor is homogeneous and that the capitalist enjoys complete information concerning worker attributes. The effectiveness of capitalist command over workers depends ultimately on the capitalist's power to terminate the labor contract. The problem for the capitalist is to devise a control strategy that will minimize the cost (in wages and surveillance) of a unit of actual work done. All else being equal, the worker will work harder the higher the probability that nonwork will be detected, and the greater the income loss suffered through being fired.

In general, for a given amount of labor actually performed, the employer will face a tradeoff between paying the worker a higher wage and subjecting the worker to more intense (and hence more costly) surveillance. The reasoning is as follows. Suppose, for simplicity, that the penalty for being caught working at a level of intensity less than that dictated by management is termination of contract (firing the worker). Then, an increase in the wage will raise the *cost* to the worker of being fired, while an increase in the level of surveillance will increase the *probability* of detection. A decrease in the wage rate will necessarily require an increase in surveillance to maintain a given "expected cost of working below standard intensity" and to elicit the same unit of work performed. It follows from standard economic reasoning that the capitalist will maximize profits by choosing a wage rate and a level of surveillance cost to balance these costs against the associated gains in work intensity.

It remains to be shown that the locus of command in the firm will affect the allocation of resources, and hence that the exercise of power in the capitalist enterprise must be considered socially consequential. Why might we expect this to be the case?

Costs of surveillance exist whatever the locus of command: no matter who hires whom, some system of control is necessary to discourage self-interested dawdling on the job. But we may provide two reasons why these costs would be lower when the locus of command resides in workers themselves. Individuals identify more completely with the goals of an institution when they are involved in participation in its governance and when it is perceived as operating in their interest. Empirical evidence supports this position.[21] A shift in the locus of command to workers is likely to lower their desire to resist work. Because each worker in a worker-controlled enterprise is harmed when other workers nap on the job, coalitions among workers aimed at increasing the costs of surveillance will be weaker and less stable, thereby reducing the individual worker's opportunity to waste time with impunity. In general, the costs of surveillance will be lower in this situation, as it is in the interests of each worker to discourage below-standard work intensity on the part of others.

In other words, the change in the locus of command from capital to labor may be expected to reduce the wage and surveillance costs of generating a given level of labor performed. Even assuming no change in the cost of a unit of surveillance, and assuming the same wage (representing for each worker the cost of being fired), there could be a substantive saving in surveillance costs simply because less surveillance would be required. (A simple reduction in surveillance, leaving the cost of job loss unchanged, will not generally be the optimal strategy for the worker-controlled firm to follow, but this does not affect our argument.) The intent of this discussion is to show not that capitalist production is wasteful (although it does suggest this), but rather that it is public or, more specifically, that because the locus of command in the firm matters it represents the socially consequential exercise of power. The labor commodity proposition, which implies that the locus of command is not socially consequential, must be rejected.

We must, however, deal with one reasonable objection to our analysis. If democratic production decreases the costs of eliciting labor, why would not the capitalist transfer command to workers in order to maximize profits? Such a transfer, should the capitalist maintain control over the net revenues of the enterprise, would increase the workers' *ability* to resist work by virtue of their more complete control over the production process, without decreasing the individual and collective *incentives* to resist work, as these incentives are predicated upon their sharing the proceeds of increased output. In effect, the cost of eliciting labor might in this case increase rather than decrease and the worker-run but capitalist-owned firm might make lower profits than the conventional capitalist enterprise.

Power, Production, and Competition

The influence of the labor commodity proposition extends far beyond its service in hiding the power of capital. It also is routinely and effectively employed to provide arguments that undermine the democratic critique of the capitalist economy. The labor commodity proposition justifies the undemocratic and hierarchical organization of work on grounds of economic efficiency; it denies that racial, sexual, or other forms of discrimination are compatible with market competition; it interprets unemployment as the voluntary choice of workers unwilling to accept the market valuation of their services. But these justifications are theoretically invalid; they implicate traditional economic theory in substantive predictions quite at variance with empirical evidence. We shall see that our attention to the political aspects of the labor exchange avoids these problems.

The argument that democratic forms of work must be economically inefficient is based on the following logic. Capitalists are forced by competitive pressures to minimize costs. If the labor commodity proposition were true, then the real price and quantity of labor services would be determined in the sphere of market exchange, and cost minimization would clearly entail the utilization of optimal technologies and a technically efficient organization of production. If democratic decision making were efficient, it would thus be chosen by market forces alone. Moreover, it would follow that an aspect of the production process would be altered by a change in the ownership or decision-making structure of the firm only if this change altered input or output prices. Hence a politically induced shift to democratic decision making could alter the social organization of production only at the cost of lower productivity. But, of course, it follows by *precisely the same reasoning* that owners of capital would have no interest in concerning themselves with the control of production! Yet in fact there is an intimate and undeniable association between control of wealth and control of production in all capitalist countries. The neoclassical argument must be incorrect; we shall see why subsequently.

Turning to the question of discrimination, the labor commodity proposition implies that the same competitive pressures toward cost minimization which lead the capitalist to avoid paying more for a ton of coal than the minimal price consistent with securing the supply would impel the employer to seek the lowest price of an hour of equivalent labor, preferring to hire women rather than men, or blacks rather than whites, should their wages (for equivalent levels of productive activity) be lower. Those who, for racist, sexist, or other reasons, persist in hiring high-priced white male labor will be eliminated by competition. (This is a reaffirmation of Friedman's position, cited in chapter 2.) Nevertheless, there is convincing evidence that differences in wages among races and between sexes both persist over time, and yet cannot be accounted for adequately in terms of differences in productive capacity. Again, the implications of the labor commodity proposition are at variance with the facts of economic life.

The labor commodity proposition bears a further implication: any unsold units of labor must be considered to be voluntarily withheld from the market. For example, when there is a glut of shirts on the clothing market, the excess supply can generally be eliminated if the seller is willing to lower the price. By this reasoning, unemployment must be considered voluntary, based on a refusal to work for a lower wage. Involuntary unemployment could still occur as the result of frictions in the labor market adjustment process, but we would have no more reason in the long run to expect excess supply than excess demand in the labor market. Yet there is a consistent tendency for capitalist economies to suffer significant levels of unemployment even in situations in which institutional constraints on wage reductions are weak or inoperative.

Our model of the labor exchange addresses these shortcomings of the labor commodity proposition by noting that the production process may be represented by two relationships. The first is appropriative: the combination of labor with nonlabor inputs to produce a given output. The second is distributive: the employer's effort to allocate resources toward inducing an increased level of work intensity, and garnering an adequate portion of the net revenue generated by the enterprise. The neoclassical economic theory of production addresses the appropriate relationship under the rubric of production functions; but it pointedly ignores the distributive relationship.

The problem of labor intensity arises, we should stress, not because labor is naturally unpleasant, as the theory of the "disutility of labor" from Adam Smith to the present would have it. Rather, the way in which the worker experiences work, and the resulting motivations, resentments, and resistances derive in important measure from the social organization of the production process itself. Indeed, the social structure of the capitalist production process—especially its authoritarian and exploitative form—induces conflict over the organization and intensity of work.

The market in labor serves to determine not a market-clearing wage but rather the power of the employer in implementing his profit-maximizing strategies. Recall that the employer's major formal power over the worker is the right to fire. The proper behavior of the worker must be induced, in the last instance, by the threat of firing, which clearly depends on job scarcity and hence on the state of the labor market. (The employer also has the prerogative to promote or not to promote. The same argument could be made using the threat of nonpromotion in place of the threat of firing.)

The employer may raise the cost to the worker of pursuing a nonwork strategy by any one of the following three counterstrategies: (1) raising the expected cost of losing one's job; (2) raising the probability of being fired if detected pursuing a nonwork strategy; and (3) raising the probability of being detected if pursuing a nonwork strategy. By investigating the application of these strategies, we may understand why the three implications of the labor as commodity view of production—efficient production, no discrimination, and no involuntary unemployment—are false. Let us consider each.

The probability that a nonwork strategy will be detected by the employer depends on the organization of work and the efficacy of the capitalist's surveillance system. The capitalist can organize the work process so that each worker's performance is more visible and measurable, for example, through the use of such production techniques as the assembly line. Even when such techniques are less efficient in the input–output sense, they may be profitable due to their ability to secure a high level of labor input (effort). Similarly, the capitalist can divert resources from production into surveillance—in the form of careful accounting, electronic equipment, surveillance personnel, and the like. In either case, the claim that cost-reduction pressures render capitalist production efficient must be rejected. When less efficient production methods allow more effective or less costly systems of labor control to such an extent that the unit cost is lower than more efficient but less easily controlled processes, the capitalist will adopt the least costly and less efficient process. Where employers deploy costly strategies of labor extraction the link between cost minimization and efficiency is broken.

Next, consider the probability of being fired if a nonwork strategy *is* detected. For simplicity we represent this probability as depending on the unity of the work force; if firing a worker will incite a strike or slowdown by all workers, the capitalist will think twice about it. In general, the degree of unity of the work force depends on its racial, sexual, age, educational, and other divisions—including differences in wages and hierarchical status within the firm.[22] The discriminating capitalist may facilitate the unencumbered firing of workers and otherwise weaken workers' bargaining power by encouraging division, invidious distinction, and hierarchy, even when such policies are inefficient because they entail using, say, racial criteria for job assignment bearing no relationship to workers' productive capacity. Discrimination is thus consistent with rational profit maximization in a competitive environment.

Consider finally the employer's strategy of raising the cost to the worker of being fired. Because both the expected duration of the worker's unemployment and the level of unemployment benefits are beyond the control of the firm, the only way the employer can raise the cost of dismissal to the worker is to pay the worker more than that wage which would make the worker indifferent to the possibility of being fired. But if the profit-maximizing wage is higher than the worker's next best alternative, other workers who currently lack jobs would also prefer to have a job at that wage rather than remaining unemployed. And if this is the case, such workers are involuntarily unemployed according to any reasonable sense of the term.

Job scarcity implies involuntary unemployment, and vice versa.

Profit maximization and labor market equilibrium, even under the most stringent assumptions of atomistic competition, do not lead to market clearing. The microeconomic basis of both Keynes's notion of "involuntary unemployment" and Marx's concept of the role of the "reserve army" in the class war between labor and capital are thus elucidated by a model in which the specific character of the labor exchange, especially the nature of the enforcement costs and motivational elements involved, is taken explicitly into account.

Despite the explanatory insights afforded by our model of the labor exchange, the model appears to suffer from an anomaly of its own. It predicts that democratic worker-owned firms, by virtue of their lower surveillance costs, should be capable of producing more efficiently than capitalist firms. Hence they should outcompete capitalist firms on competitive markets. The first part of this argument is correct. Indeed there is substantial evidence that worker-controlled firms are both more productive and give rise to higher levels of work satisfaction than capitalist-controlled firms.[23] What then prevents the spontaneous emergence of democratic forms of work organization? In addressing this question we confront the second dimension of capitalist power: the command over investment. We shall see that the command over investment has a symbiotic relationship with the command over production.

The Power of the Purse

It is the apparent divorce of property and power that justifies the liberal designation of the capitalist economy as private. The novelty of this apolitical conception of property can hardly be overstressed. It certainly would have surprised a Russian noble, whose estate, as late as the nineteenth century, could be measured indifferently in acres or in souls. It might even perplex those today not steeped in liberal social theory, for in many European languages the word *landlord* (for example, *padrone*) refers equally to boss and head of household. Yet liberal social thought restricts the influence of the wealthy to their superior buying power and possibly to their influence over the state.

Joseph Schumpeter provided an elegant demonstration of this liberal view in an essay written before World War I.[24] He noted that among people involved in the production process, "the directing and the directed" are "subject to the same rules," and neither commands production in any real sense. Schumpeter went on to demonstrate that the evolution of new technologies and new forms of social organization obeyed the same logic. New projects—whether technological or organizational—will flourish according to their ability to meet existing market demands effectively. Those new projects that meet this criterion will readily be extended credit by the economy's financial institutions to cover start-up costs. And as a bank may be considered but another capitalist firm, Schumpeter's earlier argument concerning the irrelevance of the structure of command applies here too. Projects that meet consumer demands in a cost-effective manner will proliferate; those that do not will be squeezed out. Hence neither wealth nor control of existing productive firms or banks confers command. The innovator does indeed exercise power, because his or her action—if successful—changes the structure of the economy; nevertheless the ability to do so stems not from wealth or hierarchical position, but from the creative act of innovation and from the market-worthiness of the innovation itself. Schumpeter's argument is thus an extension of the asset neutrality proposition.

By this logic, no group of workers, having formed a democratically run enterprise, need suffer any special disabilities in doing business on account of their lack of wealth. The absence of a booming worker cooperative sector in advanced capitalist economies appears to the liberal economist as evidence of their inferior efficiency. But this argument is logically flawed, and it is even inconsistent with other aspects of liberal economic theory.*

First, survival in competitive markets is based on profits, not efficiency, and, as we have suggested, the two are different. The difference can be seen by noticing that for a given wage rate profits depend on the amount of net output produced per hour of labor employed. This in turn depends

---

* The two observations that follow are hardly an exhaustive treatment of the subject. It might be added that to the extent that the viability of democratic production forms is enhanced by a long-term learning process—both in the skills of democratic decision making and more fundamentally in the evolution of new values—the present viability of a worker cooperative form of production understates its long-term viability. And the survival of any production form depends more on its present operations than on its future prospects. Also, to the extent that the skills and values appropriate to a democratic workplace are learned outside the workplace itself—in families, schools, and elsewhere—a democratic form of production might be highly effective if generally adopted and supported by other social institutions but less so or perhaps not at all if operating in isolation.

on two quantities, the amount of net output produced per unit of work actually done and the amount of work done per hour of labor hired. Output per unit of work done might plausibly be said to measure efficiency, but the amount of work done per hour (or what might be termed the intensity of labor) is a better index of employer control. If worker-controlled firms choose to impose a less arduous pace of work, but succeed in organizing the production process more efficiently than their capitalist competitors, they may still end up with lower profits and hence fewer resources for engaging in the long-term competitive struggle despite their superior efficiency.

Second, the profits of a worker-controlled firm depend on how much the enterprise must pay to borrow the money necessary to start up production (barring the anomalous case of an independently wealthy group of workers!). Precisely because workers lack ownership of capital to begin with, they will have to pay more to borrow what they need, thus further disadvantaging the worker cooperative in the competitive game.

This point is important enough to develop at greater length. Banks, and others who have the means to finance business enterprise, demand either direct business control or adequate collateral in return for loans. In either case, power is contained within the circle of the wealthy. Democratic forms of work organization are not usually funded by the wealthy because lender control is precluded by definition, and adequate collateral is lacking by virtue of the unpropertied status of the vast majority of working people.

So universal is the association between asset ownership and control of business that many may wonder why we belabor the point. But the recognition of this association is quite absent from traditional neoclassical economics. According to the asset neutrality proposition, capital markets are virtually "perfect": all individuals have equal access to credit, no matter what their social position and personal assets. Were this the case, we would expect that the captains of industry would consist of random combinations of capitalists, trained managers, technical staff, and workers. Barring some genetic superiority of the well-to-do, we would certainly not expect the control of economic life to be vested in the propertied. Yet such is clearly the case. Why?

The problem of the capitalist as supplier of funds clearly resembles that of the employer as supplier of wages. In both cases money is paid "up front" in return for some expected but not always enforceable quid pro quo services. In both cases the supplier of funds must worry about both the capacity and the will of the recipient to deliver these services. And the lender of funds, like the employer, can secure compliance mainly by monitoring as well as by raising the cost of malfeasance to the recipient. Accordingly, the lender demands some voice, direct or by representation, in controlling the actions of the borrower. The link between ownership and control enters precisely at this point.

In the case of the worker-controlled firm, opportunities for control by lenders are minimal for two reasons. The workers' lack of collateral implies that lender and borrower will have largely divergent interests in risk management. And democratic decision making by workers precludes significant outside control.

The profit-maximizing bank or other lender will thus refuse to loan money to the workplace democracy—or they will only loan it at higher rates. The skeptic may doubt that a difference in borrowing costs could bear the weight of so crucial an explanation as the failure of democratic firms to eclipse capitalist enterprise. Nor do we intend the financial argument to stand alone, for it would be mistaken to dismiss the difficulties presented by the workers' lack of marketing networks, by the inexperience with democratic decision making fostered by a lifetime of work in hierarchical economic organizations, and even by the structure of a technology whose development over two centuries (if not longer) has been attuned to gaining acceptance within a centralized and autocratic pyramid of economic power.

But before we set aside the financial argument, consider the following arithmetic. A new worker-run cooperative might expect to pay an interest rate in excess of a home mortgage, because the property (industrial equipment and structures) being purchased with the loan, unlike a home, has a very limited resale value should the worker firm fail and its assets be repossessed by the bank. The difference in borrowing costs for the worker firm and its corporate competitor (based on U.S. experience) may be in the neighborhood of 4 percentage points of interest, resulting in an equivalent difference in the net profit rates of the two firms (after the payment of interest). If the two firms—corporate and democratic—begin with the same capital stock, and regularly invest all of their profits, the 4 percentage point difference in the net profit rate will result in the corporate firm being twice as large as the worker cooperative in less than two decades. Long before this, the advantages of size—both technological and other—would likely prove decisive in the competitive struggle.

Our argument implies the eclipse of worker-controlled firms, even if bankers share our conviction that these firms are at least as efficient as their capitalist competitors. That most banks do not share this conviction merely heightens the barriers that democratic forms of work organization must surmount. We shall see in the next section that even the lenders' perceptions of the relative efficiency of alternative forms of business organization—and the degree of efficiency of these forms itself—are influenced albeit indirectly, by the third dimension of the power of capital: the power over state policy.

Free to Move

The substantive economic power of both bosses and the wealthy seems undeniable even within the terms of the perfectly competitive models commonly used by liberal economists. Nothing in the real world is likely to disabuse us of the suspicion that capital is power. An inspection of daily life in any capitalist economy quickly reveals that a relatively restricted group of individuals—not enough to fill a large university lecture hall—exercise far-reaching control over the major decisions affecting the lives of all: production, pricing, investment, product innovation, plant location, and the like.

However, there would appear to remain one telling argument in the arsenal of capitalism's defenders. Even if it is true that capital confers substantive power, one might suggest, it does not follow that, in a society with a liberal democratic state such power is unaccountable. Given the juridical sovereignty of the state, it is always open to a democratic majority to reverse decisions made in the "private" economy, or even remove the prerogatives of capital altogether, should this majority find itself in disagreement with the general tenor of the economic performance or social prerogatives entailed by the capitalist economy. For instance, if nonownership prevents communities and worker organizations from going into business, a democratically empowered citizenry retains the option of making credit available, or even of redistributing property itself. Is it not reasonable, then, to consider the power of capital in a liberal democratic society as conditional upon the will of the people?

The premises of this argument might be faulted, of course, for it is far from obvious that on important questions concerning the prerogatives of capital the political system of any of today's liberal democracies conforms to the idealized democratic principles that presume that the "majority of citizens" can simply vote down the interests of business. The vastly superior ability of the owners of capital to finance electoral and referendum campaigns, to shape public opinion through political advertising, and to sustain effective lobbying efforts is sufficient in most cases to reject the aforementioned line of defense as little more than a vacuous apologia.

But the argument is not only empirically wrong. We shall see that even in a society whose government meets the liberal democratic ideal, capital has a kind of veto power over public policy that is quite independent of its ability to intervene directly in elections or in state decision making. This power derives from the effectiveness of what has been termed *capital strike*.

A simple version of the argument may be readily summarized. The electoral prospects of an incumbent government depend on the general performance of the economy in the period preceding the election, particularly the level and growth of employment and personal income. The overall performance of the economy, in turn, depends on the level of investment. The level of investment in any given country depends on the anticipated domestic profit rate compared with expected returns in the rest of the world, and compared also with returns to noninvestment uses of capital.[25] Therefore, the adoption of public policies that reduce the expected rate of profit also tend to reduce the electoral prospects of the incumbent government.

The power of capital—its command over state policy—thus derives not so much from what it does but from what it might not do. As in many other situations, power resides with the party that can effectively (and without great cost) withdraw resources and thereby inflict large costs on an opponent. The withdrawal of investment does not presume the collective action of capitalists: each may decide not to invest solely on the basis of everyday and totally autonomous calculations of expected profitability. Nor does the capital strike argument presume that capitalists seek to affect government policy.[26]

The power of capital is based in large part on the fact that it is free to move. In this respect, as in the fact that no collective organization or even intent is required for a capital strike to be effective, capital is quite unlike labor. Capital is owned by people and alienable from them; it can be invested or withdrawn or sent around the world by nothing more than the touch of a computer keyboard. Labor is embodied in people. The withdrawal of labor services from an employer requires an alternative source of income, which workers generally lack. The withdrawal of labor from an entire economy requires the costly and often jarring and politically or culturally obstructed physical movement of the workers themselves.

But our dogged defender of the claim that the power of the capitalist is indeed accountable will respond that the sovereign state may change the rules. If a majority of the citizenry feels that alternative forms of production are desirable, and finds their realization thwarted by business opposition and capital strike, they are certainly free to limit the outflow of capital to the rest of the world and to undertake the public investment necessary to make up for the withdrawal of private investment.

The practical obstacles to this kind of democratic revolution should not be underestimated: the possibility of capital strike renders gradual movement toward an alternative economic system vulnerable to disruption, but the precipitous inauguration of a new economic system will certainly entail significant costs as well. Chief among these would be the necessary process of learning how to organize and function in a new system of production. But we know from the history of the formation of the working class in advanced capitalist societies—as in the poor countries today—that the development of the skills, attitudes, and values consistent with a novel economic system is not a matter of years, but of decades and even generations. Learning how to make a new economic system work well requires not only time but experimentation.

Through capital strike, the owners of investable resources have the power to interrupt those processes of learning and experimentation that are necessary in order to initiate a fundamentally new economic system. Writing at the depth of the Great Depression, John Maynard Keynes understood this well. In an article titled "National Self-Sufficiency" he wrote:

> Each year it becomes more obvious that the world is embarking on a variety of political-economic experiments, and that different types of experiments appeal to different national temperaments and historical environments. . . . No one can tell which of the new systems will prove itself best. But . . . we each have our own fancy. . . .

Keynes recognized that the world mobility of goods, services, and investment would sharply limit national experimentation:

> We do not wish, therefore, to be at the mercy of world forces working out or

trying to work out some uniform equilibrium according to the ideal principles, if they can still be called such, of *laisser faire* capitalism. . . . We wish—for the time being at least and so long as the present transitional experimental phase endures—to be our own masters. . . . We all need to be as free as possible of interference from economic changes elsewhere in order to make our own favorite experiments towards the ideal social republic of the future.[27]

The presumed sovereignty of the democratic citizenry fails in the presence of capital strike. The fallacy of the accountability argument is instructive, and one to which we will return. By abstracting from the process of learning and focusing on the process of choice, liberal social theory reaffirms the accountability of power. But once learning is seen as an indissoluble aspect of choice—as we shall insist in chapter 5—the argument becomes untenable. The capitalist economy, in short, not only fosters the exercise of unaccountable power, it also thwarts those forms of political learning-through-choosing by means of which democratic societies may come to deepen their fundamental political commitments and capacities.

Conclusion: Power and Agency

Liberal political philosophy is thus curiously at odds with liberal economic theory. The former heralds the individual as an agent empowered to transform his or her world; the latter favors an economic system in which agency is so compromised as to be little more than a false promise for all but the few. Michael Sandel captures this fragility of agency in liberal theory when he writes "Liberalism . . . makes agency an article of faith rather than an object of continuing attention and concern, a premise of politics rather than its precarious achievement."[28] By rendering invisible the power of capital, liberal economic theory has contributed more to the legitimation of powerlessness than to making good its claim of universal agency.

Democratic accountability of economic power cannot be secured by a transformation—no matter how radical—of the structure of the economy alone. Nor do we choose to confine our democratic critique of liberal democratic capitalist society to the manner in which the power of capital undermines the liberal promise of autonomous and effective action by individuals and groups. Democracy, like domination, knows no single home but is a characteristic of the entire ensemble of social relationships that make up society. To these broader concerns we now turn.

4

Structure: The Mosaic

of Domination

POWER may be wielded in numerous ways. Historically, armed force has been a central pillar of power, as liberal theory rightly stresses. But the arsenal of domination goes beyond the gun. Control of the tools with which we produce our livelihood and the words that give our lives and loyalties their meanings have been no less central to the exercise of power.

Debates among Marxian and liberal theorists concerning the roots of domination have tended to adopt an impoverished conception of power. The liberal concern with the despotic state is matched in its narrowness by the Marxian concern with class domination. Each ignores the undeniable insights of the other; both give scant theoretical attention to forms of power that cannot be reduced to either state despotism and class. The most ubiquitous of these excluded forms of power is the domination of women by men.

Equally important, the grand debates between the liberal and Marxian political traditions skirt a central concern of democratic theory, the relationship between power and freedom. Democracy promises the collective accountability of power, but it promises another, more constructive concept as well; namely, the ability of people to effectively carry out their individual and common projects unencumbered by arbitrary constraint. For the liberal, this positive side of power—agency—is rendered minimally, as political liberty and the freedom to contract with whomever one pleases. Both of these liberal forms of freedom represent the absence of constraint rather than personal or collective empowerment. They are, in Isiah Berlin's apt terminology, "negative freedoms." For the classical Marxist, agency is the ability of an emerging class to carry out a historic project dictated by the onward march of the productive forces of society. Neither the liberal nor the Marxian definition encompasses the vision of people and of a people free to be the architects of their own personal and social histories.

We will address the problems raised for democratic theory by these partial conceptions of power in this chapter and in chapter 5, which considers the question of the individual and agency. Here we will develop a conception of power, the structures of social domination, and the resistance to domination capable of understanding the historical dynamics of diverse forms of power—patriarchal, state, class, or other. We will analyze the reproduction of patriarchal domination both as a central issue of democracy in its own right and as an illustration of our approach.

This approach will provide a lens with which the clash of rights (chapter 2) and the political nature of the economy (chapter 3) may be brought into a common focus. Chapter 2 presented the historical trajectory of liberal democratic capitalist societies not as the product of a unified logic expressed in an economically determined set of laws of motion, nor as a teleological movement of modernization pulled by the magnet of enlightenment, but rather as the result of the contradictory possibilities of two conflicting tendencies, the expansion of personal rights and the expansion of property rights. Chapter 3 demonstrated that the economy is a political arena in an everyday sense of that term, and that within that arena the ownership of the productive apparatus of a society confers a form of democratically unaccountable power. We concluded that the heightening of conflict concerning the extension of a democratic conception of personal rights to the economy, if not inevitable, is a probable next phase of a by-now well-established historical trajectory.

The underlying logic of our argument contrasts in two important ways with dominant conceptions in social theory. First, though we affirm that historical change is structured, systematic, and hence understandable in more than simply empirical terms, we reject the notion that either stability or change obeys a single logic, whether of enlightenment, modernization, or the advance of productive capacities. Underlying this denial is our second fundamental commitment, a rejection of the concept of power as unitary; it is the notion that power emanates from a single source in society that provides the bedrock of what might be called the unitary conception of history.

We believe that an alternative conception of power, social structure, and history can make better sense of the historical clash of rights in liberal democratic capitalism and the political nature of the economy. The next two sections develop such a conception of power, in terms of the following five propositions.

First, power is heterogeneous, wielding a variety of weapons, yielding to a host of counterpressures, and obeying no single logic. Here we focus on the distinct forms of domination and solidarity based on class, state, and gender.

Second, power is not an amorphous constraint on action but rather a structure of rules empowering and restraining actors in varying degrees. These distinct sets of rules may be embodied in concrete institutions (for example, the World Bank), in linguistic convention (as in the generic term *man*), in unwritten custom (for example, primogeniture), in legal practice (as in the formal recognition of collective bargaining for wages), and, as we have seen, in more general conceptions of property and personal rights.

Third, the perpetuation of any power structure is generally problematic. Further, a structure of power is secured or toppled not only by history-making collective struggles, but more prosaically by a complex societywide web of everyday individual action and compliance.

Fourth, distinct structures of power—be they the liberal democratic state, the patriarchal family, the capitalist economy, or other—are not merely juxtaposed, they are bound together in a common process of social reproduction. Each one may contribute to the survival of another; or they may foster mutually corrosive and subversive impulses.

And fifth, because people's lives are generally governed by more than one distinct power structure—for example one may be a worker, a wife, and a citizen—we experience power as heterogeneous, and are often able to bring the experiences within one system of power to bear in the pursuit of our projects within another. The clash of rights, based on impressive ability of elites and democratic movements alike to extend rights from one sphere of society to others, is the most important historical example of this transportation of practices from one social realm to another.

We refer to our approach as a historical-structural model of power. As we deny the usefulness of a general theory of power and its reproduction, we will seek to develop these five propositions in a particular historical setting; that is, the liberal capitalist nations of Europe and North America over the past two centuries.[1]

A Political Conception of Family, State, and Economy

It has become fashionable, in reacting against the traditional unitary conception of power, to profess a richly textured alternative notion—an idea of power as likely to be illuminated by the study of words and symbols as of armaments and property. Michel Foucault, for instance, writes:

> The analysis, made in terms of power, must not assume that the sovereignty of the state, the form of the law or the overall unity of a domination are given at the outset. . . . Power is everywhere. . . .[2]

This acute and welcome sensitivity to the ubiquity of power, however, can easily slip into treating power per se as domination, and replacing a critique of domination with a diffuse critique of authority of no particular use to democratic social movements. Thus Thomas Wartenberg notes, in a perceptive analysis of Foucault's attempt at deconstructing power, that

> at the political level, this problem asserts itself in Foucault's failure to distinguish different types of repressive societies. . . . Though all social systems do exist by means of a structuring of human beings to meet the needs of that system, we need to have a way to talk about how much pain such structuring inflicts upon the creatures for whom it exists.[3]

We also need, we might add, a way to talk about the *structure* of power in order to assess its *accountability*.

Our conception of power is at once a theory of domination and a theory of structural change flowing from collective resistance to domination. It is at the same time a structural theory and a theory of social action. Marx, in criticizing Ludwig Feuerbach, lamented the fact that materialist thought tended to denigrate action in favor of structure: "Hence it happened that the active side, in contradistinction to materialism, was developed by idealism."[4] Analogously, structural theories of power often support a conception either of unquestioned, monolithic, uncontested domination or of the mechanistic inevitability of the collapse of domination.* The commonplace observation that structures do not reproduce or destroy themselves but are perpetuated or overturned by *what people do* finds no place in most structural theories. The active side of power is more fully developed by theories of choice.

Theories of choice, however—for reasons we will address in the next chapter—generally fail to provide an adequate account of the forms of collective action central to an active and historical conception of power. By developing the relationship between domination and solidarity, we seek to avoid both the individualism of choice theories and the presumption of a pregiven logic of either stability or crisis in structural theories. More positively, we will embrace the fundamental tenet of structural theories—that individual action is highly regulated—in a framework that insists that the historical dynamics of the structures regulating choice are themselves the result, however indirect and unintended, of individual action.

Vertical relationships of superior to subordinate, of employer to worker, of man to woman, of despot to subject, of white to black, provide the raw materials with which people construct the corresponding horizontal structures of social bonding—class consciousness, democratic nationalism, racial unity, and the like. (This rudimentary statement of the conditions of collective action simply generalizes Marx's insight that the structure of exploitation might provide the conditions for the unification of the exploited. We will turn to this issue in some detail in chapter 6.) These structures of social bonding allow people to forge from their individual experiences of oppression (and those of other people) an ensemble of cultural and organizational tools upon which collective action may be based.

The active side of power surely includes the exercise of domination by the powerful and the complicity of the oppressed in their oppression. But it also includes revolutionary collective action: forging communicative and organizational tools of bonding from the cacaphony of discourses to which the mosaic of domination gives rise, and putting these tools to use in trans-

---

* Many who have stressed the centrality of power (Marxists, anarchists, humanists, and others) have courted the danger of ultimately reducing history to the mechanical unfolding of a system of power's pregiven logic. As a result, the prospect of emancipation has often been sought either in the indomitable and freedom-loving human spirit, or in the structurally given inevitability of systemic collapse. However, we see no need to pin our democratic hopes either on human nature or on the accident-prone character of the structures that dominate our lives. The ubiquity of unaccountable power does not imply its invincibility.

forming structures of power. The clash of rights in liberal democratic capitalism, in particular, has seen both the collective action of the dispossessed in pitting personal rights against the privileges of wealth, race, and gender as well as the counterstrategies of the privileged in shoring up patriarchal rights, property rights, and "skin privilege."

Recognition of the heterogeneity of power invites a more searching analysis of the way in which distinct spheres of social life regulate social action in such a manner as to produce systems of domination *and* the possibility of their elimination.

Power is the capacity to render social action effective. It is coextensive with neither the state, nor with physical force, nor with face-to-face command.[5] Power may be exercised through the ability to overcome the resistance of others—as in Max Weber's conception—but it may equally be exercised through the ability to avoid resistance, either through control over which issues become contestable or through influence over others' wants, sentiments, desires, or, more generally, objectives.[6]

Power is exercised through social action. But what is action? By an action or a practice we mean an active intervention on the part of an individual or a group, with the project of transforming some aspect of social reality the object of the action. An action may be considered from a variety of aspects. When the object (the thing to be transformed) is part of the natural world, we speak of the practice as *appropriative*: labor is, among other things, an appropriative practice. When, however, the object of the practice includes the rules of the game themselves—that is, the stabilization or transformation of a structure of social relations—we speak of the action as *political*. Appropriation and politics do not exhaust social action. We will, for instance, consider a practice as *distributive* to the extent that its object includes the distribution and redistribution of positions and prerogatives within a given set of rules of the game. Finally, when the object of a practice includes the transformation or consolidation of the tools of social discourse, we will term the action *cultural*. (From this point of view, chapter 6 represents an extended analysis of cultural practices.)

Political practices, then, are actions that seek to manipulate the rules of the game in some sphere of social life, in order to achieve some desired end. Political action, for example, may seek to alter not the rules of the state, but the rules governing gender or race relationships. And, quite obviously, political action may seek to alter one set of rules as a step toward transforming another structure, as in the time-honored demand of workers

97

to democratize the state so as to have the power to alter the structure of the economy.

We focus on three general forms of the asymmetrical exercise of power: domination through the monopoly of the means of coercion, through the exercise of property rights, and through the operation of gender-based privilege. These are certainly not the only forms of domination observed in modern society. Race, ethnicity, religion, language, and region, among others, have served as major bases of social oppression and loci of bitter conflict. We focus on these three forms of domination not because other forms are less important where they occur, but because they are less general, affecting particular liberal democratic capitalist societies in widely differing degrees and in quite distinct manners.*

Each of these three forms of domination may be considered to be a means of regulating social action. Thus, in three distinct ways, action is structured by a specific set of rules of the game: (a) the forms and rewards of participation of individuals in a practice are socially regulated; (b) the range of feasible alternative forms of practice are socially delimited; and (c) the potential effectiveness of distinct types of practice are socially mediated.

We refer to each of these distinct sets of rules of the game as *sites* of social practice. In the liberal democratic capitalist societies we are considering, the liberal democratic state, the capitalist economy, and the patriarchal family are sites, each possessing a distinct set of rules of the game governing the appropriative, political, cultural, and distributive practices occurring within them.

A site is a region of social life with a coherent set of characteristic rules of the game. It is distinguished not by what is done there (appropriation of nature, politics, culture, reproduction), but by the manner in which whatever is done there is regulated by a set of social rules. We distinguish an economy from other spheres of social life by the fact that its rules of the game confer socially consequential power, sanction participation, and distribute rewards, on the basis of property rights. Slave, feudal, capitalist, and state socialist economies represent distinct forms of property relations defining the rules of participation in the appropriative, political, and other social practices. Some forms of what might be termed communal society, and hypothetical

---

* Our analysis of domination in liberal democratic capitalist societies is situated on a level of abstraction between "capitalist society in general" or "patriarchal society in general" and particular concrete societies such as the United States in the post–World War II era. A more concrete study would require attention to other axes of domination, in the case of the United States, race and imperialism in particular.

classless societies as well, may be deemed to lack an economy in our sense, just as some kinship-based social systems lack a state. Though this may appear to be an oddity, it reflects a substantive commitment that must still be regarded as a hypothesis: property-based systems structuring social practices (economies) share some common characteristics and historical logics not exhibited by other means of structuring appropriative and other practices.

We have already defined the capitalist form of the economy as a system regulating the production of commodities for exchange using wage labor and private ownership of the means of production. These structural characteristics of the capitalistic economy give rise to a number of relatively well-defined social regularities dictating the decline or expansion of particular forms of activity and the range of feasible and infeasible individual and group strategies. Examples range from the obvious—that consumers may not generally consume more than their income or that firms incurring losses fail—to less transparent macroeconomic relationships such as that between the level of employment and the rate of profit. According to our definition of a site, the status of an economy as "capitalist" depends on the nature of these rules; it does not matter whether the production process produces goods or services, agricultural or industrial goods, day-care centers or nuclear power.

The state is no less amenable to such a structural definition. We define the state generically, with Max Weber, in terms of its structural position in the monopolization of the means of coercion.[7] The liberal democratic form of the state is characterized by generalized civil liberties and universal adult suffrage, by a substantial separation of the state from control over the allocation of labor and the investment of the surplus product, by an open and competitive system of political parties, and by formal rules of participation granting rights to virtually all citizens. These basic principles give rise to rules of action in the liberal democratic state: parties that lose elections may not continue to hold office, votes may not be purchased or sold, and the like.[8]

In a similar manner, we view the patriarchal family as a system of rules in which social positions are organized according to gender, age, and kinship in such a way to confer special privileges on adult males.[9]

An illustration of the relationship between sites and practices appears in figure 4.1. This figure depicts our basic assertion: in general, *each* site in society structures, in a manner distinctive to the site, *all* varieties of social practices. The notion that sites are defined by rules rather than functions

FIGURE 4.1

Sites and Practices: Some Examples

Site	Practice			
	Appropriative	Distributive	Political	Cultural
Capitalist Economy	Workers Convert Ore into Steel	Employer Lowers the Real Wage	Union Wins Control over Monitoring Work Safety	Factory Supervisor Wears Tie and Jacket
Liberal Democratic State	Municipal Workers Generate Electricity	Government Closes Tax Loopholes	Women Fight for the Right to Elective Abortion	President Appoints a Woman to the Supreme Court
Patriarchal Family	Wife Makes Dinner	Children Ask for Larger Allowance	Wife Demands Share in Family Budget Decisions	Wife Objects to Being Called "Mrs. John Doe"

should not be construed to imply that the nature of rules does not specify to a significant extent the types of activities that occur at a given site. The rules of the liberal state dictate that it both possess a monopoly on the means of coercion and not control capital accumulation. The nature of kinship and the widespread prohibition on the marketing of both people and sexuality (for example, slavery is forbidden and prostitution is restricted) imply that the family will likely be the locus of child rearing and sexual relations. This in no way weakens our point that politics, production, and culture are not site-specific activities. Our conception of the economy as political is thus a special case of the more general proposition that each site possesses its unique structure, in the sense that each organizes in a substantively distinct manner the array of political practices taking place within it.

In contrast to the conception illustrated in figure 4.1, much of contemporary social theory suffers from what we term the *isomorphism of sites and practices*. In this view, a particular *practice* is uniquely associated with a particular *site* of which it is ostensibly characteristic; the economy with appropriation and distribution, the state with politics, and family, church, and media with culture. This identification of structure and function is promoted by the arbitrary academic boundaries of the contemporary social sciences, and it is fostered by social appearance as well. Maurice Godelier writes:

> It is only in certain societies and particularly in capitalist society, that [the] distinction between functions comes to coincide with a distinction between institutions. . . . [T]he capitalist mode of production . . . for the first time separated economics, politics, religion, kinship, art, etc., as so many distinct institutions.[10]

But we maintain that Godelier's remarks are a more apt description of liberal social theory and academic convention than of the nature of social life under capitalism.[11]

We say that a group wields socially consequential power when the structure of a site and the manner in which it interacts with other sites systematically privileges its projects over the projects of other groups.*

A relationship of domination is one in which a structure allows socially consequential power to be employed against the wills and efforts of those affected thereby. More succinctly put, domination is a form of socially consequential yet democratically unaccountable power. The power of capital in the capitalist economy is by this reasoning a form of class domination. The power of state elites even in formally liberal democratic societies may also be a form of domination to the extent that the entire nexus of social institutions governing the various sites in society do not secure the accountability of state power. The privileged access of men rather than women to desirable jobs, physical security, and social esteem likewise constitute evidence of patriarchal domination.

It would be fruitless to attempt to trace the source of a form of domination to any particular site. Patriarchal power is, of course, related to the family in the nominal sense that the family-based terms of kinship, age, and gender provide the semantic tools for the description of the structural locations of a patriarchal structure such as wife, male family head, minor child and the like. But in the absence of an analysis of how, where, and toward what ends

---

* We do not minimize the difficulty of applying this—or indeed any other—definition of domination. Chapter 3 constitutes an example of one such application involving an investigation of the structural principles governing the effectiveness of the practices of capital and labor in a capitalist economy. In many cases, the presence of domination in a social relationship may be more difficult to detect, its positive identification awaiting an open challenge to the rules of the game for illumination of its most fundamental principles. We do not think, however, that this definition of domination is any more problematic than commonly used concepts of equality of opportunity, exploitation or, for that matter, net national product.

adult male power is exercised and its structure reproduced, not much more can be said. Therefore, the patriarchal family need not be the main locus of the exercise of male power or the critical arena for its reproduction.

The statement that the power of capital is rooted in the economy refers to little more than the nature of capital as a class defined by the ownership of the means of production. The statement may point suggestively to a central aspect of the reproduction of this form of domination—the ability to withhold investment of the surplus product—but it is incomplete. The effectiveness of this form of power and indeed the manner in which it might be exercised depends no less critically on the structure of the state than on the structure of the economy.

We conclude that, if distinct forms of power are to be made accountable or even rendered intelligible, they must be brought together, as it were, in the social whole. Only then can we understand how power operates, how powers both complement one another and clash, and how structures of domination are consolidated, eroded, and transformed.

Reproduction, Contradiction, and Change

The timeless analysis of structure might represent different forms of domination as radically distinct, as simply adjacent vertical forms much like skyscrapers on an urban skyline. Yet a historical analysis of structure cannot avoid their integral dynamic relationships, for each structure of power is involved in the history of the others. The manner in which rights in property and rights of citizenship have jointly expanded in sometimes complementary and sometimes contradictory ways is an important example of this general phenomenon.

The way that a social system of interacting sites is reproduced or transformed is the key to understanding the unity of a social whole. If, as we have suggested, the sites that make up society are defined by their rules, the unity of the society as a whole is defined by its characteristic processes of change and stasis, or what Marx somewhat grandiosely termed its "laws of motion." Society, we suggest, is a reproductive unity: each site within society, however distinct the forms of power it structures, depends upon its neighboring sites for its own continued existence.

The capitalist economy does not reproduce itself. This observation goes considerably beyond the oft-noted dependence of the reproduction of the structure of the capitalist economy on the state. It is uncontroversial that a state external to the system of capitalist production is needed both to enforce contractual relations and to provide social infrastructure precluded by the atomistic character of economic action. Less well understood is the dependence of the reproduction of the capitalist economy on a distinctly non-capitalist family. The production of the most central of all inputs in the capitalist economy, labor-power itself, logically must take place outside of capitalist production. Why is this? In contrast to slave economies, in a capitalist economy labor-power is inalienable—one's capacity to labor cannot be owned by another—it cannot be sold as a commodity by a capitalist producer. It can only be sold—or rather, rented—by the person embodying it. But in this case, parents, wives, or other producers of labor-power cannot have property rights in the worker, and hence must have reasons other than the maximization of profits through exchange for producing labor-power.[12] Other sites—state and family—are no less dependent on the joint effects of the entire ensemble of sites for their reproduction.

Our focus on reproduction does not convey a presumption of stasis; we attribute no theoretical status and certainly no causal or explanatory power to the "reproductive needs" of any structure.[13] More pointedly, there is no reason to infer that the practices of those seeking to consolidate a set of rules will have the intended effects and will predominate over those seeking to change them. Our concept of a reproductive whole suggests simply that the structures defining society *might* be reproduced, not that they will be.

Social systems also exhibit specific structural vulnerabilities which often chart their historical dynamic. For this reason we represent society as a *reproductive and contradictory totality*. In other words, the very structures that render society a reproductive unity often tend to require their mutual dynamic structural adaptation and dislocation.

The reproduction of a structure is never automatic; it is the result—not always intentional—of the collective and individual projects in which people engage. Reproduction of relationships of domination can be accounted for by the tendency for rules that predominantly benefit one group to provide this group with the resources necessary to secure its reproduction. Resources devoted to the reproduction of rules may take the form of police costs and costs of controlling the process of production as well as resources devoted to promoting understandings and sentiments consistent with the perpetuation of the existing order. We term these resources the *enforcement costs* of a structure.[14] The extent of the enforcement costs depends on both the opportunities for resistance and the forms of solidarity and alliance supported by the heterogeneous collection of sites making up society.

The ability of a dominant group to command the resources necessary for the enforcement of the rules depends in part on the rules themselves, of course. First, the rules influence the general availability of goods and services by the manner in which they structure appropriative practices, supporting varying degrees of waste or effectiveness in the production process. Second, the rules organize those distributive practices which determine how much of the social product will be effectively commanded by the dominant groups in society. And, third, the rules structure those political and cultural practices which influence the extent and effectiveness of resistance to the rules.

Because rules regulate both appropriative and distributive practices and because it is the amount of resources at the command of the dominant groups, not the size of the total social product, which is critical in the ability of a group to reproduce or alter the rules, there is no presumption that rules will be efficient in the usual sense. This is because rules that are very effective in structuring efficient or technologically dynamic appropriative practices may corrode the ability of the dominant groups in society to command the resulting increases in output. For example, Keynesian demand management proved very effective in securing the full utilization of labor inputs in production and rapid technical change, but the resulting labor scarcity undermined capital's bargaining power, squeezed profits, and jeopardized the reproduction processes of the capitalist class structure.

The principle of survival of structures is not that the fittest is the most efficient, but that the fittest most securely places adequate resources to cover the enforcement costs entailed by this particular structure in the hands of those who benefit from the status quo.[15]

With Marx, we believe that the most fundamental structural changes in our society flow from contradictions inherent in its structural constitution. But we also believe that the traditional Marxian or "dialectical" conception of social contradiction is inadequate. According to the dialectical conception, a new social formation emerges as a structural unity whose social relations are geared toward the reproduction both of its defining institutions and of the positions of its dominant groups. As it develops, such a society necessarily produces, as its antithesis, conditions dedicated to its destruction. Normally these conditions are taken as reflected in the existence and power of social groups (classes) standing to benefit from the inauguration of a new social order. These conditions, moreover, ostensibly gather strength as society matures, and eventually lead to its downfall.

This Hegelian paradigm is inspired by a biological conception of maturation and change, which can be applied to society only if we accept a lineal notion of social evolution. It is furthermore inextricably linked to a mechanistic view of history, in that it reduces practices to the effects of structures and hence sees human action as little more than the proximate cause of social dynamics whose essential determination is pregiven.

Yet the concept of contradiction remains valuable for understanding social dynamics. Indeed, we have implicitly employed the notion of a *structural* contradiction in our analysis of the clash of rights in chapter 2. We saw that distinct sites within a given society tend to generate, by virtue of the rules of the game by which they are defined, social practices that undermine the reproduction of society, or one or more of its sites. The necessary conditions for the perpetuation of a given structure may be simply inconsistent, as when the reproduction of a structure requires both A and B, but B requires both C and not A. We term this a *structural contradiction*.

Structural contradictions are especially likely to occur when society exhibits heterogeneous centers of contested power involving multiple forms of social domination. In this case, the rules governing distinct types of social asymmetry in different sites are unlikely to be mutually supportive if their applicability is not confined to their site of origin. For this reason both dominant and subordinate groups frequently seek to transport practices characteristic of one site to another in which they seek to undermine dominant forms of power. The demand for the democratic election of workplace managers or the lunch counter sit-ins are examples of this, as is the successful late-nineteenth-century attempt by business groups in the United States to extend the judicial concept of liberty to include the right to free contract unimpeded by government interference.

Dramatic examples of social conflict over where which rules should apply have arisen in recent years as feminists have challenged patriarchal privilege. Instead of deploying a distinctly feminist concept of the good society against male domination, feminists have more often employed the radical potential of liberal democratic and even capitalist rules.

The Sex-Gender System and
the Reproduction of Domination

"Households, like decks of cards, have suits and hierarchies," writes Nancy Folbre, "their members are almost always differentiated by gender and by age."[16] And, continuing Folbre's analogy, although the deck is constantly being shuffled, the hierarchies and suits remain. To understand patriarchy is to explain how the privileges, powers, and meanings attached to the suits and the hierarchies of the household are variously perpetuated and transformed not only in the family, but throughout society.

The centrality of the reproduction of patriarchy as a concern of social theory may be questioned at the outset, of course, but only by resort to two of the more dubious staples of conservative thought through the centuries. Among those who interpret patriarchal domination as "natural," no less than among those who represent the patriarchal family as a structure of altruism and reciprocity, the problem of patriarchal domination as a socially contrived arrangement evaporates, and with it the problem of how it is perpetuated.

Accepting patriarchal structures as forms of domination, by contrast, poses a dual problem. How do specific patriarchal forms emerge, evolve, and disappear? If patriarchy takes distinct forms, by what reason may we posit its unity across time and space? We will first draw upon contemporary feminist theory to attempt a response to the second question, and then turn to the first, proposing not a general theory of patriarchal reproduction, but rather an interpretation of the reproduction of one among its major forms in contemporary society.

Our conclusions may be summarized at the outset. Patriarchy is a system of domination that is distinct from both class and state power. Male dominance is a form of social relationship occurring in virtually every sphere of social life. The patriarchal family is one of the fundamental sites of social practices that constitute contemporary liberal democratic capitalist society. This site has its own rules of the game which regulate kinship, sexuality, and the gender-based division of household labor.

The reproduction both of the patriarchal family and male dominance throughout society—which together might be termed the patriarchal system—is secured through the action of those who seek to perpetuate and deepen its associated privileges and gender identities. In contemporary liberal democratic capitalist society, two fundamental aspects of this reproduction process appear to be particularly important. First, the sexual division of labor in child rearing creates strongly divergent patterns of personal development in men and women. Second, labor-market discrimination against women and the fact that the labor of child rearing is remunerated primarily through redistributions within couples renders women economically dependent on men.

However, the twin expansionary logics of personal and property rights in state and economy challenge this reproduction process, because neither personal rights nor property rights provide anything but the most arbitrary recognition of male privilege as a rule of the game. Thus the meanings and personality developments associated with the sexual division of labor in child rearing are countered by what might be termed the "de-gendering" potentials of liberal discourse. Similarly, although labor-market discrimination against women appears to exhibit no tendency to decline through the autonomous working of market forces, it is vulnerable on the same grounds as racial discrimination and other asymmetries in personal rights, and hence is extremely susceptible to political opposition within the logic of the expansion of personal rights.

Our representation of the patriarchal family as a set of gender-, age-, and kinship-based rules owes much to the work of Gayle Rubin and Heidi Hartmann and those who followed their leads.[17] The first commitment of this approach is to reject the view of the family as a unit, or as a homogeneous actor with common objectives. As in early liberal political theory, in contemporary neoclassical economics the terms *family* and *individual* are often used interchangeably. Milton Friedman writes, "As liberals, we take freedom of the individual, or perhaps the family, as our ultimate goal in judging social arrangements."[18]

Friedman's apparently casual apposition is far from innocent. Indeed, it elides one of the most profound contradictions in liberal social theory. The liberal commitment to seeing individuals as intentional actors pursuing strategies toward the achievement of their chosen ends is given full reign in representations of the state and at least partial scope in the consumption sphere of the economy. But it does not extend to the kitchen, the nursery, or the bedroom. The family has a special status in liberal thought: the status of an organic whole. The family is "represented" in the political arena by a family head and in the marketplace by a housewife; both putatively make choices that represent a balanced aggregation of the wants and needs of family members.

The unity of this organic whole is secured either by a natural dependence (in early formulations) or by the overarching order conferred by an altruistic family head (in the "new home economics"). How can family altruism and the liberal commitment to instrumental action be reconciled? The effective exercise of altruism by the family head raises the familiar "free rider" problem: why do not family members simply exploit the altruism of the head? The solution is offered by Gary Becker in his celebrated "Rotten Kid" theorem. The Rotten Kid theorem is to the neoclassical theory of the family what the Invisible Hand theorem is to the neoclassical theory of the market economy. Becker's theorem holds that if the family head is benevolent, then, under certain conditions, it is in the interests of even selfish family members to *act* as though they too are benevolent. But Becker's solution can hardly be regarded as adequate; Folbre writes:

> In trying to explain why individual family members do not free ride on the benevolence of others, Becker resorts to the concept of a benevolent dictator . . . the joint utility function assumes that the only power holders in the family are altruists and the only rotten family members are those who wield no effective power. In other words, Becker allows for rotten kids, but not for rotten parents, rotten husbands, and rotten wives.[19]

Quite apart from the despotic connotations of the family head viewed as altruist, the special treatment of the family in liberal theory appears to be no less arbitrary than the liberal representation of the economy as private, in contradistinction to the public state. "There is something paradoxical," writes Folbre, "about the juxtaposition of a naked self-interest that presumably motivates efficient allocation of market resources and a perfect altruism that presumably motivates equitable allocation of family resources."[20]

By contrast, contemporary feminist theory represents the family not as a unified actor, but as a terrain, or—to borrow Hartmann's term—"a locus of gender, class, and political struggle." We believe that this insight is enhanced by our representation of the patriarchal family as a site with particular rules of the game which overlaps with other sites with distinct and heterogeneous rules. This model allows the theory of the collective struggle against domination, pioneered by Marx in the case of class exploitation, to inform an analysis of patriarchy, without gender relations being reduced to an effect of class.[21]

Structure: The Mosaic of Domination

The patriarchal family's manner of regulating age, gender, and kinship relations is not pregiven, but rather is continually being renewed and transformed, in part through political and cultural practices both within the family and without. Nor are the actors themselves pregiven: the variety of practices structured by the patriarchal family—ranging from household labor to what Ann Ferguson terms "sex-affective production"—are critically involved in shaping everything from our physical makeup to our capacities, identities, and sentiments.

We do not believe that patriarchy can be adequately represented as a "mode of production," and we suspect that attempts to focus on "labor" or "production" as the analytical key to understanding gender, age, and kinship relations will prove unduly limiting. The attraction of these alternative formulations is their stress on the importance of the productive activities of women and children (for example, Folbre's illuminating work on household labor and demography), their ability to illuminate distinctive aspects of practices structured by patriarchal relationships (for example, Ferguson's insights on sexuality), and their capacity to deploy such conceptual tools as surplus labor time and exploitation, which have proven exceptionally valuable in other contexts.

Yet we find labor and production a restrictive conceptual grid, one inviting an exaggerated attention to issues of exploitation and economically conceived interest and tending to favor an instrumental rather than a constitutive conception of action. In this we agree with Rubin who advocates the concept of a sex-gender system as a necessary theoretical innovation in light of the failure of classical Marxism to handle gender-based forms of domination:

This failure results from the fact that Marxism, as a theory of social life, is relatively unconcerned with sex. In Marx's map of the social world, human beings are workers, peasants, capitalists; that they are also men and women is not seen as very significant. By contrast, in the maps of social reality drawn by Freud and Levi-Strauss, there is a deep recognition of the place of sexuality in society, and of the profound differences in the social experience of men and women.

Rubin later adds that

the subordination of women can be seen as a product of the relationship by which sex and gender are organized and produced. The economic oppression of women is derivative and secondary. But there is an economics of sex and gender, and what we need is a political economy of sexual systems.[22]

In defining the patriarchal family as a set of rules we obviously intend something different from the everyday notion of the family as a set of personal relationships among kin. Patriarchy, like class, certainly involves face-to-face relationships. The interactions between men and women, like those between boss and worker, are often experienced as a "one on one" contest. But the patriarchal family also regulates relations between men and women as groups and provides the material for both solidarity and competition among men and among women.[23] Thus the patriarchal family is a set of rules governing not only members of what are commonly termed "families," but of single people, gay and lesbian couples, and others.

The ubiquitous historical importance and distinct nature of these age-, gender-, and kinship-based rules motivates our generic concept of the family as a distinct site. But not all such rules may reasonably be termed patriarchal. And even those clearly characterized by one or another form of adult male dominance exhibit an otherwise staggering diversity. The expression "patriarchal society" is, therefore, akin to the expression "class society."[24] It refers to a particular form of domination without specifying its structure in detail, and without indicating its specific processes of reproduction and transformation. Indeed, distinct forms of patriarchy may be as different from one another as are capitalism, feudalism, and other distinct forms of class society.

Equally important, distinct forms of family structure coexist in every society. For example, both the rules of the game and the manner in which they are reproduced or altered differ significantly between white and black families and between families in differing class positions.

The development of concepts adequate to an understanding of the specific forms of patriarchy is still in its infancy. Ferguson, for example, has suggested that in the United States we may distinguish at least three forms corresponding to more or less distinct historical periods: father patriarchy, husband patriarchy, and public patriarchy. The distinct nature of different forms of patriarchy may be variously represented, but we believe that one of the most perceptive ways is to model the reproduction processes of each. For example, in Ferguson's terms, father patriarchy may be conceived to have been perpetuated primarily through the patriarchal inheritance of property, and husband patriarchy may be considered to be reproduced through the labor-market privileges of adult males.[25]

Note that the latter statement, though plausible enough in its own right, flies in the face of both liberal and classical Marxian economic theory. As we have seen, both theories presume that the process of competition among cost-minimizing capitalists will tend to eliminate labor-market discrimination and would therefore render patriarchal domination little but a tottering anachronism. Father patriarchy might well be reproduced through property inheritance and correspondingly property inheritance may be reproduced by patriarchal control over women's sexuality, as Engels suggested in his work on the family; nevertheless, no similar reproductive nexus is apparent where fathers are not owners of the land, tools, and other means of livelihood of other family members. And as Marx and Engels realized, the distinctive characteristic of the capitalist epoch proper is the severing of most families from ownership of the means of production, thus radically weakening the reproductive mechanism identified by Engels. It is for this reason that Marx and Engels anticipated the "withering away" of the proletarian family.

If patriarchal domination in the capitalist era is reproduced through economic dependency, it must find in the labor market an analogue to the forms of female dependence earlier made possible by patriarchal inheritance of productive property. But the Marxian theory of labor markets, no less than the neoclassical, is unremittingly hostile to this project.[26] It is partly for this reason that the problem of the perpetuation of contemporary patriarchy has posed such problems in the Marxian tradition, and prompted such theoretical innovation among Marxist feminists in particular.[27]

But, as we have seen, the views that capitalist competition would tend to eliminate discrimination against women (the neoclassical version) or homogenize workers (the Marxian version) are based on the apolitical representation of the economy that follows from treating labor as an object rather than a form of social action embodying not only appropriative, but political, distributive, and cultural practices as well. Our reconstruction of the political foundations of production and exchange in the preceding chapter provides a radically different conclusion: that discrimination against women is part of a viable divide-and-rule strategy for capitalist employers, and that for this reason competition among profit-seeking capitalist firms is as likely to enhance it as to eliminate it.

We do not conclude, therefore, that capitalism *must* reproduce patriarchy, but only that it *might*. No more substantive statement can be made without a more fully developed interpretation of the process of reproduction of patriarchal domination.

Many of the insights of the recent literature on the reproduction of patriarchy may be framed using our representation of patriarchy as one of several overlapping sites involving contrasting rules of the game and heterogeneous power. Patriarchal rules are not reproduced by actors merely acting out the script written by their social roles; they are consolidated or altered by groups of people carrying out intentional projects. Patriarchy is reproduced partly because those who benefit from it have the power to prevent the rules from being changed. Moreover, the patriarchal family does not generally secure the conditions for its own survival. The reproduction of patriarchy depends upon actions taken in the state and in the economy at least as much as in the family.

But most centrally, far from being a foregone conclusion, the reproduction of any form of patriarchy is always in doubt and is constantly rendered problematic by the forms of solidarity and intervention made possible by the heterogeneous structure of power in society. Indeed, the patriarchal system within liberal democratic capitalism is an excellent example of a contradictory structural system in action. The patriarchal family is directly stabilized by the legal structure of family relations and the differential access of men and women to employment in the capitalist economy. But indirectly these neighboring sites also supply the raw material for undermining fundamental forms of patriarchal authority.

The process of reproduction and transformation of contemporary patriarchy is best understood, we believe, within this framework. A comprehensive treatment would require attention to the diversity of patriarchal structures among different races and classes—we will briefly illustrate our approach through a consideration of two important lines of argument, one psychoanalytic and the other primarily economic.

Nancy Chodorow's ground-breaking work on mothering provides a valuable interpretation of the reproduction process.

> All sex-gender systems organize sex, gender, and babies. A sexual division of labor in which women mother organizes babies and separates domestic and public spheres. Heterosexual marriage, which usually gives men rights in women's sexual and reproductive capacities and formal rights in children, organizes sex. Both together organize and reproduce gender as an unequal social relation.[28]

The expression of gender personality in adulthood, Chodorow argues, commits men and women alike to defending and reproducing the very family structure through which this personality is nurtured. This explains the tendency for social continuity in the interpersonal relationships which underlie and reproduce the patriarchal family. Central to the formation of gender personality, says Chodorow, is the fact that parenting is mostly mothering:

> Girls and boys develop different relational capacities and senses of self as a result of growing up in a family in which women mother. These gender personalities are reinforced by differences in the identification processes of boys and girls that also result from women's mothering. Differing relational capacities and forms of identification prepare women and men to assume the adult gender roles which situate women primarily within the sphere of reproduction in a sexually unequal society.[29]

The psychoanalytical bases for this position are the "asymmetries in family experiences, growing out of women's mothering, [which] affect the differential development of the feminine and masculine psyche."[30] Of particular importance is the greater difficulty that boys have in developing a masculine identity in a society in which the prime parenting is done by women: "A boy, in order to feel himself adequately masculine, must distinguish and differentiate himself from others in a way that a girl need not—must categorize himself as someone apart."[31]

Despite the almost exclusive focus on parenting, Chodorow does not propose an autonomous family-based theory of reproduction.[32] The central explanatory term in Chodorow's argument—sexual division of labor in parenting—itself is strongly reinforced by discrimination against women in the capitalist economy. Where women systematically receive less pay than men, and where part-time work is particularly low-paying, it makes little economic sense for men to do most of the work of parenting, or even to share equally in parenting.

A clear implication is that the sexual division of labor in parenting is critically involved in reproducing sexual inequality in society at large, and vice versa. Chodorow's argument is devoted primarily to explaining the reproduction of the sexual division of labor in child rearing rather than telling why this is an unequal division of labor that reflects not only a sexual division of tasks but a hierarchy of power as well. The fact that men operate in the public sphere does not by itself provide the required explanation unless the domination of the private sphere by the public is explained. Analogously, the power of capital over the state is not explained primarily by the fact that owners of large firms operate in the state sphere, but rather by the structural links between ownership and state policy.

Other strands in the theory of the reproduction of patriarchal domination address this issue more directly. These include support for public policies that enhance the power of men over women, and restrictions on both reproductive rights and rights of sexual preference. Violence against women, the de facto toleration of rape, wife beating, and sexual harassment, as well as the widespread treatment of these crimes as either permissible or less egregious than other forms of violence undoubtedly play both a practical and symbolic part in perpetuating gender inequality. The toleration of a high level of violence against women is particularly remarkable given the tendency of states to guard jealously their monopoly on the use of violence.[33] We will focus here, however, on the relationship between economic dependence and the reproduction of contemporary patriarchy.

A Marxian approach to women's economic dependence, we note at the outset, simply will not work: the subordination of women is a clear-cut case of domination not reducible to the transfer of surplus labor time, and hence incomprehensible from the perspective of the theory of exploitation. The subordination of women, whether in the form of patriarchy, property in women, or simply a general sex-gender ascriptive system, is present in the vast majority of societies, and in a wide variety of regions of social life within them. It represents a system of domination in the precise sense that it places effective power disproportionately in the hands of men. But this system of domination is quite compatible with men's enjoying no particular economic privilege therefrom. Men and women may work the same number of hours and enjoy the same living standards. Yet male power may be reproduced through such varied means as a male monopoly on bearing arms, or a prohibition of female mobility, or even a prohibition (as in colonial New England) of female property ownership.

This is not to argue that a transfer of surplus labor time from women to men does not occur quite widely.[34] Rather, the reproduction of the system of domination may not be dependent upon such a transfer, and hence the process itself may not be comprehensible within the frame of reference of exploitation alone.

More important than an economic transfer between women and men, we believe, is the differential status experienced by single women and women in couples. Women's restricted access to the capitalist labor market along with the status of the heterosexual couple as the most effective system of income redistribution in contemporary society places women in a position economically dependent on men. The critical aspect of this dependence in understanding the perpetuation of male dominance is not the economic privilege—more consumption or less work—it may afford to men but the superior power it gives men in their relationships with women.

This model of women's economic dependence has been developed most fully by Elaine McCrate:

> Feminists have typically argued that women have been dependent on men for physical protection, emotional and intellectual approval, and economic support. If we focus on the economic dimension of feminine dependence, we quickly observe that "getting a husband" occupies a position in feminist theory on women's oppression which is analogous to "getting a job" in Marxian theory of capitalism.[35]

It follows from this model that what might be termed the free marriage market, like its labor market counterpart, is a structure that effectively ensures the dependency of one of the contracting parties. McCrate argues that marriage is

> an institution in which family conflicts are resolved undemocratically, and often unequally, because of individual men's power over their wives. Their power is derived in large part from their gender-based advantages in access to a livelihood, that is, from the corresponding economic penalties imposed on women who live independently of men.[36]

Clearly, the degree of dependence of each party to this bilateral relationship depends on the relative costs that each would experience should the relationship end. Correspondingly, the relative power of men and women considering entering a relationship is strongly affected by the relative gains each would experience by shifting from a single to a couple status. The economic aspects of these costs depend on a wide variety of influences, among them public policy, the effects of aging on perceived sexual attractiveness, the politics of housework (including the distribution of consumption and housework within the household), the relative wages or other access to income of men and women, the availability of paying jobs for men and women, the number of children and extent of effective parental child-support payments in the case of separated couples, the availability of governmental child-support payments and other public income support, and the availability of alternative couple partners. If job opportunities for women were increased, or if state-provided child-support payments were to rise, the relative independence of women would increase on the average.[37]

Like Chodorow's theory of parenting, McCrate's economic dependence model points to the importance of the sexual division of labor and the subordinate position of women in labor markets as central to the reproduction of patriarchy. McCrate's model focuses particular attention on the multi-faceted nature of this reproduction process, drawing upon practices not only in the family but in the state and the economy as well.[38] On the integral part played by the state in the reproduction of patriarchal domination Nancy Folbre remarks,

> In the contemporary U.S., one occasionally hears the argument that feminists have contributed to the rise of the female-headed household by promoting State interference in family life. Yet the State interfered in family life from the very outset of U.S. history, not to strengthen the family per se, but to strengthen the power of elder men (with the exception of Black men) within it. . . . Patriarchy has gone "public" in the sense that employers and the State have proved as reluctant if not more than individual men to help out with the kids.[39]

But the intervention of the state and the workings of the economy need not act to reproduce patriarchy. As patriarchy occurs within the context of a system of heterogeneous power, disruptions in its reproduction process may emerge—often unexpectedly or unintentionally—from a wide variety of sources. For example, the lower wages paid to women as a result of discriminatory employment also have the direct effect in a profit-oriented economy of expanding the range of jobs available to women. While low wages continue to be a source of women's economic dependence, expanding job opportunities enhance their bargaining power. Correspondingly, while state elites expand income support programs hoping to quiet both public concern over economic inequality and reduce the threat of social unrest, social welfare programs have the effect of enhancing not only poor women's economic independence, but that of all women.[40]

These fissures in the edifice of patriarchy are made possible by the heterogeneous nature of the rules of the various overlapping sites that constitute liberal capitalist society. The structure of these rules and their associated discourses do not, by themselves, threaten the reproduction of patriarchy. But they do provide ample tools to be deployed against patriarchy. The logic of opposition to patriarchal privilege, no less than its reproduction, may be illuminated by representing society as a collection of sites of social practice embodying a heterogeneity of power.

Conclusion: Markets, Dramas, and Contests

Among the more compelling metaphors for society is the market. States are viewed as bartering protection and justice for tax revenues, social interactions are termed exchanges, society is considered a social compact, and even such intimate institutions as marriage are deemed contractual. Perhaps the popularity of this metaphor is due to the impressive reach of markets into daily life. For whatever reason, society is represented as a set of consensual contractual obligations, bound together by a minimal legal structure and such conventional symbolic forms as language, money, and dress.

This view admirably captures the intentional aspect of human activities reflected in the act of choice, but it ignores structural determination; the systematic way in which the rules of the game produce social outcomes independently of the wills of the actors themselves. We sense that something is amiss when Milton Friedman writes that a "free private enterprise exchange economy" may be considered to be "a collection of Robinson Crusoes" in which "since the household always has the alternative of producing directly for itself, it need not enter into any exchange unless it benefits from it. . . . Cooperation is thereby achieved without coercion."[41] We have argued in the preceding chapter that the conventional view of exchange is inadequate even to explain labor markets and credit markets. By extension we are dubious of the light to be shed by regarding society as a vast system of exchanges.

Opposing the exchange metaphor is a structuralist alternative: society is a play in which we act out a script written "behind our backs" as it were. Actors are attached to roles (that is, they occupy social positions) which they have learned (through socialization) and which they play more or less adeptly (normally or deviantly). Relations of hierarchy and subordinacy are written into the script, and justice depends on whether the casting is fair (meritocratic or ascriptive). Freedom, in this view, is virtually an illusion.*

This view, though finely attuned to the often-opaque origins of our intentions and the unseen limitations on the effectiveness of human projects, fails to provide a convincing account of the impressive dynamism of social

---

* We present the theatrical metaphor in Parsonian language, but a Marxian variant also exists: society consists of social relations among producers and nonproducers, together with a superstructure of cultural forms justifying these relations; individuals and groups then act out the class positions that they occupy. We return to this Marxian "expressive theory of action" in chapter 5.

relations. The theatrical performance itself is a continual transformation of the script. There is no separate place of convocation, distinct from the performance itself, at which the actors struggle not within, but over, the plot. The play and its transformation take place at the same time, on stage; if society is a theatrical performance it is one inspired by Luigi Pirandello's *Six Characters in Search of an Author*.

We propose a richer metaphor: society is a contest, or better, an ensemble of games. The game analogy is immediately attractive as it evokes both action and structure: the game of chess, for instance, is both an activity (playing chess), and a structure (the rules of chess.) Unlike the games referred to in everyday language, however, we participate in most of the games that make up society not by choice but involuntarily.

We integrate choice, structural determination, and history by conceiving of realms of social action as games in which both the rules and the players are continually transformed. In adopting the game as our metaphor, we commit ourselves to treating social relations as rules governing the strategic behavior of relatively autonomous social individuals and groups.

The rules of the various games define the meaning and effectiveness of action on the part of the players, but these rules are in turn altered by the players themselves. We refer to this aspect of the game as *recursive*, as it is played and replayed continuously, the rules of the game themselves being one of the stakes of the game.

Because of the recursive nature of the rules of the game, history counts. When the players change not only the rules but themselves as well, social choice is decisive and exhibits a degree of finality not understood in contractual and theatrical theories. Historical time, unlike the logical time of most social theory, is in principle irreversible. In a world of historical time—the world we inhabit—it is not exactly true that you cannot go back, but to get back to where you were you cannot simply reverse your tracks; rather, a new route is usually required.

Social action generally cannot be reversed, in the first instance, because the result of action is the transformation of the rules of the game, and hence the very conditions of social choice. But perhaps more important, the *constitutive* character of social action—the fact that social actors are transformed by their very acts—entails that social choice transforms not only the rules of the game, but the subjects of social life themselves.

Further, essential to our view is that society is not a single game, but a series of interacting games, each with distinct rules. It is the plurality of the games that most clearly distinguishes our historical structural concept of power from the Marxian mode of production. The Marxian approach privileges one structure—class—while accounting for others primarily as the effects or the conditions of existence of class. We accept the possibility of the dominance of a particular structure—of the absolute state in sixteenth-century France, of class in early twentieth-century Great Britain, of patriarchy in colonial New England, for example—but the relationship among structures cannot be posited in advance of a study of the reproduction processes of each.

Because individuals are invariably players in more than one game—family, state, and economy, for example—we say that the games are *overlapping*, often giving rise to conflicting strategies and jurisdictions concerning the range of application of incommensurable rules. (A society might by chance exhibit only one set of rules, of course: prestate kinship-based societies or some form of totalitarian dictatorship come to mind. However, we doubt that this possibility is of concrete importance.) The games that constitute a society may be considered overlapping in another sense as well: the historical perpetuation of the rules of any of the games depends upon the structure of the entire ensemble of games.

Finally, the recursive, overlapping, constitutive games that make up society are *asymmetrical*. The rules of chess make it immaterial who plays with white and who with black; the rules of the games that make up society, however, generally confer systematic advantage on one group of players or another. We can of course imagine societies structured by symmetrical games; we do not consider domination an expression of the human condition. The asymmetry of the games is the key to our understanding of domination.

The asymmetric, recursive, constitutive, overlapping game metaphor allows us to assert the centrality of domination without asserting its inevitability or immutability.[42]

The recursive and asymmetrical features of social games support a view of politics quite different from the dominant pluralist conception of American political science associated with the work of Arthur Bentley, David Truman, Robert Dahl, and others. In our conception the rules generally work to the advantage of well-defined groups and to the disadvantage of others. Partly for this reason the survival of the rules is always problematic. By contrast, pluralist theorists tend to take the basic structures of social interaction as so widely agreed upon or at least ineffectively opposed as to be given. Robert Dahl expresses this conviction in the final chapter of his celebrated *Who*

Governs. Concerning the stability of liberal democratic rules he notes,

> Over long periods of time the great bulk of citizens possess a fairly stable set of democratic beliefs at a high level of abstraction. . . . Most citizens assume that the American political system is consistent with the democratic creed. . . . To reject the democratic creed is in effect to refuse to be an American.[43]

Not surprisingly, if the rules are taken as given, politics is reduced to a distributional struggle over resources. Arthur Bentley, the father of the American pluralist school, expressed this view well: "My interest in politics is not primary, but derived from my interest in economic life, and . . . I hope from this point of approach ultimately to gain a better understanding of economic life than I had succeeded in gaining hitherto."[44] By contrast, in our conception political practices are aimed at changing or stabilizing the rules governing resource distribution and human development. What pluralists often call "politics"—the process determining "who gets what, when, and how," in Harold Lasswell's phrase—we term distributional practices. The political actors in the pluralist view tend to be interest groups; in ours they are created from the bonds of solidarity of those sharing a common of oppression. Our point is not that interest groups are unimportant, but that the pluralist focus on their interplay provides a narrow and occluded vision of the historical evolution of social structure and may even fundamentally misunderstand its chosen objects of analysis, such as conflicts over income distribution.

Making society more democratic involves more than the progressive elimination of the familiar forms of domination: it means making people's political practices effective, and more nearly equally effective, thus rendering the process of structural change subject to democratic accountability.

Structures change because people change them. Making good the promise of the democratic accountability of social change demands an understanding of why and how people change or fail to change the rules that govern their lives. This understanding in turn requires a more searching treatment of individual choice and collective action.

5

Action: Learning

and Choosing

AMONG liberalism's enduring contributions is its rich conception of individual action. Whatever its defects, the liberal view of individual choice will continue to serve as a key point of departure for democratic theory. But we have noticed the curiously compromised status of the liberal theory of agency. The roots of this defect in liberal theory, we shall see, lie not in simply overlooking patriarchal privilege, the power of capital, and other forms of domination, but in more fundamental commitments.

These commitments may be suggested by a brief consideration of two generally ignored pages from the tradition of liberal political philosophy, one from Jeremy Bentham and the other from Thomas Hobbes. Both may be passed over as mere oddities reflecting nothing more than the idiosyncrasy of genius, but we believe they are considerably more suggestive of the nature of the liberal paradigm itself.

In 1787, Jeremy Bentham, the father of utilitarian liberalism, proposed an ingenious plan for a circular building, which he called the Panopticon. Bentham believed the structure could become the model for prisons, factories, schools, houses of correction, homes for deserted young women, nurseries, lunatic asylums, and even chicken coops. The structure was, he said, "a way of obtaining power of mind over mind in a quantity hitherto without example." The building provided simultaneously for the isolation of its inmates and their continuous surveillance. Overlooking no detail of lighting, wall color, and materials, Bentham designed the edifice so that the central surveillance kiosk afforded a view into each cell (to which was also connected a listening tube) without allowing the inmates to view the warders. Bentham suggested that his design would be well suited to a harem, for it would minimize the number of eunuchs required. The idea was originally directed toward more prosaic ends, however: his younger brother had devised it as a model for a factory being built for the Russian Prince Potemkin.[1] Robin Evans comments:

> Operationally the closest approximations to Bentham's principle are to be found in certain building types developed for aviaries and menageries. . . . his convict plan was parallel most closely to the architecture of zoos.[2]

That liberalism is a theory of order as well as of freedom can hardly be counted against it, and that one of its leading thinkers devoted his energies to systems of control and correction bespeaks a healthy realism, not a theoretical flaw. But Bentham's plan reveals more than an interest in order, it suggests a divided world in which rational and moral agents exercise a just and intrusive tutelage over the irrational and the dependent. It evokes not only the Enlightenment vision of human perfectability but also the later Victorian notion that the "white man's burden" was to civilize the colonial populations of the world.

One senses here not simply the ugly overtones of the pretensions of a chosen few, but a rather primitive conception of the process of development of human sentiments and capacities. This may be suggested by an unjustly obscure passage from Hobbes. In developing the concept of the state of nature, Hobbes asks us to "consider men as if . . . sprung out of the earth, and suddenly, like mushrooms come to full maturity, without any kind of engagement with each other." Christine Di Stefano comments,

> Hobbes uses his state of nature construct to eliminate factors such as socialization, education, and other means of "cultivating" human beings. . . . Mushrooms do seem to spring up overnight; they grow rapidly in the wild and require no special tending. . . . [Mushrooms] reproduce quietly and apparently asexually. . . . This feature of the metaphorical image allows us to accept . . . one of the most incredible and problematic features of Hobbes's state of nature. And it is this: that men are not born of, much less nurtured by, women, or anyone else, for that matter.[3]

Other feminist theorists have noted the absence—or the invisibility—of women in the masterworks of the liberal political and philosophical tradition.[4] It is wrong to assume that the lack is simply an oversight, perhaps due to nothing more than the origin of these works in an era more egregiously dominated by men than today, and easily rectified in our more enlightened times. Rather it reflects a fundamental commitment of liberal theory, not to gender domination per se, but to an insupportably limited view of agency, choice, and the formation of the human subject. We earlier identified this conception as the partition of learning and choosing. In setting aside the process of human development in favor of a fictional subject who hatches full-grown, Hobbes is no different from later liberal theorists. Amy Gutmann favors understatement when she observes, "Education seems to present special difficulties for all liberal theories."[5]

As a result, the modern liberal conception of the individual has a defect that renders its model of choice incompatible with democratic theory. This is the assumption that the individual enters into a choice situation with externally constituted goals—the "preferences" of neoclassical economics, and the "interests" of political science. Whenever the problem of agency arises, and hence whenever considerations of liberty and democratic accountability apply, individuals can be taken as given. This handy fiction makes the argument for individual liberty extremely simple and elegant— consider, for instance, the following well-known passage from John Stuart Mill's *On Liberty*:

> The only purpose for which power can be rightfully exercised over any member of a civilized community against his will is to prevent harm to others. His own good . . . is not a sufficient warrant.[6]

But by the same token the fiction undermines the defense of popular sovereignty. To take preferences as given allows us to recognize democracy's contribution to the proper aggregation of wants through the counting of votes, but it obscures the contribution of democratic institutions to human development—their unique capacity to foster in people the ability intelligently and creatively to control their lives. Liberalism tells us that people make decisions. But the liberal conception of action must be reconstructed to recognize that decisions also make people.[7]

Of course the liberal model of the individual recognizes that preferences and capacities are formed somewhere. Its error is to assume that when individuals are in the process of becoming, problems of agency and choice are absent. For instance, Mill's famous proclamation of the inviolability of individual preferences cited earlier is followed immediately by the less frequently cited proviso:

> It is, perhaps, hardly necessary to say that . . . we are not speaking of children or of young persons below the age which the law may fix as that of manhood or womanhood . . . [who] . . . must be protected against their own actions. . . . For the same reason we may leave out of consideration those backward states of society in which the race itself may be considered as in its nonage. . . . Despotism is a legitimate mode of government in dealing with barbarians, provided the end be their improvement.[8]

Mill here erects an opposition between "choosers" on the one hand and "learners" on the other, and justifies a system of relations of domination and subordination between the former and the latter. (The logic of Mill's argument in no way depends upon the particular examples he has chosen— "children" and "barbarians"—and is scarcely discredited by what we might now consider a racist choice of terminology in apparently referring to non-European societies.) This opposition is characteristic of liberal discourse in general. Choosers are the knights in shining armor of liberalism, whereas learners represent a residual category—individuals whose statuses do not include, and whose behavior does not support (be it temporarily or *in perpetuum*), the right of free choice; in short, learners are those who are not deemed to be rational agents.

The status of chooser has always applied in liberal discourse to educated, propertied, white male heads of households, and variously through history to others. The status of learner has always applied in liberal discourse to children, prisoners, the "insane," and the "uncivilized." It has also applied variously to women, servants, workers, and specific races and cultures which, by virtue of their biological constitution or social station, are deemed to be more or less permanently denied the status of rational agent.

The learning–choosing opposition, in addition to permeating liberal consciousness, is reflected in the very taxonomy of the traditional social sciences. Economics and political science deal with choosers, and exhibit scant concern for the formation of wills; sociology, anthropology, and psychology deal with learners in the process of formation of wills, which lies outside the logic of choice. Perhaps it is for this reason the maximizing models of economics found a ready welcome in political science but have yet to make serious inroads into the other social sciences.

FIGURE 5.1

Liberal Partitions and Favored Social Institutions

	Social Sphere	
Action	Private	Public
Learning	Patriarchal Families	Hierarchical Schools
Choosing	Competitive Markets	Democratic Elections

If we combine the learning–choosing partition with the private–public distinction analyzed in chapter 3, we arrive at four basic types of action accessible to liberal theory: learning in the private sphere, choosing in the private sphere, learning in the public sphere, and choosing in the public sphere. Contemporary liberals prescribe a set of favored social institutions for the regulation of each type of action, some of which are illustrated in figure 5.1.

The crux of the liberal learning–choosing partition can be summarized by reference to figure 5.1. First, institutions deemed educational or correctional are exempted from scrutiny according to the principles of rational agency, freedom, and choice. Within the liberal discourse one does not ask, for instance, whether schools are democratic. Because such favored institutions of learning as families and schools are not required to be accountable to their participants, central forms of domination governing personal development are obscured. Second, liberalism relegates choice to an arena of personal autonomy ostensibly devoid of developmental potential. Although favored liberal institutions—market and ballot box—are praised as sensitively attuned to expressing the wills of consumers and citizens, this sensitivity fails to extend to a most central area of personal control; that is, the choices determining how individuals are to develop their preferences, their capacities for social participation, and their abilities to make informed decisions. Liberalism claims that the marketplace and the ballot box allow people to get what they want. But liberalism is silent on how people might get to be what they want to be, and how they might get to want what they want to want.

This defect in the liberal model of action helps us understand how the golden age of free trade and the "democratic revolution" also saw the birth of compulsory education, conscription, colonialism, and other systems of institutional dependence and social control to an extent unparalleled in human history. Our point here is hardly to mourn some fictitious idyllic past when popular forces impressed upon society a free and democratic structure of personal development. Forms of domination (class, ethnic, patriarchal, religious, and other) clearly underlay personal formation in pre-capitalist Europe and America. Indeed, the expansionary tendency of personal rights has doubtless undermined many such ancient forms of oppression. We suggest, rather, that it is in the nature of the learning–choosing partition systematically to obfuscate the issue of domination in human development; that the liberal state cannot account for its own manner of imposing preferences is simply a case in point.

In our view, learning and choosing represent polar categories of a more general form of social action. In place of the archetypal "child" and "adult" of liberal theory, we say that the individual constitutes preferences and develops personal powers through acting in the world. This model thus supplements Mill's vision of the rational chooser with Marx's conception of the formative power of action. Marx, in *Capital*, stressed that labor is "a process between man and nature, a process by which man . . . acts upon external nature and changes it, and in this way simultaneously changes his own nature."[9]

Our unification of learning and choosing, in rejecting the traditional status of the child also thereby rejects the status of adult. Those traditional liberal defenses of liberty based on the sanctity of individual preferences are thus severely compromised. When individuals are at once choosers and learners, the boundaries between liberty, popular sovereignty, and legitimate authority become blurred. Some simple examples illustrate our point. Ought the producer or consumer determine the nature of a service delivered? If the consumer is considered a chooser, the service is called a commodity, and consumer sovereignty is deemed to hold. If, by contrast, the consumer is considered a learner (for example, a child), the preferences of others count. Schools, for instance, teach what children *should* know, not what they *wish* to know. If we reject the learning–choosing dichotomy, however, we must search for new principles to resolve the issue. How do we deal, for example, with the case of the craft that considers not only what consumers want, but what will also contribute to the development of consumers' capacities to appreciate? What about students who fully accept the notion of learning and perhaps even revere the superior wisdom of their teachers, but wish to participate in making educational policy? These, we submit, are not anomalous cases. They are the rule, not the exception to the rule.

The use of a becoming-by-acting model of individual choice provides a postliberal democratic theory not with a set of ready-made political slogans but with a challenging intellectual enterprise: how might the centrality of individual choice and the commitment to liberty and popular sovereignty be preserved, while at the same time the myths of the autonomous individual and the fully formed chooser are rejected?

We address this problem by recognizing that personal development is in general best served through an interaction of two strategies. They are exercising one's freedom to choose independently of collective sentiment, and entering into mutual, reciprocal, and participatory action with others to achieve commonly defined goals. These two strategies are precisely Albert Hirschman's twin notions of "exit" and "voice."[10] The critique of the liberal model of action in terms of exit and voice is simply stated. By taking preferences and interests as pregiven, liberalism equates agency with exit. Individuals exercise their rights through market and ballot box. Both present a "menu" of alternatives, of which the preferred can be chosen by the individual in social isolation. The power of the chooser is limited to his or her ability to abandon a product or a political party—that is, to "exit." The market economy and the liberal democratic state, then, stress exit to the virtual exclusion of voice, and representation to the virtual exclusion of participation. The balance of exit and voice, upon which personal development depends, is thus not permitted to develop.

The instrumental theory of action of course simply bypasses these concerns, for it cannot accommodate the insight that we become who we are in part through what we do. Because economic activity is so much of what we do, it has a powerful influence on who we are, an influence almost entirely ignored in liberal theory. But only at the risk of being historically irrelevant can a viable theory of democracy elide the complex relationship between economic organization and the evolution of sentiments and capacities favoring or jeopardizing democratic self-government.

Exit, Voice, and Markets

Markets allocate resources. Market systems may be evaluated according to how efficiently they perform this function. Markets are also a way of life; they may also be evaluated according to what kind of life this is and in particular what kinds of human development it fosters. A democratic critique of markets must therefore ask how markets promote or erode a democratic culture. To do so requires a reconsideration of the theory of exchange parallel to our reconsideration of the theory of production in chapter 3.

Exchanging goods in markets is not altogether unlike exchanging greetings, kisses, or blows. Goods and services are indeed allocated through market exchange, but the exchanging parties are themselves transformed or reproduced in the process. The becoming-by-acting model treats exchange as an interaction among subjects shaping human development. Indeed, there is a strong analogy between exchange and language, in that both represent forms of social discourse which shape who we are and who we might become.[11] The point is a familiar one to anthropologists. Marshall Sahlins writes:

> If friends make gifts, gifts make friends . . . the connection between material flow and social relations is reciprocal. A specific social relation may constrain a given movement of goods, but a specific transaction—"by the same token"— suggests a particular social relation . . . the material flow underwrites or initiates social relations.[12]

We might add—contrary to Adam Smith's adage that it is our natural proclivity to "truck and barter"—that if traders make trades, trading makes traders.

The constitutive aspect of exchange in precapitalist societies has been seen as essential to social cohesion and peaceful resolution of conflict. Following Claude Lévi-Strauss, Gayle Rubin writes,

> The marriage ceremonies recorded in the ethnographic literature are moments in a ceaseless and ordered procession in which women, children, shells, words, cattle, names, fish, ancestors, whale's teeth, pigs, yams, spells, dances, mats, etc., pass from hand to hand, leaving as their tracks the ties that bind.[13]

Exchanges obviously do much more than allocate goods and services. Indeed they may not even do that at all. Again Sahlins:

> Sometimes the peace-making aspect [of exchange] is so fundamental that precisely the same sorts and amounts of stuff change hands: the renunciation of opposed interest is in this way symbolized. On a strictly formal view the transaction is a waste of time and effort. . . . They do, however, decidedly provision society: they maintain social relations, the structure of society.[14]

The exchange process need not cement social unity, however. It may as well be an explosive centrifugal force, eroding social relationships and courting social dissolution. Karl Polanyi took this view of what he called the "disembedded" market economy of the nineteenth-century European capitalist nations:

> The disembedded economy of the nineteenth century stood apart from the rest of society, more especially from the political and governmental system. In a market economy, the production and distribution of material goods in principle is . . . governed by . . . the so-called laws of supply and demand, and motivated by fear of hunger and hope of gain. Not blood-tie, legal compulsion, religious obligation, fealty or magic creates the sociological situations which make individuals partake in economic life. . . . Such an institution could not exist for any length of time without annihilating the human and natural substance of society.[15]

It is exactly the anonymity of the market that renders it so attractive when considered from the standpoint of instrumental action and so ominous when considered as a formative influence on human development. The liberal economist Charles Schultze finds the market "the most important social invention mankind has achieved," in part because it effects an admirable detachment: "Market-like arrangements . . . reduce the need for compassion, patriotism, brotherly love, and cultural solidarity."[16] Another neoclassical economist, James Buchanan, describes the workings of the market by analogy to "a roadside stand outside Blacksburg":

> I do not know the fruit salesman personally, and I have no particular interest in his well-being. He reciprocates this attitude. I do not know, and have no need to know, whether he is in direst poverty, extremely wealthy, or somewhere in between. . . . Yet the two of us are able to complete an exchange expeditiously, an exchange that both of us accept as "just." . . . We transact exchanges efficiently because both parties agree on the property rights relevant to them.[17]

But what if the market arena of self-interested and anonymous interaction reduces not only the need for compassion, but the sentiment itself? What kind of traders does capitalist trading make? More important, as we will see presently, what kind of citizens does the capitalist economy foster?

In short, exchanges are far more than a simple transfer of ownership. They are complex social relationships, the character of which depends on whether the parties in an exchange are individuals or groups, and in the latter case, how these groups are constituted by the process of exchange;

129

on the degree, nature, and structure of information concerning the objects exchanged; on the degree of communication, cooperation, and collusion among the parties; on the extent to which the terms of the exchange are externally enforced as opposed to fixed by the social relations of the exchanging parties; on the extent to which parties to the exchange are concerned with one another's discretionary behavior, and the degree to which they are capable of affecting this behavior; and finally on the resources possessed by the parties to an exchange that can be used to ensure favorable terms of exchange.

In liberal economic theory, by contrast, social exchange is reduced to an abstract contractual transaction: the transfer of fully specified property titles between two parties, the terms of which (the price) are taken by the participants as exogenously determined. The preceding considerations show this notion to be a special case which, although it applies to many exchanges, does not represent the critical ones. It is not surprising that the traditional economics textbooks tend to use as examples shoppers at the supermarket choosing between apples and nuts. More complicated exchanges and arguably the most central exchanges of modern economic life, such as those determining the terms of trade between boss and worker, between lender and borrower, or between buyers and sellers of different nations, explode the paradigmatic boundaries of liberal political science and economics, and the boundaries of the learning–choosing partition as well.

A constitutive conception of exchange must therefore reject the time-honored productivist ontology. According to that view, what economic life is *about* is the production of things—how it is done, by whom, for whom, and who shares its fruits. By contrast, a constitutive theory of the economy must address not only the question of who gets what and why, it must also ask who gets to become what and why. A theory that focuses exclusively on production runs the risk of seeing economic activity as simply a process of *getting* rather than also a process of *becoming*. The ontology of a democratic economic theory must encompass learning as well as labor, the production and reproduction of people as well as the production of things.[18]

The Economy Produces People

Once the pregiven nature of preferences is rejected, it is clearly inconsistent to consider a society to be democratic when the rights of popular determination and individual choice do not extend to the social relations through which preferences themselves are formed. This principle is of course recognized in liberal doctrine, but only in a dichotomized learning–choosing form. For example, compulsory education is held accountable through the democratic character of government, and such "private" institutions of preference formation as churches, the various communications media, and proprietary educational institutions are held accountable through the freedom of market choice and voluntary association.

Philosophical critiques of the liberal treatment of the economy have, reasonably enough, centered on questions of distributional justice and allocational efficiency. The learning–choosing partition, however, sheds additional light upon the shortcomings of the liberal justification of capitalism. Liberal discourse clearly presents the economy not only as a set of private institutions, but as a sphere of social life within which "choosing" rather than "learning" occurs. This notion is sanctified in liberal economic theory which, following the liberal economist Lionel Robbins, defines economics as "the science which studies human behavior as a relationship between given ends and scarce means which have alternative uses." This is the source of the commonsense notion of the economy as a site that produces *things* according to the *preferences* of its participants.[19]

But the economy produces people. The experience of individuals as economic actors is a major determinant of their personal capacities, attitudes, choices, interpersonal relations, and social philosophies. Individuals develop their needs, powers, capacities, consciousness, and personal attributes partly through the way they go about transforming and appropriating their natural environment. Moreover, individuals and groups regulate their own development in part to the extent that they succeed in controlling their own labor. Thus under ideal circumstances, developmental practices form an essential and intentional element of production itself. Our critique of the capitalist economy in this respect is that it renders the developmental practices of workers in production relatively ineffective and sharply circumscribed while giving broad scope to educational practices of employers, and that the effects of these arrangements, both intended and unintended, are antithetical to the development of a democratic culture.

To the extent that the experiences of production constitute an important learning environment, then, the despotic character of the capitalist economy obstructs the ability of liberal democratic capitalism to foster generalized popular control over personal development. If, as we argued in chapter 3, the economy is a public sphere generally unaccountable to its participants, these participants will not possess the social power to control their own development either as workers or, insofar as development through work suffuses their personalities and capacities, as citizens and family members. The problem concerns not only the dubious status of a liberal capitalist society as democratic but the ability of such a society in the long run to support and reproduce even minimally the liberal democratic systems of state decision making. This broader claim requires a sustained investigation of the relationship between the capitalist economy and democratic culture.

By democratic culture we mean a broad diffusion of politically relevant information, skills, and attitudes of political effectiveness, as well as the availability of forms of discourse conducive to the effective functioning of democratic institutions. A frequent claim of the defenders of liberal democratic capitalism is that it promotes precisely such a democratic culture. These claims, based on arguments dating from Tocqueville, Jefferson, and James Harrington, cannot be summarily dismissed. The discourse of individual rights, the near-universal spread of literacy, the extension of social interaction to ever-wider circles of contact, the consequent destruction of many forms of patriarchy, parochialism, and political deference are all integral to democratic culture, and at least in some measure they are promoted by the extension of the capitalist economy.

But we find the claim that capitalism supports the generation and regeneration of democratic culture not altogether persuasive. Our arguments for a critical reconsideration of this claim concern the division of labor within the capitalist enterprise and the market.

Consider, first, the experience of production as it may affect the formation of people and communities. Our analysis of the organization of the labor process within the capitalist enterprise suggests that it may be a powerful influence on human development, one that is antithetical to the production of a democratic culture.[20] Tocqueville, Adam Smith, and even Adam Ferguson, Smith's mentor, foresaw similar dangers well before the birth of the Marxian tradition.[21]

Action: Learning and Choosing

A modern restatement of the argument may begin by noting that under conditions of capitalist production the division of labor within the enterprise quite generally exhibits four relevant characteristics. These are the minute fragmentation of tasks, the separation of the conception of tasks from their execution, the hierarchical control of the labor process, and the assignment of persons to positions on the basis of race, sex, age, and academic credentials. These four characteristics would appear to promote the *opposite* of a democratic culture, as they concentrate information, information processing, and decision-making skills at the narrow pinnacle of a pyramidal structure. At the same time, the structure of capitalist production promotes a sense of political ineffectiveness, and assigns to racial, sexual, and other differences a set of hierarchical meanings that are as inconsistent with tolerance and respect as they are hostile to the forms of solidarity and cooperation necessary for effective political action.

But can these antidemocratic effects be traced to the specifically capitalist structure of production? Each of the four characteristics might well be taken as a lamentable manifestation of the technically or genetically determined requirements of efficient production. These would then presumably appear in any system, and thus would present natural rather than social limits to democratic accountability.

If labor were like any other input in the textbook rendition of neoclassical economics, and its use were governed simply by costlessly enforced contractual relations, the liberal counterclaims would be compelling. But as we have seen in chapter 3, the neoclassical representation of labor is incoherent: it cannot make sense of even the most rudimentary facts and enduring tendencies of the capitalist economy such as unemployment. It is precisely the noncontractual aspect of the relationship between boss and worker (the extraction of labor from the worker) that simultaneously explains the above-mentioned four characteristics of the labor process and forces a divergence between efficiency and profitability even under competitive conditions. The minute fragmentation of tasks and the separation of conception from execution make individual workers dispensable (and hence susceptible to threat of dismissal) by restricting the areas of production involving high levels of skill and expertise; fragmentation renders the worker's activities more susceptible to measurement and supervision. The hierarchical control of the labor process, whatever its technical properties, is required to enforce the delivery of labor services, and the assignment of persons to positions on the basis of race, sex, age, or academic credentials serves to legitimate the hierarchical division of labor and divide workers against each other. It is on this basis that we can claim that the hierarchical structure of the labor process is consistent with a competitive equilibrium of profit-maximizing noncolluding capitalists, but it is not reducible to the imperatives of technical efficiency in production.[22] We are thus permitted to say that these characteristics of the division of labor within the enterprise are not the result of technological requirements or genetic limitations and that they are (at least in part) the results of the specifically capitalist structure of production even in its idealized competitive form.

If the antidemocratic nature of the labor process has been all but ignored by advocates of the liberal democratic argument, the other major facet of the coordination of the division of labor in capitalist society—the private and decentralized coordination of the activities of the producers of diverse commodities through the medium of markets—has provided its foundation. It is true, to be sure, that since Tocqueville few liberal theorists have made much of the relationship between markets and culture. Where the issue has been raised, as in Milton Friedman's classic defense of markets, it has been to assert that markets inhibit prejudice, censorship, and the arbitrary use of power. This argument, which, as Albert Hirschman has pointed out in *The Passions and the Interests*, may be traced to Montesquieu, is a compelling one. But it is so partial that it is radically misleading.[23]

The strength of the argument lies in the anonymity and range of choice offered in markets, which explain, to return to Friedman's example, why the consumer of bread does not know whether it was produced by "a Negro, by a Christian or a Jew." The shortcoming of the argument consists in overlooking the relationship between markets, political participation, and the formation of a democratic culture.

Demonstrating this shortcoming is quite straightforward. A democratic culture is produced and reproduced through the activities that people undertake. Perhaps the most important of these activities is democratic politics itself. Under what conditions will people engage in learning democratic culture by doing democratic politics? Clearly, the answer is where such opportunities exist and where there are incentives to participate. The incentives to participate will be greater where something important is at stake, or to put it differently, where the opportunity cost of not participating is high.

Markets minimize the cost to the individual of not participating in democratic political practices, for markets promote exit over voice and hence provide an alternative to political participation as a means toward achieving desired ends. The extensive reliance upon markets thus undermines the conditions conducive to a high level of participation and a vibrant democratic culture. If most important social outcomes are generated by market processes, the stakes of democratically constituted decision processes are severely circumscribed. That markets might undermine democratic political participation through limiting the stakes and reducing the opportunity costs of not participating is perhaps not surprising. For it is precisely this reduction in the "need" for collective decision making that is so much applauded in liberal social theory.

Perhaps an example will make our point clear. Consider the disgruntled parent of an elementary-school student seeking to rectify the inadequacy of the curriculum at the neighborhood public school. Assuming that the parent's suggestions have been ignored, he or she may organize others to elect a new school board, or may threaten to do so. Or he or she may withdraw the child, curtail competing expenditures if possible, and send the child to a private school with the preferred curriculum. The opportunities open to the parent are voice or exit. Markets inhibit participation by ensuring that the option of exit is always present, thus undercutting the commitment to voice.

The example may appear limited, but it is not. The person who feels strongly about street crime or air pollution can either organize to improve the social and physical environment, or can "shop" for a community with a more desirable bundle of characteristics. The disgruntled individual with limited resources and less mobility can buy an air conditioner, or a gun.

In short, the issue of market versus nonmarket decision making, which is traditionally seen as an "economic" debate to be decided on grounds of allocational efficiency, must also be political and cultural. The issue cannot be resolved in favor of market or planning, we submit, for the same reason that a reasonable political philosophy does not choose between liberty and popular sovereignty.

The capitalist economy, then, produces people; and the people it produces are far from ideally equipped with democratic sentiments and capacities. The instrumental conception of action, which has diverted liberal attention from this problem in the evaluation of economic structure, is no more auspicious as a basis for a theory of specifically political action.

Representative Government and Constitution of Interests

The instrumental conception of politics was presupposed by Hobbes's justification of monarchy and Locke's arguments for republican government, dating back to Machiavelli and what Quentin Skinner aptly termed the "crucial disjuncture between the pursuit of virtue and the achievement of success in political affairs."[24] But contrary to the instrumental view of politics, political action—like economic action—creates as much as it satisfies needs. Individuals act and groups are structured on this presumption. Understanding political action thus requires that we reject the instrumental conception in favor of the notion of becoming-by-acting.

Our objections to the instrumental conception of politics parallel our reservations concerning instrumentalism in economic theory. First, by abstracting from the formation of wills and the process of human development, this conception extols exit and denigrates voice, and hence reduces democratic government to representative government. By devaluing political participation (or rather, reducing participation to the act of registering one's preferences—voting), it counsels against politically empowering forms of community association which lie between the individual and the state itself.

The liberal approach thereby effectively identifies the democratization of a sphere of social life (such as the economy), either with its organization according to principles of unimpeded exit or with its assimilation into the liberal democratic state. As a result, the liberal mind has difficulty expanding the menu of democratic choices beyond the conservative reliance on the market and the social democratic disposition toward an enlarged state. The affirmation of the desirability of heterogeneous forms of social power, each governed by an interaction of exit and voice, is thus precluded by the instrumental conception of political action.

Second, the instrumental conception of political action fails to account for political behavior, for it supplies no coherent account of collective action. Throughout history groups have banded together to implement common projects for social change, often against the grain of dominant social institutions. The instrumental theory of action is incapable of explaining this most basic of political phenomena. It is perhaps for this reason that Robert McNamara, the man who introduced the marginalist calculus of cost-benefit analysis to the U.S. automobile industry, was unable to understand, when he became Secretary of Defense in the 1960s, why the Vietnamese fighting U.S. intervention in their nation did not simply drop out of the struggle when he raised the costs by massive bombing.

Mancur Olson has shown that, within the terms of the instrumental conception of action, self-regarding uncoerced individuals will enter into joint relations to meet common ends only under the most stringent of circumstances. Insofar as there are costs of participation, and given that each individual will benefit from the success of the project whether or not he or she contributed to its success, it behooves each to refrain from participation. In Mancur Olson's words,

> unless the number of individuals in a group is quite small, or unless there is coercion or some other special device . . . rational, self-interested individuals will not act to achieve their common or group interests. . . . These points hold true even when there is unanimous agreement in a group about the common good and the methods of achieving it.[25]

It of course follows from this argument that self-interested individuals will not engage in such life-threatening acts as making revolution, fighting for democracy, or engaging in civil disobedience to secure civil rights. One may respond that these heroic forms of behavior may elude the grasp of the liberal model of political action, but the vast bulk of normal political activity is amenable to its analysis. However, according to Olson's logic, the "free rider" problem haunts even such mundane arenas as electoral politics: in general, instrumental action will induce the individual even to refrain from voting in a liberal democratic society. Clearly, the costs of voting in terms of time and energy spent in the process, as well as that expended in obtaining the information necessary for reasoned choice, will generally exceed the expected contribution of one person's vote to the probability of a favorable outcome of an election.

That contemporary liberal political theorists are nonetheless content to assume that voting is rational contrasts sharply with a fundamental proposition of contemporary liberal economic theory. In the theory of competitive markets each actor is assumed to take prices as given—to act, as the textbooks put it, as a "price taker." The logic behind this assumption is that although the actors' decisions (say, to produce a larger quantity of output, if the actor is the management of a firm) will have some effects throughout the economy, and will in general affect all prices, these effects are so small in a market of many buyers and sellers that they may safely be ignored. (Literally, they are so small that it would be irrational—unprofitable in our example—to take them into account.) But by similar reasoning these actors would never vote, as the effects of the single vote in an electorate of many voters would be too small to justify the cost of the action.

Of course, it may be objected that there is nothing in the instrumental conception of politics to require that the objectives of individuals be self-regarding. Indeed, the term *citizen* itself in liberal discourse suggests an individual status transcending self-relating concerns. It may be thought that insofar as individuals altruistically identify with the concerns of a social grouping—be it a special interest group, a social class, the nation, or even the whole of humanity—the free rider dilemma posed by Mancur Olson disappears.

This objection, however, misses the mark: the Olson paradox does not depend upon the self-interested character of individual preferences. For it is quite clear from the logic of the free rider argument that as long as participation is costly, the precise content of the preferences of the individual are irrelevant. Whether the benefits of participation take the form of personal gain, satisfaction of the needs of a group of which the individual is a member, or compassion for the well-being of other groups of which he or she is not a member, the individual will calculate in a parallel manner the benefits and costs of participation, and in general refrain from participation.

But individuals do participate voluntarily in a variety of social practices, including voting, demonstrating, striking, and promoting charity, out of both self-relating and altruistic motivations. Nor is it reasonable to question whether even altruistic individuals take into account their own costs of participation; for example, the soldier volunteering for a combat mission has not generally been accused of devaluing his or her own life. The most fruitful method of explaining such behavior, we maintain, involves abandoning the instrumental conception of action itself—and in particular jettisoning the notion of preconstituted or exogenously given preferences.

According to the principle of learning through choosing, by contrast, individuals and groups in general participate not merely to meet preexisting ends, but also to constitute themselves, or to reaffirm themselves, as persons and groups with particular and desired attributes.[26] It follows that preferences are as much formed as revealed in the exercise of choice. Individuals choose in order to become, and the nature of the opportunities given for the expression of choice affects the formation of wills.

One does not merely register one's preferences in giving to charity or voting; rather, one constitutes and reaffirms oneself as a charitable person or a good citizen. Similarly, in volunteering for combat the soldier is not merely registering a preference for victory, nor even expressing a capacity for bravery; volunteering for combat constitutes and reaffirms the soldier's character as brave. The woman who joins a demonstration against domestic violence is not simply or possibly even primarily seeking a greater measure of physical security; she is participating in the redefinition of "woman" and so reconstituting herself. Finally, the worker joining with others to overcome class oppression is not simply opting for one social outcome as opposed to another; he or she is in addition affirming his or her status in social life, and his or her dignity by virtue of, or even despite, that status.

More is at issue here than the philosopher's venerable concern with the most felicitous representation of intention, action, and the individual. The instrumental conception of politics renders liberalism indifferent or hostile to the formation of those loyalties and social bonds upon which a vibrant democracy must depend. This is nowhere more clear than in its devaluation of decentralized autonomous communities.

Samuel Bowles & Herbert Gintis, Democracy & Capitalism (NY: Basic Books, 1987).

Learning, Loyalty, and the Political Community

Thomas Jefferson believed that republican government required the proliferation within the state of "small republics" in which each citizen would become "an acting member of the Common government." "These little republics would," Jefferson hoped, "be the main strength of the great one."[27] Hannah Arendt comments,

> If the ultimate end of revolution was freedom and the constitution of a public space where freedom could appear, . . . then the elementary republics of the wards, the only tangible space where everyone could be free actually, were the end of the great republic whose chief purpose in domestic affairs should have been to provide the people with such spaces and to protect them.[28]

Today one might go further and insist that these democratic communities should not be the creature of the state: a democratic society must foster the proliferation of vital and autonomous self-governing communities standing between the individual and the state.[29] This is true for three reasons. First, as we have noted, participation in self-government is a form of democratic learning. Second, the expanding power of even a democratically elected state is always a potential threat not only to personal autonomy, but to popular sovereignty as well. The isolated individual—as voter or as buyer of commodities—is relatively powerless to resist the claims of the state, and is greatly empowered by the availability of a rich selection of collective forms of democratic social action not beholden to the state. Just as capital has assiduously cultivated barriers to state intervention in the economy—the institutions securing the mobility of capital and the power of capital strike being foremost among them—so too must democrats rely on the construction of partial barriers to the interventions of even the most democratic of states. The democratic communities that make up these barriers—whether they be workplaces, neighborhoods, or educational institutions—constitute a collective form of liberty not so different from the concept of *libertas* which expressed the collective sovereignty of the city-state in Machiavelli's Florence.

Third, because a democratic politics relies on voluntary compromise and empathy, it requires at least a minimal identification of the citizen with public life, and with some notion of collective interest. The quality of these identifications is of course central to the functioning of democracy, because they may range from benign love of one's neighborhood or commitment to one's fellow workers, to virulent racism or bellicose nationalism. We could not agree more with Charles Taylor, who says that "what modern society needs . . . is a ground for differentiation, meaningful to the people concerned, but which at the same time does not set the partial communities against each other, but rather knits them together in a larger whole."[30] The alternative to a democratic pluralism, in our opinion, is a vacuous universalism which courts anomie and its twin, totalitarianism.

Far from fostering such a democratic pluralism, liberal capitalism has produced a political wasteland stretching between the individual and the state. The problem, according to Hannah Arendt, is not the scale of social life, but its substance: "What makes mass society so difficult to bear is not the number of people involved, but the fact that the world between them has lost its power to gather them together . . . and to separate them."[31] But the era of the ballot box and the marketplace did not so much destroy the intervening communities as it did disempower and depoliticize them. As a result the state came to monopolize politics.

Political life prior to the liberal capitalist era was hardly democratic. But as Charles Tilly has shown, it exhibited a generous array of communitarian political activities. Writing about France, Tilly observes:

> The eighteenth century had its own repertoire. The anti-tax rebellion, the movement against conscription, the food riot, the concerted invasion of fields or forests were the most distinctive forms of revolt. . . . [A] great deal of . . . collective action went on either through deliberate (although sometimes unauthorized) assemblies of corporate groups which brought forth declarations, demands, petitions or lawsuits; or via authorized festivals and ceremonies in the course of which ordinary people expressed their grievances symbolically.[32]

Political action was often based on highly integrated communities. It was not focused exclusively on the state and it often took forms that we might today consider more cultural than political. As characteristics of these "premodern" political forms, Tilly notes

> a tendency for aggrieved people to converge on the residence of wrongdoers and on the sites of wrongdoing rather than on the seats of power . . . ; the rare appearance of people organized voluntarily around a special interest, as compared with whole communities and constituted corporate groups; the recurrent use of street theatre, visual imagery, effigies, symbolic objects and other dramatic devices to state the participants' claims and complaints; and the frequent borrowing . . . of the authorities' normal forms of action . . . often amount[ing] to the crowd's almost literally taking the law into its own hands.[33]

The nineteenth century saw the emergence of a new state-centered political repertoire; the highly political but local community-based charivari and the food riot gave way to the national vote and the demonstration at the courthouse. Coinciding with the extension of suffrage, the eclipse of older forms of political action was no doubt due to the effectiveness of national electoral politics as a form of action. But it also owed much to the manner in which markets and particularly the mobility of labor in the emerging capitalist economy worked to erode the traditional corporate and residential communities that had formed the basis of the earlier repertoires.

The demise of precapitalist corporate communities, however, was not simply the inexorable result of the logic of the market; in some arenas it was a deliberate objective of liberal state policy. This can be most clearly seen in what Gerald Frug calls "the liberal attack on city power," characterizing the withdrawal of the chartered freedoms of the medieval town.

The deliberate erosion of city autonomy, writes Frug, was "but an example of the more general liberal hostility towards all entities intermediate between the state and the individual, and thus all forms of decentralized power."[34] The medieval town was "a corporation, an intermediate entity which is neither the state nor the individual, neither political nor economic, neither public nor private, yet which has autonomy protected against the power of the state."[35] Interestingly, before the nineteenth century in England and America both businesses and cities were corporations, there being no distinction in this respect between private and public functions.

The paradigmatic partitions of liberalism, and its resulting idiosyncratic conceptions of freedom, would end this confusion. During the course of the nineteenth century the two forms of corporation were distinguished. The chartered freedoms of the cities were eliminated in the interests of rational and orderly government, and the private corporate status of the business entity was secured in the name of economic progress.

The attack on the city is illustrative of a more general liberal opposition, one that was often motivated by the prosaic self-interest of the actors but is nonetheless deeply supported by liberal discourse itself. "Every example of group power," comments Frug, "permits the power wielder to invade the spheres of both the individual and the state, and is thus subject to the same liberal attack as has been waged against the cities."[36]

In noting the demise of "the numberless indefeasible chartered freedoms" of the precapitalist era, Marx captured well the peculiarities of the ascendent liberal concept of freedom:

> The bourgeoisie, wherever it has got the upper hand, has put an end to all feudal, patriarchal, idyllic relations . . . it has drowned the most heavenly ecstasies of religious fervor, of chivalrous enthusiasm of philistine sentimentalism, in the icy waters of egotistical calculation. It has resolved personal worth into exchange value.[37]

But Marx perhaps underestimated the capacity of capitalist society to spawn novel collectivities, for in practice liberalism was not so much hostile to corporate bodies as opposed to the particular forms that these took prior to the ascendency of capital.

Where the rural community and the chartered city once provided the basis for an active and participatory—if often parochial and intolerant—political life outside the state, the dominant institutional innovations of liberal democratic capitalist society—typified by the school and the modern corporation—are deemed either arenas of tutelage and hence of legitimate autocratic rule or private spheres beyond the ken of politics altogether.

Thus it is not corporate bodies per se but a participatory political life outside the state arena which was eclipsed in the liberal capitalist era. In part this is the case because political actors and especially state elites never accepted the instrumental conception of politics so fully as to take the cultural environment entirely for granted.

The great liberal thinkers themselves did not pretend that choice based on instrumental action could form the universal model of social practice. Obligation, loyalty, love, shame, civic virtue, and a host of other sentiments and commitments were variously held to be essential influences upon social action. Even Bernard Mandeville, who shocked his eighteenth-century readers with *The Fable of the Bees*, did not envision that private greed would yield public virtue in all realms of society; instead he focused on the economy.[38] Early liberal economic thinkers—notably Smith and Bentham—showed a lively interest in both the learning and choosing aspects of economic life, pondering the kinds of human beings that the emerging capitalist system would produce and advocating institutions to guide and correct this process. The celebrated ability of markets to reconcile individual interests and collective rationality—or at least to substantially attenuate the contradiction between the two—was always viewed as conditional on a kind of morality and moral action. We cannot agree more with Denis O'Brien on this point:

> While the classical writers were the earliest fully to appreciate the allocative mechanism of the market, and the power, subtlety and efficiency of this mechanism, they were perfectly clear that it could operate only within a framework of restrictions. Such restrictions were partly legal and partly religious, moral and conventional; and they were designed to ensure the coincidence of self and community interest.[39]

The early liberals recognized that the perpetuation of these moral, religious, and conventional commitments could not be taken for granted. But later views, especially those inspired by the instrumental theory of action exemplified by neoclassical economics, came to embrace a much simpler conception: the exogenous individual. Custom, community, and commitment might still be the bedrock of social interaction, but liberal thinkers—rejecting Edmund Burke's activism on behalf of tradition—increasingly saw these as the result of a more or less historical legacy rather than as the outcomes of ongoing projects of cultural reproduction. Accordingly, the problem of the reproduction of a culture consistent with the workings of the market, the ballot box, and the other institutions favored by liberalism dropped from theoretical debate.

To some extent the eclipse of cultural practices as a theoretical concern has flowed from the logic of liberal discourse itself. By couching its fundamental principles in terms of an individual and asocial conception of rights, liberal discourse makes it difficult to express solidarity and cooperation as goals of political practices. With the ascendency of liberalism, observed Otto Gierke, the "sovereignty of the state and the sovereignty of the individual were steadily on their way towards becoming the two central axioms from which all theories of social structure would proceed, and whose relationship to each other would be the focus of all theoretical controversy."[40] The sole forms of social solidarity explicitly sanctioned in liberal discourse are nationality, based on common citizenship, and kinship, based on the family. It is perhaps for this reason that among the most effective forms of "the politics of becoming" in some advanced capitalist countries today are nationalism and the antifeminist defense of the patriarchal family.

Paradoxically, the disappearance from *theoretical* discussion of the problem of cultural reproduction in the nineteenth century coincided with a growing awareness that heightened labor mobility, urbanization, economic dynamism, and other outcomes of the growth of capitalist economy itself had undermined many traditional bases of morality and social control. Just as the issue of cultural reproduction fell from theoretical view, it began to assume immense practical importance in the minds and work of the growing army of reformers and administrators who since the nineteenth century have attempted to construct state surrogates for the rapidly eroding family, neighborhood community, craft guild, church, community, and the like. The result was the erection of compulsory schools, asylums, and prisons on an unprecedented scale during an era that prided itself on tearing down other walls in the interest of economic freedom. These costs of enforcing the liberal capitalist order have continued to mount in the twentieth century.

A fundamental problem of liberal social theory, then, is that it takes as axiomatic the reproduction of those cultural, moral, and economic conditions which are necessary to make good the normative claims made on behalf of its favored institutions. In the absence of vital communities standing between the individual and the state, liberalism's cherished political principle, liberty, is experienced more as loneliness than as freedom. And the putative allocative efficiency of the market is challenged by the proliferation of enforcement costs arising from the exercise of instrumental self-interest in a conflict-ridden economy inhabited by strangers.

In its more modern variants liberalism is thus not only temperamentally ill-disposed but conceptually ill-equipped to address the problem of the forms of learning promoted by the spread of markets and elections as the dominant framework for choosing. Nor is liberal theory capable of offering an assessment of the competing claims of democracy, liberty, or other objectives in how this interaction of learning and choosing might best be governed. Indeed, the two forms of action are considered to be polarities almost literally disjointed in time (or at least in age).

Marxian social theory, which has taken the social construction of the individual as axiomatic, might be thought to provide an alternative conception of the individual and of social action capable of addressing the concerns of democratic culture and community. But for quite different reasons, this is not entirely the case.

Direct Democracy and the Expressive Theory of Action

Scorning the notion of the exogenously given individual, Karl Marx championed the view that people produce themselves through their social practices. Building on the concept of the socially constituted individual, he provided a theory of social action of historically unprecedented sophistication. Relations of dominance and subordination, he argued, are the stuff of which collective action is made. Class relations, he stressed, are not only relations of domination, but of bonding as well—and hence they are the potential foundation of common political action. Yet these insights were not developed in a way that might overcome the weaknesses of the liberal theory of action. Nor, as we shall see, do they provide an adequate basis for a reconstructed theory of democracy. In particular, Marx treated interests as prior to and ultimately as determinants of action:

> The question is not what this or that proletarian, or even the whole of the proletariat at the moment considers as its aim. The question is *what the proletariat is*, and what, consequent on this *being*, it will historically be compelled to do.[41]

145

Interests are pregiven because they are firmly rooted in historical necessity.

The Marxian tradition does not, however, simply reproduce the liberal theory of action. It solves the problem of collective action by inverting the liberal error. It elevates "voice" and promotes a conception of spontaneous, unstructured popular sovereignty. At the same time, it scorns the "exit" mechanisms of market and ballot box, and hence provides little conceptual support for those decentralized and representative political institutions critical to the practical achievement of a democratic order. The Marxian model of the individual is grounded in what we term as *expressive conception of action*; that is, the notion that individual behavior is an expression of collective membership. According to the expressive theory of action, individuals behave according to their class, gender, national, ethnic, and other social positions.

Missing from the Marxian model is the notion of choice. In Marxian theory, a social group possesses a set of interests, of which its members may have more or less true consciousness, and of which their action is an expression. Choice, as merely an expression of social position, has neither explanatory nor moral significance. As a result, the structural prerequisites of freedom and democratic accountability have been severely slighted.

A consequence of this denegration of individual action as a conceptual category has been a lack of interest among Marxian economists in developing the microeconomic logic of even their most fundamental propositions. The demonstration of the celebrated tendency of the profit rate to fall as a result of a rising organic composition of capital, for example, typically does not ask if any profit-maximizing noncolluding individual capitalist firm would ever choose to install new technologies in the manner posited by the theory. Okishio and others have demonstrated that when this rather elementary microeconomic question is posed, the tendency collapses.[42]

Even in the absence of a theory of choice and individual action, however, the commitment to democracy enjoys a solid lineage in Marxian tradition. Marx himself conceived of communism as a completion of the development of democratic institutions. In the *Grundrisse*, for instance, Marx interprets the passage from feudalism, to capitalism, and finally to communism, as the progressive realization of democratic institutions:

> Relations of personal dependence . . . are the first forms of society in which human productivity develops. . . . Personal independence founded on *material* dependence is the second great form. . . . Free individuality, which is founded

on the universal development of individuals . . . is the third stage. The second stage creates the conditions for the third. . . . Universally developed individuals, whose social relationships are subject . . . to their own collective control, are the product . . . of history.[43]

Yet the precise social institutions regulating this "collective control" have remained elusive in the Marxian tradition. Friedrich Engels's assessment is typical of the Marxian rejection of the state as an instrument of such control:

The society that organizes production anew on the basis of a free and equal association of the producers will put the whole state machine where it will then belong: in the museum of antiquities, side by side with the spinning wheel and the bronze ax.[44]

If not to the state, might we then turn to a more informal conception of grass-roots popular initiative? Marx and Engels's political ideal, the Paris Commune, was clearly such. In Engels's words, "Well and good, gentlemen, do you want to know what this dictatorship [of the proletariat] looks like? Look at the Paris Commune. That was the Dictatorship of the Proletariat."[45] And Lenin, before and even during the Russian Revolution, spoke in reverential terms of popular initiative: "the nation's millions . . . are creating a democracy on their own, *in their own way*, without waiting . . . for a parliamentary bourgeois republic . . . [which] stifles the independent political life of the *masses*."[46]

The Marxian critique of representative democracy is not a critique of democracy, but of representation. By treating direct popular expression as the ideal type of accountability, Marxian political theory falls within that tradition which takes representation as a withdrawal from social engagement.[47] Jean Jacques Rousseau is here typical:

Sovereignty . . . cannot be represented; it lies essentially in the general will. . . . Every law the people has not ratified in person is null and void. . . . The people of England . . . is free only during the election of members of parliament. As soon as they are elected, slavery overtakes it, and it is nothing.[48]

This hostility to representative government is rooted in a vision of society in which politics is totally integrated with daily life, and hence in which the public–private dichotomy disappears. The very notion of representation, by implying the possibility of voluntary withdrawal from the public realm, becomes a moral threat. In the romantic tradition, Lucio Colletti suggests, morality does not govern politics, but politics itself is the solution to the moral problem. . . . man's nature can be actualized only "in and through society." . . . freedom is no longer liberal freedom or individual freedom "from" society, but freedom realized in and through the latter.[49]

The liberal defense of freedom requires a sphere of social life that is both private and moral. Yet in the tradition of Rousseau, Marx, and Lenin, the private–public separation is an imperfection that disappears in the course of social emancipation. Indeed, in the socialist tradition the private emanates from capitalist property relations, and hence is an expression of alienated social being. Marx, as Leszek Kolakowski has observed,

> regards the emancipation of man as . . . made possible by the identification of private with public life, the political with the social sphere . . . what Marx desired to see was a community in which the sources of antagonism among individuals were done away with. This antagonism sprang, in his view, from the mutual isolation that is bound to arise when political life is divorced from civil society.[50]

The romantic notion of direct democracy thus precludes the possibility of a reasoned defense of representative institutions.[51] Further, the tradition of direct democracy is based ultimately upon the denial of the realm of the private. Because individuals, in the expressive theory of action, are tokens for the groups to which they belong, individual rights in opposition to popular will become a contradiction in terms, as the individual is nothing outside the grid of social relations and collective participation. Deviates are, at best, bearers of "false consciousness," and at worst, as the expression goes, "class enemies."

Ironically, the Marxian theory of collective action is no more capable of dealing with the free rider problem than is its liberal adversary. Rather than explaining why individuals would engage in collective action, it simply displaces the problem of individual action altogether. The expressive theory of action recognizes collective behavior, but it cannot explain the individual rationality of such behavior. The Marxian tradition is thus reduced to ad hoc and empirical observations concerning when, under what conditions, and in what forms collective action will take place.

Of course, it might be argued that individuals are not rational choosers. People die for their countries and in giving birth to their children, they work for their families, and defend their communities. Why question their capacities to behave according to their group interests? We respond that interests are not causally prior to practices. Rather, the interests of a group will in general depend, among other things, upon the membership of the group, its internal discursive and structural organization, and its location in an ecological system of social actions.

This critique of the expressive theory of action is clearly parallel to the preceding critique of the liberal instrumental conception of action. In both cases that which is held to determine behavior (individual preferences, group interests) is shown to be at least in part the product of behavior. In both cases we are pushed to look more deeply for the explanation of behavior. For instance, it may generally be in the interests of workers to have higher wages, but whether it is in the interest of domestic workers to ally with foreign workers against their common employers, or ally with their employers to discriminate against foreign workers, cannot be determined a priori. We do not suggest that interests are "subjective" or otherwise lacking in substance. Our argument holds even if interests could be reliably inferred from an analysis of social structure—so long as the composition of social practices, including their discursive and organizational character, are included as elements of this structure.

Moreover, in rejecting the notion that a given social order has a unique successor (for example, capitalism necessarily follows feudalism, and socialism necessarily follows capitalism), we abandon the notion that a group of individuals, however similarly placed in terms of social position, possesses a unique set of objective interests which they can discover but cannot create. In the terminology of game theory, this is equivalent to asserting that the games which constitute social life have no "core." The core of a game is a partition of all participants into groups of one or more members with pooled resources and strategies, so that no individual has an interest in leaving his or her group, and no group has an interest in enticing others to join it. To say that society has no core, then, is to assert that there are no natural boundaries to group membership, and no intrinsically optimal strategies for a given group of social actors.

Of course, groups do develop common projects, and individuals often act in concert with the groups to which they belong. Such behavior simply cannot be explained within the expressive theory of action. A constitutive theory of action—one moving beyond individual action to treat the bonding of individuals in group practices—is required for a satisfactory treatment of social behavior.

As a result, one of the key terms of political philosophy, "interest," must be reconsidered. The concept of "interest" is inherently ambiguous, involving both the notion of what people *in fact* desire, and what they *ought to* desire. In liberal theory the two are conflated, as the principle of choice implies that people should get what they want. But the two uses of "interest" are also conflated in Marxian theory because, according to the expressive theory of action, workers will eventually come to act on the basis of what is historically necessary for the success of their class, which in turn is normatively required for social progress. We argue that there is no unique resolution to the problem of the "is" and the "ought," so that interests both explain and are explained by social action.

Conclusion: Collective Action, Privacy, and Liberty

How can collective action be explained in a framework eschewing an expressive theory of action? We propose a model that extends the notion of becoming-by-action developed earlier in this chapter.

Individuals identify with others because others are integral to their individuality, and they act with others not only to get but to become.[52] The key to understanding collective action, we believe, lies in the observation that ends are *not* pregiven, and hence that there is a constitutive aspect of social interaction. In other words, individuals enter into practices with others not only to achieve common goals, but also to determine who they are and who they shall become as social beings. The liberal and Marxian models of individual behavior both fail because they posit action as oriented toward the satisfaction of ends existing prior to social action, rather than resulting from it—in the liberal case from pregiven individual wants, and in the Marxian case from historically determined group interests. Groups cannot act as groups, in these conceptions, because individuals derive nothing from action and belonging themselves. By contrast, the notion of becoming-by-acting asserts that individuals constitute themselves in important part through their joint projects.

The constitutive aspect of social interaction starts from the fact that individuals are recognized (in their own eyes and in the eyes of others) by their acts. The self as a social self is in continual need of definition, validation, and recognition through action.[53] Just as objects are known by their properties, so one's self is known by one's behavior. To be brave is to act bravely. To be charitable is to give charitably. To care about peace is to vote for peace or to demonstrate against nuclear war. These acts are not merely instrumental to the achievement of given ends, they register and create character. Action expresses identity and influences personal development; but action also *is* identity and *is* personal development. The motivation for participation in practices, despite the fact that instrumental rationality and the dominant rules of the game militate against such behavior, is rooted in the constitutive character of action.

We have traced the shortcomings of liberalism to its twin partitions, private versus public and learning versus choosing. But simply to reject these twin pillars of liberal discourse in favor of a theory of the constitution of the individual through practices and a theory of the political nature of the economy and class relations hardly represents an adequate response to the centrally important questions to which liberal theorists originally proposed their unfortunate dual dichotomies as answers.

Privacy and liberty remain focal concerns of the political philosophy of any democrat. Michael Walzer correctly notes, "We greatly value our privacy, whether or not we do odd and exciting things in private."[54] But if the liberal concept of the exogenous origin of wills is to be rejected, as it must, and along with it the inviolability of individual preferences, on what basis will liberty be defined and defended? And if the ownership of productive property no longer provides a coherent basis for the division of society into a public state and a private economy, as it surely does not, how then will a concept of the private be defined and defended?

We have suggested that individual preferences be treated both as socially conditioned and susceptible to development through individual choice. Individuals affect their own becoming, as well as that of others, through their actions. Therefore, choice serves the dual objectives of getting and becoming. Indeed, we believe that a broadened conception of choice and liberty may be defensible precisely on the grounds of its ability to facilitate learning, a position that recalls Mill's unduly ignored and more limited defense of liberty as a necessary precondition of learning. But such a model must encompass not only the logic of the individual learner and chooser, but the manner in which people act together toward their common ends.

6

Community: Language, Solidarity, and Power

LIBERAL AND MARXIAN social theory have conspired to depict personal rights as the indelible expression of bourgeois individualism. Liberalism contributes to this interpretation by taking rights as self-referencing, atomistic, and asocial. Marxism complies by taking the liberal analysis at face value, and further dismissing personal rights as mere ideological expressions of an underlying structure of class privilege. Yet rights are fundamentally social in nature, and they can embody a deeply democratic commitment. "It is a paradox of liberty," writes the Marxist historian Eric Hobsbawm, "that it became the slogan of those who needed it least and wanted to deny it to those who needed it most."[1]

Personal rights are neither liberal, nor reactionary, nor revolutionary; they are neither an ephemeral veil of privilege nor the lever of revolutionary change; they are neither prior to society nor its mere reflection. Personal rights are simply part of a discourse, a structure of communication and political action which has been a ubiquitous medium of social solidarity and conflict in Europe and North America since the rise of nation-states. This discourse has been deployed in popular struggles for the expansion of liberty and democracy, and has been used by elites to justify private property and a restricted franchise.[2] In contemporary capitalism, the discourse of rights thus belongs to no specific class or group and corresponds to no integrated world view. There is, of course, a specifically liberal conception of rights, including the private–public and learning–choosing partitions as well as the natural character of the patriarchal family. But this is only one stage in the development of a more general discourse of rights, extending from the seventeenth-century assertion of aristocratic privilege over royal pretension to contemporary demands for workplace democracy, equal opportunity, economic security, and the right to control one's body.

Even those who concede that the language of personal rights may be adapted for use by radical democrats frequently argue, however, that the discourse of rights is so quintessentially individualistic that its extensive use in promoting a democratic society is at best an expedient fraught with the danger of reproducing an anachronistic and essentially privatistic political world view. Marx was of this opinion.

> None of the supposed rights of man . . . goes beyond the egotistic man . . . that is, an individual separated from the community, withdrawn into himself, wholly preoccupied with his private interest and acting according to his private caprice.[3]

This objection is based on the widely shared notion that a political discourse is a reflection, however indirect and removed, of an underlying intellectual edifice. In this view, the discourse of rights, no matter how extensively it may be altered for expedient political or didactic purposes, remains but a reflection of an essentially bourgeois and elitist political philosophy.

We shall argue, by contrast, that political discourse (including language and other communicative symbolism) reflects neither shared consciousness nor social ideology.[4] A discourse is a set of tools. People use these tools to forge the unities that provide the basis for their collective social practices. As such, the tools of discourse are a mechanism for the formation of group action. The content of a discourse is simply the constellation of uses to which it is regularly put. The meaning of rights, in turn, is precisely their socially structured deployment in social action. Lacking an intrinsic connection to a set of ideas, words, like tools, may be borrowed. Indeed, like weapons in a revolutionary war, some of the most effective words are captured from the dominant class.

Discourses and struggles over discourses—over the way words are used, which flags are borne, and so on—are thus a key to understanding the formation and solidarity of collective social actors. The importance of discourse is easily overlooked by both liberals and Marxists; by the former because they ignore the centrality of collective action, and by the latter

153

because they believe that collective actors—classes—are not the outcome of social struggles but rather the expression of economic structures.

But politics consists critically in the formation of the "us" and the "them" which define the boundaries of collective social action. In the process of creating and transforming the "us" and "them" of politics, words, gestures, monuments, banners, dress, and even architectural design play parts no less important than one's status as an owner of the means of production, a worker, or a mother. Indeed, the ability of any of these terms designating a common location in a social structure to evoke a sense of common cause or opposition is itself the product of centuries of social conflict over discourse.

The radical democratic potential of the discourse of rights has always been the manner in which rights enhance people's capacity to label unwarranted privilege and illegitimate authority, and thereby to isolate a "them" and to mobilize a democratic "us." Sean Wilentz's study of the early-nineteenth-century working class in New York illustrates this point:

> In almost every conceivable public context and some private ones as well the subjects of this book turned to the language of the Republic to explain their views, attack their enemies, and support their friends. . . . [F]aced with profound changes in the social relations of production, ordinary New Yorkers began to reinterpret their shared ideals of commonwealth, virtue, independence, citizenship, and equality, and struggled over the very meaning of the terms.[5]

This is not the only use of the discourse of rights, as we shall see.*

Language and Social Reality

Money talks. Tradition speaks for itself. The barrel of a gun has its own uncanny persuasive power. Yet democratic institutions have often been won by people who are not wealthy, for whom traditional values protect the powers that dominate them, and who have faced the coercive force of a hostile state. How is this possible? Is there another force capable of pro-

---

* Our defense of the discourse of rights as instrument of progressive social change should not be viewed as support for the notion that a philosophy of rights can be the sole basis for a theory of the good society.

ducing social change that does not reduce to money, tradition, and physical coercion? There is, of course. It is the power of numbers—of people sharing a common project and acting in unison toward its achievement.

The power of numbers is vacuous in the absence of unity. Language is critical to democratic social change because, in the absence of wealth, without the support of tradition, and militarily weak, a democratic social movement depends upon political discourse as its synthesizing force.

Like guns and money, discourse is a social force with a character of its own. Political discourse cannot be understood as a reflection of "ideas" in people's heads, "meanings" adhering to ideological world views, or as tokens of "consciousness" to be relegated to the sphere of "ideology." As Ludwig Wittgenstein has stressed, "Words are not a translation of something else that was there before they were."[6] The importance of the structure of discourse as an element of social dynamics is normally vastly understated in social theory. This understatement is based, we suggest, on a fundamental misunderstanding of the categorical position of communication in relation to consciousness and culture.

Language is normally thought of as a conduit between inner and outer states. Speech is treated, both in popular thought and in much of social science, as the public version of an individual's psychic condition. Speaking and writing are seen as expressions of thoughts, feelings, opinions, and attitudes—in short as revelations (more or less veritable) of psychological states. Discourse is thereby consigned to a marginal status in social action akin to the role of the typewriter in creative writing. According to this view, discourse is an indicator of consciousness, consciousness being the true object of explanation or intervention. There is thus no substantive role for the structure of discourse itself in explaining social life.

The treatment of communication as a conduit from inner to outer states has a respectable philosophical lineage, in the form of what William Alston calls the "ideational theory of meaning."[7] For example, we find in Hobbes's *Leviathan* that "the general use of speech, is to transfer our mental discourse, into verbal; or the train of our thoughts, into a train of words."[8] The notion of language as a means of translating private into public discourse approaches a theory of meaning itself in the writings of John Locke, according to whom "words, in their primary or immediate signification, stand for nothing but the ideas in the mind of him that uses them."[9]

At the core of this doctrine lies the untenable assumption that human action is the expression of ideas, of which communicative action is but a reflection. But if action is an intervention into the world geared toward achieving particular human projects, there is little basis for the privileged status of "ideas" in discourse. When a father tells a child, "Go to your room!" we may construe intentions, emotions, and desires, but hardly ideas. What ideas are represented when a head of state says, "The nations of the world are engaged in the common task of constructing a future of peace"? We see in such verbalization not ideas but particular forms of transforming the world.

There are even more serious problems with the translation theory of language. Are ideas logically prior to language? Let us perform an experiment. Take three groups of social science initiates, and provide each with a distinct set of words and rough definitions to supplement their everyday language. Give the first group the terms *function, norm, structural differentiation, role,* and *pattern variable*. Give the second group *marginal productivity, Pareto optimality, utility function,* and *supply and demand*. Give the third group *libido, projection, superego, trauma,* and *catharsis*. Plunk them down in Chicago and ask them to explain poverty and crime. Will their "ideas" be unaffected by their "tools"? We think not.

In this example, it is probable that over time some concurrence will appear between ideas and words used to express them. Moreover, if allowed to choose from a less restricted selection of terms, some social actors will develop a creative selectivity in harmonizing ideas and words on the one hand, and personal projects on the other. But the privileged position of the idea will have disappeared. (We do not wish to assert the contrary of the translation theory. Ideas are not merely the manifestation of the forms of discourse which are available for its expression. Individuals regularly find the tools of discourse inadequate—even misleading—for the expression of ideas. They then attempt to transform the tools of discourse available to them.)

Let us consider another case. When has a student been properly initiated into a science? Is it when he or she has come to believe its major propositions? No, for creative work as often as not takes the form of destroying as well as validating commonly held beliefs concerning the interactions among the terms of the science. Initiation occurs when one's experience is translated into the lexicon of the science, even when the substantive interrelations and the very significations of the terms may have been altered. A science is often held together more by its terminology and its paradigmatic practices than by its ideas.

Community: Language, Solidarity, and Power

In the twentieth century, philosophers of language moved from considering language as conduit between states of mind and their public expression to considering language as a neutral system of conventions for the transmission of information. In the hands of Gottlob Frege and his successors, for example, ideational theories of meaning were forsaken in favor of viewing meaningful communication as forging valid linkages between "senses" (meanings) and "references" (things to which meanings apply). Language was thus taken simply as a tool for expressing facts, and political discourse became a mix of nonsense and scientifically verifiable assertions. Precluded was its treatment as either a potentially creative force in social change or an object of social conflict.

Sense and reference approaches to language, however, are as misleading as translation theories in dealing with the social impact of discourse. In society meanings are not fixed, they are prizes in a pitched conflict among groups attempting to constitute their social identity by transforming the communicative tools that link their members together and set them apart from others. Moreover, we cannot readily treat language as a conventional tool for relating sense to reference. The conventional sense of some words is straightforward. A *duckling* is a baby duck and a *bachelor* is an unmarried adult male. Here conventional sense works because we are able to find synonyms: we translate one word into another. But this succeeds only when there is a preexisting "other word" into which the given term can be translated. What, for instance, is the conventional sense of the words *good*, *game*, or *green*? Competent speakers are quite capable of using and interpreting these words. But is there some entity that can be called their "sense"? There is no such entity.

Several philosophers within the analytic tradition (for example, Ludwig Wittgenstein and J. L. Austin) have formulated alternative approaches of direct relevance toward understanding this insight.[10] Wittgenstein holds that words are defined by their uses in a series of overlapping discursive games. In his own words,

> Think of the tools in a tool-box: there is a hammer, pliers, a saw, a screw-driver, a rule, a glue-pot, glue, nails and screws. The functions of words are as diverse as the functions of these objects . . . the meaning of a word is its use in language. . . . Of course, what confuses us is the uniform appearance of words when we hear them spoken or meet them in script and print. For their *application* is not presented to us so clearly.[11]

157

In particular, social discourse does not reflect a realm of ideas serving as a coherent representation of social reality. Rather, as Wittgenstein has emphasized, language is a "form of life" in which words are deeds and understanding is knowing how to *do* certain things. Except in formalized and scientific contexts, words do not have senses, but a series of related uses in overlapping spheres of social activity. They are subject to different (though perhaps related) rules in each.

That the concerns of J. L. Austin lie in directions parallel to those of Wittgenstein is evident in the title of his major work, *How to Do Things with Words*. For Austin, however, the criticism of sense and reference theory focuses on the restricted categories of speeches with which it can successfully deal. Communication, Austin stresses, can be reduced neither to the transmission of information nor to the assertion of fact or value. To speak is in the first instance to constitute a fact rather than to state a fact. To say "I predict victory" is not to assert anything, but to predict something. To say "With this ring I thee wed" is to consummate an act, not to transmit information; in this it differs radically from the statement "I married him last month." Other words that have this "performative" character are *christen, vow, bet, warn, concede, assert, condemn, demand,* and *deny*.[12]

The implications of these insights for the analysis of political discourse are profound. The structure of discourse, we are led to understand, supplies a vocabulary, including for instance such terms as *liberty, freedom, right, man,* and *citizen*. But these terms do not stand for ideas, meanings, or concepts. Rather they are tools with uses and with specific ranges over which they may be applied. Struggles over discourse concern the terms admitted to the vocabulary, as well as the how, when, and where of their application.

Indeed, discourses go beyond words to include such aspects of communication as flags, uniforms, and architectural form.[13] When the radical Philadelphia militiamen in the mid-1770s resisted wearing conventional uniforms, favoring hunting shirts, which they said would "level all distinctions" within the militia, they were engaging in a struggle over discourse.[14] Indeed, as Clifford Geertz suggests in his study of the nineteenth-century Balinese state, language itself may at times be a relatively subordinate form of discursive bonding:

> The Balinese, not only in court rituals but generally, cast their most comprehensive ideas of the way things ultimately are, and the way that men should

therefore act, into immediately apprehended sensuous symbols—into a lexicon of carvings, flowers, dances, melodies, gestures, chants, ornaments, temples, postures, and masks—rather than into a discursively apprehended, ordered set of explicit "beliefs."[15]

Nor should it be inferred that the primacy of nonlinguistic forms of discursive relations are characteristic of premodern societies alone. For, as Eric Hobsbawm has observed, the consolidation of the modern nation-state involved the wholesale invention of novel symbolic discourses.

It is clear that plenty of political institutions, ideological movements and groups—not least in nationalism—were so unprecedented that even historic continuity had to be invented. . . . It is also clear that entirely new symbols and devices came into existence as part of national movements and states, such as the national anthem, the national flag, or the personification of "the nation" in symbol or image, either official, as with Marianne and Germania, or unofficial, as in the cartoon stereotypes of John Bull, the lean Yankee Uncle Sam and the "German Michel."[16]

In sum, the tools of discourse have uses that are transformed through practices and transported from one arena of social life to another in the course of social conflict.[17] We treat discourse as a contested structure constituting social life rather than reflecting it, and as framing social action. J. G. A. Pocock is surely correct in noting that "any formalized language is a political phenomenon in the sense that it serves to constitute an authority structure."[18] And Clifford Geertz, reflecting on nineteenth-century Bali, observes that

statecraft is a thespian art. But there is more to it than this, because the pageants were not mere aesthetic embellishments, celebrations of a domination independently existing: they were the thing itself. . . . The state ceremonials of classical Bali were metaphysical theatre: theatre designed to express a view of the ultimate nature of reality and, at the same time, to shape the existing conditions of life to be consonant with that reality: that is, theatre to present an ontology and by presenting it, to make it happen—make it actual.[19]

Initiation into the various discourses through which individuals are bonded together in a collective practice occurs through participation. The tools of discourse represent possibilities for the creative execution of personal and collective projects, and they acquire their force through their ability to unite people in action.

Consciousness, Discourse, and Social Bonding

The dubious notion that language is a conduit for the public expression of consciousness perfectly complements the Marxian theory of action as an expression of one's objective social position. Together the translation theory of language and the expressive theory of action engender an anthropomorphic conception of collective social practices. According to this view, individuals act jointly through their common interests and consciousness; the behavior and discourse of each individual is an expression of these common interests and consciousness. Thus the group is effectively treated as though it were a single mind with multiple corporeal representations. The problem of solidarity—the bonding of individuals together in collective practices—is thereby trivialized.

But the anthropomorphic model of collective social action cannot be sustained: the notion of the group as a collective individual is untenable even as a suggestive fiction.[20] Groups and their interests do not exist fully constituted prior to collective action: politics is as much the creation of collectivities and their erosion as it is a clash among given groups. The successful organization of a collective practice is thus seen to serve a double function; it must lead to effective interventions in the world, and at the same time it must secure its own integrity through the bonding of its members.

It thus becomes critical to understand the forces involved in maintaining the unity of collective practices. Indeed, the centripetal forces threatening the viability of a collective action may themselves contribute directly to the formulation of its goals and the character of its social interactions. The decision of a union to strike, for example, may be made more with an eye to its effects on the solidarity of its members than the ostensible economic objectives of the action. Bonding is constitutive of, rather than merely instrumental to, social action. In this conception, the deployment of a specific discourse, the liberal discourse of rights, for example, will shape the character of collective action and can have a major effect on the dynamics of social change. The tools of discourse facilitate practices, while in part constituting them through the forms of bonding and division they foster and through the limitations they place on the expression of goals and the means of their attainment. The nature of these limitations has not been adequately studied.

Community: Language, Solidarity, and Power

We shall here suggest some possible elements of such an approach.

The effectiveness of an alliance of individuals depends on the degree of internal unity and depth of commitment of its members, the resources the members can make available to the group, and the linkages the alliance can forge with other groups in implementing its projects. The raw materials of such commitment in general are a common social position of members (class, race, sex, region, nation, religion) vis-à-vis a structure of domination in society, and a shared system of communicative and organizational practices in society. Marx was undoubtedly correct in taking common life circumstances and particularly the shared experience of a common form of oppression as the basis of social solidarity. This indeed is the basis of the Marxian concept of class as a tool of historical analysis.

But if common social position precedes social action, solidarity and common interest (both its existence and content) come into being only through concrete communicative and organizational practices. Just as discourse is not the reflection of consciousness, so the discursive practices of political life are not the expression of pregiven interests inhering in the social position of actors. First, the criteria of group membership, and hence its social composition, cannot be determined a priori. A multiplicity of "us and them" divisions is possible in any social order.* Second, members of any group inevitably have conflicting perspectives based on differences in race, sex, ethnicity, region, industrial and occupational position, age, and other attributes which may appear tangential to the group's central projects. The nature and extent of unity, then, is itself a product of the constitution of bonding through discourse and organization. Finally, because of the essentially indeterminate and open-ended character of the structured contests that constitute society, and because of inherently incomplete information, no clearly dominant or unique strategy will be derived from the common social position of its members. Where ambiguity is present, the internal structure of a practice—in particular the discursive tools available to it—will decisively affect the character of its projects.

But the converse is true as well. Because the structure of discourse affects practices, discourse itself inevitably becomes the object of social struggle. It is characteristic of tools, the tools of discourse included, that they may be detached from their origins, to be modified and applied elsewhere. Elements of a political lexicon—such as the discourse of rights—do not relate to one

* Indeed this is the inescapable conclusion of our earlier representation of society as a game without a core.

another in inherently given ways. They do not have essential meanings. If they did, the formation and dissolution of collective action would be far more predictable than it is.

Making history is often a matter of making language. But discourses are more often borrowed or stolen than created de novo. Faced with a restricted political vocabulary, political actors appropriate and transform tools that even hostile forces have labored to develop. We are in complete agreement with Eric Foner, who writes,

> One of the keys to social change is a change in the nature of the language itself, both in the emergence of new words and in old words taking on new meanings. . . . [Thomas Paine helped] to promote revolution by changing the very terms in which people thought about politics and society. . . . Paine was one of the creators of [a] secular language of revolution, a language in which timeless discontents, millennial aspirations, and popular traditions were expressed in a strikingly new vocabulary. . . . Paine helped to transform the meaning of the key words of political discourse.[21]

Even radical social change is thus often couched in terms that obscure its discontinuity with the past. Marx, writing about mid-nineteenth-century France, noted this tendency:

> And, just when [people] appear to be engaged in the revolutionary transformation of themselves and their material surroundings, in the creation of something that does not yet exist, precisely in such epochs of revolutionary crisis they timidly conjure up the spirits of the past to help them; they borrow their names, slogans and costumes so as to stage the new world-historical scene in this venerable disguise and borrowed language.[22]

Examples of this dynamic abound. The language of representative government, created in eighteenth-century France by supporters of the aristocracy in their struggle with the crown, was appropriated by the Third Estate after 1789. The treatment of labor as the sole source of value, developed in England by Locke and later by David Ricardo to aid the emerging capitalist proprietors in their struggle with the landed interests, was appropriated later by socialists in the British working class, leading to its hasty abandonment and rejection by supporters of the bourgeoisie.[23] The language and organizational forms of the revolutionary workers in France in 1848 reached back to before 1789, drawing on the guilds and other corporate practices of the Old Regime, as well as those of the *sans culottes* of revolution.

Indeed, revolutionary consciousness was most pronounced among the skilled workers in those trades that had spawned the *confraternities* of the Old Regime. In the words of William Sewell,

> The new socialist vision the workers were developing in 1848 was founded on a very old sense of craft community. . . . Under the old regime, corporations were legally sanctioned bodies, and their language and institutions recapitulated the hierarchical premises of the traditional monarchy. But after the Revolution [of 1789, these corporations] . . . developed into the cells of revolutionary democratic and socialist movement in 1848.[24]

Along with Gareth Stedman Jones's work on nineteenth-century British labor history, Sewell's analysis of the nineteenth-century French working class is among the few careful attempts to take discourse seriously as it interacts with social class in producing social change. He is particularly concerned to chart the reciprocal nature of the interaction of social position and language. In treating the July Revolution, for instance, Sewell notes that

> it was not until the weeks following the Revolution of 1830, when workers attempted to formulate their demands publicly, that they became clearly aware of the limitations of their idiom . . . the corporate idiom as it existed in 1830 was without moral or even cognitive force in the public sphere; if workers were to make public demands, they would have to do so in a new vocabulary.[25]

But he quickly adds that this new vocabulary retained critical elements of the old and at the same time transformed the tools of discourse which the workers found it necessary to assimilate.

> Beginning around 1831, workers in various trades began to recast their corporation as "associations," thereby basing them rhetorically on the principles of liberty so often proclaimed as the foundation of the new regime. . . . The idea of associated production was predicated on an ambiguity of liberal discourse. If citizens possessed the right to associate freely, then they could use that right to create voluntary organizations intended to overcome the egoistic individualism and anarchy of the current liberal system.[26]

Harmony and Contradiction in the Structure of Rights

That the French workers studied by Sewell and others the world over have taken up the discourse of rights does not demonstrate its radical potential, but simply the dominance of this medium of political communication. Nonetheless, we believe there are structural reasons internal to the liberal discourse which promote the effective use of the discourse of rights toward radical ends.

The link between personal rights and individualist political philosophy cannot be denied. Personal liberty and private property empower the individual in the spheres of individual action and control of material resources, while democratic rights ensure the individual's equal access to determination of collective decisions. But liberty, property, and democratic choice appear as a harmonious unity only in opposition to corporatist and hierarchical political philosophies hostile to individual agency. Like allies in a battle, who, once their common enemy is laid to rest, begin to set at one another's throats, so too liberal rights become the basis for irreducibly heterogeneous normative claims.

The presumed harmony of personal rights and property rights appears reasonable only when their permissible *range of application* is not called into question. When the freedom of speech and press is extended to the right of equal access to education, when equal treatment before the law is extended to equal treatment before the health care system, and when freedom of association extends from political demonstrations to trade unions, we have clear-cut instances of the clash of personal and property rights. When freedom of speech is extended to workers on the job, or equal treatment is extended to women, or freedom of association is extended to gay and lesbian couples, we move toward undermining the fundamental structures of authority in economy and family.

Yet, following Wittgenstein, the sense of a right is constituted in part by its range of application—the "sphere of life" to which it applies. The very notion of an inalienable right, to take a prominent case, involves the resolution of a range-of-application conflict. The prohibition of slavery, for instance, is the removal of persons from the range of application of contractual exchange. Personal liberty is "inalienable" in the sense that the individual does not fall within the purview of property rights. Inalienable rights of this type are thus restrictions on the range of application of property rights—restrictions imposed in the name of preserving liberty.

But we may draw a more general lesson from this example. The nature of contractual exchange depends not upon *whether* there are markets, but rather upon precisely *what* is permitted to be exchanged, in return for *what* else, and under precisely *what* conditions of exchange. We applied a limited form of this principle in showing that "capital" and "labor" do not conform to the classical model of exchangeable property. But here the assertion must be considerably widened: personal rights can, and normally do, come directly into play in determining the limits of property. Exchangeable property titles are normally permitted only in given, socially determined, and legally acceptable bundles. Much attention has been paid recently to such novel "bundles" as implied warranties on consumer durables and "truth in content" regulations covering food and cosmetics. In both cases, the range of application of voluntary exchange is restricted by forcing contracting parties to contract only along predetermined dimensions (for example, an automobile dealer cannot sell a car without a warranty at a lower price, an airline cannot offer an inexpensive ticket on an accident-prone plane, and a doctor cannot give mediocre service at bargain prices). These examples may not be of great social import, but restricting the range of application of property rights through such "bundling" must not be seen as a trivial conflict of rights. The presumption of traditional economic theory that virtually any mix of goods (save of course those exempted on the basis of "inalienability") are capable of being exchanged is radically incorrect.

To see this, we need only consider a weightier sort of exchange—that between employer and employee. Why, for instance, cannot employers set up courts to fine and imprison workers? Why are not workers allowed to exchange their right to due process for a higher wage? Why are they prohibited the right to agree not to join a union as a condition of employment? Why cannot workers agree to certain types of substandard working conditions? Reflection on these and similar issues convinces us that the character of work depends not on *whether* labor is marketed, but exactly under what *conditions* and in what *forms* it is marketed.

These examples can be extended in a myriad of directions. Why cannot people sell their eyes, their votes, or their children? Why cannot people vote on who marries whom? Why are luncheonettes required to serve minorities? Why are insurance companies under pressure to treat male and female clients equally? In each of these cases, we see rights in conflict, we see this conflict as one of accepted range of application, and finally we see the character of society depending critically on how this conflict is adjudicated. Various mixes of personal and property rights, then, are in principle compatible with a slave society, a capitalist society, a workers' democracy, and other social orders exhibiting a wide variety of rules of the game.

Suppose in a score of years we find that individuals can hold shares in firms but have no rights in the control of either the process of production or investment decisions. Suppose the right of control has passed to workers, to local communities, or to decision-making bodies of types that cannot now be envisioned. Such a society would clearly not be capitalist. But it probably could be defended on quasi-liberal grounds. Would it not be tempting to argue in such a situation that the democratic control of production and investment had always been included (albeit incompletely) in the meaning of democracy? But of course nothing could be further from the truth.

Personal rights and property rights, we have determined, in general represent alternative rules of the game for making the *same* types of decisions, rather than parallel mechanisms for making *distinct* types of decisions. Not surprisingly, some of the most critical contests in the development of capitalism have involved the respecification of the *range of application* of these rights instead of their wholesale replacement by other rules of the game not expressible in terms of the lexicon of rights. The historical dimensions of these battles are illuminated by Wittgenstein's critical insight that meaning depends upon use, and that use is infinitely varied over time and space.

Social Struggle and the Discourse of Rights

Contemporary social thought virtually identifies liberalism with democracy. Yet liberal theory has followed rather than led in the emergence of democratic institutions; its key terms have been continually reinterpreted with the evolution of class, race, gender, ethnic, and other conflicts. If the discourse of rights cannot be attributed to the liberal tradition, how are we to account for its development? We shall argue that nearly every group contending for social dominance since the demise of feudalism contributed to the discourse of rights.

The notion of unitary sovereignty was itself promoted by monarchs in their struggle against decentralized feudal relations, and it provided a conceptual tool for establishing unrestrained control over all elements of the social body.[27] The next stage in the historical development of what we now term liberal discourse involved the consolidation of the nation-state in its absolutist form as a formidable system of centralized coercion, administration, and control. Central elements of what we now view as the liberal vocabulary arose as an aristocratic, and manifestly undemocratic, reaction to this situation. The aristocratic revolts of the seventeenth and eighteenth centuries in Europe developed the notion of constitutional rule, according to which sovereignty resides in the nation,[28] and the notion of representative government, according to which the aristocracy was to constitute the controlling body of government.[29] Indeed much of the political theory of the Enlightenment consisted of attempts to defend absolutism against these aristocratic threats. In the words of Carl Friedrich,

> Constitutionalism, both in England and abroad, was at the outset not at all democratic but rather aristocratic.... The movement of Enlightenment preached to the absolute rulers the necessity of rationally conducting their office so as to forestall constitutionalism. Even so enlightened a spirit as Voltaire would rather educate Frederick of Prussia than build a constitution.[30]

The aristocratic revolt, moreover, is directly responsible for such characteristic expressions of the discourse of rights as habeas corpus, trial by peers, due process of law, and the separation of powers. The supporters of Montesquieu's principles of separation of powers, for instance, in saying that power emanates from the people, meant by "the people" the French nobility. They supported the torture of dissidents, opposed religious tolerance, despised the philosophes, and destroyed the progressive Jesuit order. It is not surprising that in response to the reactionary character of the supporters of "representative government," Voltaire and his friends would support enlightened despotism.[31]

Religious dissent was also a significant addition to the discourse of rights— a fact often overlooked in the secular progressive tradition. Liberty of conscience, for instance, was asserted during the early modern revolts against the hegemony of the Catholic Church. There was nothing democratic, participatory, or representative about the early notions of freedom of conscience of Marsiglio of Padua and William of Occam, for example. As John Plamenatz has put it,

> The opponents of the papacy were not asserting the right of the individual Christian against the Church; they were asserting the right of the Church . . . against the papacy. They were not even claiming for every Christian the right to take part in running the Christian community. The delegates they had in mind [were] . . . the "natural" leaders of society.[32]

Nevertheless, by the end of the seventeenth century liberty of conscience had emerged as a right of individuals to hold and profess any opinions, as Locke so treated it in his *Letter on Toleration*, published in 1689.

The emerging commercial bourgeoisie in the period contributed little to this movement. Indeed the system of alliances giving birth to European capitalism situated the rising commercial and financial elites more often than not against the growing philosophy of natural rights. In England and France, for instance, the new merchant class in the seventeenth and eighteenth centuries was directly fostered and exploited by the monarchy as a means of state finance in its struggle against traditional elites, in return for which trade routes were protected and traders were allowed access to raw materials, resources, and foreign markets. The merchant class in this period had a direct interest in the preservation and extension of state power. They therefore had little use for egalitarian ideologies, much less the new discourse of rights which served to oppose absolutist pretensions. As attested by the writings of their intellectual supporters the mercantilists, the political philosophy of early commercial interests was neither liberal nor democratic.

In time the growth of trade and manufacture strengthened the commercial elites and rendered them increasingly intolerant of state exactions, throwing them into a position comparable to that of other social groups threatened by the absolutism. Nonetheless, only with the impending demise of absolutism (in the mid-seventeenth century in England and later in France and elsewhere) was the vocabulary of rights usurped by the rising commercial class, and transformed into demands for the independent power of propertied wealth within the framework of republican government. Lockean liberalism was the tenet of the bourgeoisie and the commercially oriented landowners seeking freedom from state exactions, as well as from the democratic pretensions of the increasingly self-conscious national citizenry. Nevertheless, this movement contributed the notion of representation based on civil equality, the abolition of estates, and the concept of meritocratic advance and careers open to talents. Finally, the professional groups (lawyers, doctors, journalists, academicians) that arose to fill the needs of state and war, beginning with the Enlightenment, contributed to our modern notions of free press, speech, and assembly.

These demands, in turn, were to become identified in the nineteenth century with the rising working-class movements, which added yet new dimensions to the discourse of rights. As we have seen, the working-class movement was directly responsible for integrating the modern notion of the freedom of association into the discourse of rights. And as we saw in chapter 2, the insertion of a democratic idiom into the discourse of rights derived from an accommodation of nineteenth-century working-class demands to the dominant bourgeois notions of representative government and laissez-faire economics. Finally, the addition of what T. H. Marshall has called "social rights" (the right to employment, medical care, job safety, and personal security) and the rights of women and minorities were even later additions to the lexicon of rights—additions falling quite outside the range of the early liberal lexicon.

The contributions of working-class movements to the expansion of personal rights has been widely undervalued.[33] Sympathetic interpreters of working-class aspirations have routinely imbued their movements with a socialist consciousness that rarely existed, and the working class's enemies have equally routinely depicted their movements as authoritarian and crassly materialistic. Eric Hobsbawm finds it necessary to stress,

> There is absolutely no doubt that the poor, the working people and the potential or actual members of labour movements spoke the language of *rights* (and still do). . . . By far the most powerful mobilizations of labour on the continent, e.g. general strikes, were for electoral reform. . . . Hence, insofar as they were politically active as movements, most nineteenth-century labour movements still operated in the framework of the American and French revolutions and their type of the Rights of Man.[34]

The repertoire of nineteenth-century working-class movements, operating with the discourse of rights, moreover, has simply been consolidated and refined in contemporary times.

The discourse of rights, then, is no more bourgeois than it is aristocratic, or Protestant, or proletarian. It has been the object of a variety of intense and cross-cutting social struggles, its progressive tendencies deriving in significant part from the contributions of dominated and oppressed groups.

Moreover, the discourse of rights has served as a source of bonding and a framework for the expression of group demands, rather than reflecting a social philosophy or a political ideology. Contemporary political discourse, to borrow a phrase that Wittgenstein applied to language in general,

> can be seen as an ancient city: a maze of little streets and squares, of old and new houses, and of houses with additions from various periods; and this surrounded by a multitude of boroughs with straight regular streets and uniform houses.[35]

Capitalist Property and the Concept of Rights

If workers have found novel and effective uses for the discourse of rights, so too have their employers. No better case of this capitalist appropriation of personal rights is their success in extending to an impersonal entity—the business corporation—the title and rights of "person."

It is common to equate corporate with personal property, and hence to view the rise of corporate enterprise as the growth of one type of personal rights in contrast to others. But the expansion of corporate property can only with great difficulty be represented as an extension of personal rights. A capitalist corporation is a "chartered freedom": a structured association of persons with juridically recognized privileges and duties. As such, it is no less a privileged political body than is a university or a trade union. Corporate property is therefore no more personal property than is a university lecture hall or a trade union pension fund.

Viewed from this perspective, one of the most dramatic aspects of capitalist accumulation is the *depersonalization* of property rights that it entails. Property rights become depersonalized to the extent that they are held by nonpersons. The process of depersonalization, the elimination of proprietorship, has been critical to the historical expansion of capital mobility, and hence to the power of capital itself. Its growth has involved the demise of the family farm and the rise of agribusiness, as well as the expansion of global multifirm and franchise enterprises, usurping the traditional position of the local restaurant, the corner drugstore, and the neighborhood food market. It includes the replacement of the family doctor by the multiservice corporate health-care delivery system, and the assimilation of the network of local newspapers into media conglomerates. These phenomena, which are usually discussed under the rubric of the concentration of property, may also be understood as its depersonalization, and hence its removal from the realm of personal rights.

The corporate enterprise's "chartered freedom" represents a striking transportation of rules from the liberal state to the capitalist economy. This is a clear case of a Wittgensteinian transformation of use: corporate groups are treated as fictive individuals, and are thus endowed with the rights that individuals in a free society alone are accorded. In mid-nineteenth-century America, for instance, the courts began a process of extending to the corporation those rights of due process which previously had applied only to real persons. In the same period, the courts instituted the still-operative fiction of considering corporations as "persons" within the meaning of the Fourteenth Amendment. With this sleight of hand, the depersonalization of property is represented as the personalization of the business enterprise. And because a "person" is incontrovertibly "private," so the internal organization of the corporation is effectively exempted from legal scrutiny as a public body. And attempts by government at regulating market exchanges were increasingly seen as invasions of liberty.[36]

The resulting centralization of capitalist power cannot, however, escape the critique of the democrat. In democratic theory, fictive persons—whether the patriarchal family or the capitalist enterprise—are simply realms of potentially unaccountable power.[37]

But is it so unreasonable to treat the corporation as an ersatz person—a pseudoperson simply representing its owners, the stockholders? We have, after all, defended representative democracy as capable of conferring substantive power upon persons. Why then deny to the corporate enterprise the status of an association accountable to its voting members, the shareholders? Would it not be more accurate to treat the corporation as a Lockean association, conferring rights upon persons in proportion to their "interest" (that is, ownership) on the collectivity? Were this the case, the treatment of corporate property as worthy of protection by virtue of personal rights might be arguable, at least under conditions of relatively broad distribution of property claims.

However, the very nature of the capitalist corporation as a limited liability association implies that stockholders will in general treat the enterprise instrumentally toward the achievement of personal ends (such as the accumulation of wealth). In this case, the logic of the free rider problem indicates that the stockholder will not participate in the governance of the corporation. This is especially the case because the degree of marketability (more formally, the low level of transactions costs) which limited liability ensures so significantly reduces the costs of "exit" to individual stockholders that they have no "loyalty" to the organization, hence no interest in exercising a voice in its governance. All but the largest investors vote with their feet—or rather their brokers' feet.

It follows that except in unusual circumstances the corporation cannot be considered accountable to any except perhaps its largest shareholders. Corporate enterprise is a locus of irreducibly unaccountable power. Everyday observation of the world of business confirms this fact. There is thus no logical reason for treating capitalist property as personal private property. But there is a powerful political reason: extending rights to the corporation as a fictive person considerably extends its power and its immunity from encroachment either by the state, by its employees, or by others whose lives are affected by its decisions.

The legal protection of capitalist property, moreover, does not flow from the recognition of the rights of persons to dominion over their possessions; rather, this protection is the fruit of the political success of capital. Business groups used the discourse of rights not only to legitimate corporate ownership, but to affirm the priority of accumulation over the enjoyment of property titles. That this affirmation is not inherent in the concept of "property right" has been convincingly demonstrated by the legal historian Morton Horwitz. In effect, Horwitz argues, between the Revolution and the Civil War the notion of property law as the interpretation and enforcement of justice began to be displaced by its conception as instrumental to commercial development:

> What dramatically distinguished nineteenth century law from its eighteenth century counterpart was the extent to which . . . jurists began to frame legal arguments in terms of "the importance of the present decision to the commercial character of our country," or of the necessity of deciding whether adherence to a particular common law rule will result in "improvement in our commercial code."[38]

This new interpretation of property rights, by contrast with the older notion of property as entitling the owner to undisturbed enjoyment, emphasized the benefits of efficiency and marketability. A major aspect of this change toward favoring "new" property over "old" property was a move from strict liability in tort, which favored existing rights over newly created rights, to what Horwitz calls "the newer 'balancing test' of efficiency."

> Property rights came to be justified by their efficacy in promoting economic growth. . . . The most important challenge to the common law doctrine [of strict liability] was the so-called reasonable use or balancing test. *Palmer v. Mulligan* [1805] represents the beginning of a gradual acceptance of the idea that the ownership of property implies above all the right to develop that property for business purposes.[39]

Thus began a movement toward the treatment of property law as an arm of accumulation—a movement which in the late twentieth century has seen jurists with increasing frequency attending conferences on economic efficiency, and the wholesale introduction into legal education of the principles of neoclassical economics. The roots of this movement, claims Horwitz, lay in the earliest decades of American independence:

> One of the most universal features of postrevolutionary American jurisprudence was an attack on the colonial subservience to precedent . . . "reason" and "principle" came to be understood not as rules or doctrines to be discovered, not as customary norms to be applied through precedent, but as a body of prudential regulations framed . . . from the perspective of "enlarged and liberal views of policy.[40]

To implement such policies, it became more and more necessary to remove the deliberation on complex economic issues from the hands of what forward-looking elites considered to be an ignorant and often hostile community. Hence the decreased reliance upon the use of juries with the advance of the new commercial spirit in the United States:

> Where eighteenth century judges often submitted a case to the jury without any directions . . . nineteenth century courts became preoccupied with submitting clear directions to juries . . . judges regularly set aside jury verdicts as contrary to law.[41]

The historical success of capital within the discourse of rights is dramatically illuminated by Robert Green McCloskey's study of the interaction of economic and political liberalism in the rise of American capitalism. For McCloskey, the privileged position accorded the unfettered power of capital in modern liberalism represents a degeneration of the liberal democratic tradition. . . . When he used the term "liberty," the early democrat meant, first of all, freedom of conscience—moral liberty—rather than freedom of business enterprise. His chief interest, in short, was in the right of the individual to realize his moral personality, and not the right to buy and sell and prosper economically.[42]

McCloskey notes that the doctrine of economic liberalism was a result of two influences in the nascent liberalism of the seventeenth century.

Democratic thought received two infusions, the first from the radical Christian democrats . . . the second from the sober-sided English middle class, bent on shaping a doctrine congenial to men of property. . . . Locke fastened on democracy the idea that the right of private property is fundamental; he set in train a materialization of democratic ideals that led ultimately to their perversion.[43]

Because of this dual etiology of liberal discourse as both reaction against the despotism of the modern state and as affirmation of the power of capital directly engendered by this state, liberalism has suffered a congenital moral indeterminacy: the equality of all before the law is also the privilege of the wealthy to exploit the dispossessed.

Conclusion

Born in the shadow of the absolutist state and in the turmoil of bourgeois-aristocratic struggles, the liberal lexicon's later development followed almost term by term the rhythm of bourgeois confrontations with the popular classes in the course of capitalist accumulation. Beginning with the negative liberties of laissez-faire economics, civil equality, civil liberties, and constitutional government, liberal discourse developed progressively to include the positive liberties of rights of association, political democracy, equality of opportunity, minimum state-supported living standards and rights to social services, as well as selected antiracist and antisexist commitments.

In short, the discourse of rights is fraught with internal tensions due to its genesis in social conflict and the consequently contradictory forms it is obliged to assume in social life. This contradictory character explains both its emancipatory potential and its seemingly limitless capacity to legitimate social inequality and undemocratic economic arrangements.

It is these contradictory potentials that have multiplied the stakes of the social conflicts associated with the erosion and demise of the post–World War II Keynesian accommodation. Our conviction is that elements of the now-dominant liberal discourse can be forged into powerful tools of democratic mobilization, a mobilization which, if successful, is almost certain in the long run to burst the bounds of the liberal discourse itself.

7

Future: Postliberal
Democracy

LIBERAL CAPITALISM banished the bondage of serfdom and slavery; it reined in the pretensions of the absolutist state; but it failed to inaugurate freedom. Its promises of the material security and liberty on which freedom depends have not been wholly empty. But neither have they been fulfilled. The liberal era has thus seen neither freedom itself nor its nemesis; at best the era may be considered, to borrow a phrase from Alexis de Tocqueville, freedom's apprenticeship:

> Nothing is more fertile in marvels than the art of being free, but nothing is harder than freedom's apprenticeship ... liberty is generally born in stormy weather, growing with difficulty amid civil discords, and only when it is already old does one see the blessings it has brought.[1]

The liberal vision of people effectively controlling their lives is not a hollow promise doomed by human nature and modern technology. Liberalism's fault lies not in overstating the possibilities for human freedom, but in failing to identify the roots of domination—those which lie in economic dependency and patriarchal authority chief among them—and in elevating a radically individual conception of autonomy to the detriment of a conception of community which might form the basis of democratic empowerment.

176

As a result, liberal theory has justified a social order whose precious accomplishments—a higher material standard of living and a kind of liberty from coercive incursions in one's private life—have been gained at the cost of a historically unprecedented accumulation of unaccountable power in state and economy.

Both the liberal state and the capitalist economy have flourished by undermining sources of personal and traditional collective autonomy. The right to bear arms—which Machiavelli and later thinkers had believed so central to popular sovereignty—was at least metaphorically traded for the right to vote. The ownership and control of land, tools, and other conditions of one's livelihood—the foundation of autonomy in the thought of James Harrington and later of Thomas Jefferson—was traded for a wage.[2] And liberalism has conspired with the imperatives of the capitalist economy to erode all collective bodies standing between the state and the individual save one: the capitalist corporation.

The promise of postliberal democracy is to reverse this development: to continue the expansion of personal rights and thus to render the exercise of both property rights and state power democratically accountable. It affirms the traditional democratic forms of representative democracy and individual liberty and proposes novel forms of social power independent of the state; namely, democratically accountable, chartered freedoms in community and work. These aspects of economic democracy, including the democratic control of investment and production, are not only desirable in their own right, they are also an increasingly necessary condition for the viability of democratic control of governments.

Democracy is necessarily a relationship among free people, and economic dependency no less than personal bondage is the antithesis of freedom. The hardheaded seventeenth-century advocates of representative government thus had a point in opposing extending suffrage to "servants" on the grounds that employees had exchanged their autonomy for a wage. The Jeffersonian synthesis of property and democracy addressed the issue of economic dependency by proposing its elimination through the extension of ownership. But Jefferson's vision went against the capitalist grain: property was not to become more generally shared but the reverse. The eclipse of small ownership by the large-scale employment of wage labor has rendered his solution archaic. The Marxian conception of socialism as common ownership and collective control of productive property suffered a similar fate: for just as Jefferson had underestimated the power of the capitalist accumulation process to corrode the economic bases of personal autonomy, Marxists typically failed to take account of the impressive ability of centralized state bureaucracy to thwart democratic accountability.

Postliberal democracy may be considered a synthesis of the Jeffersonian and Marxian visions. It affirms both the Jeffersonian commitment to decentralized control of the productive apparatus and the Marxian recognition that because production is social its decentralization cannot take the form of individual property ownership. The postliberal democratic commitment to democratic control of the economy thus amounts to a rejection of the terms of the two-century-old debate between liberals and socialists concerning the nature of property. Neither the Jeffersonian universalization of individual property nor the Marxian collectivization of private property is acceptable. What is needed is the displacement of property rights by democratic personal rights.

We conceive of postliberal democracy as more than a new set of rules of the game. It also encompasses a set of human purposes, embracing a broad vision of human development as its guiding principle. If for liberalism the archetypal human activity is choice, and for Marxism it is labor, postliberal democratic theory represents people as learners for whom both choice and labor are indispensable means toward personal development. We thus follow John Stuart Mill in celebrating Wilhelm von Humboldt's profession of Enlightenment faith:

> The grand, leading principle, towards which every argument unfolded in these pages directly converges is the absolute and essential importance of human development in its richest diversity.[3]

In contrast to traditional liberal doctrine, which supports a society of acquisition based on the exchange of property claims, postliberal democracy is a vision of a society based on learning governed by the exercise of personal rights. It presents a profound reorientation of our normative grid, an inversion of the relationship between human development and economic organization. This allows economic activity to be considered not as an end but as a means toward democratically determined forms of human development. The legitimation of this model—as well as its sense of history—is based not on accumulation but on learning, not on the ever-widening appropriation of nature in the interests of economic development but on the continuing deepening of capacities and understandings through a process of personal and social transformation in the interests of human development. Thus a new model of economic growth no less than a new model of democracy is implied.[4]

This vision of a postliberal democracy is unmistakably the product of the aspirations of the liberal era itself, yet it breaks sharply with the liberal tradition in two respects. It represents the individual as an intrinsically social being actively engaged in the continual transformation of one's own and others' capacities, sentiments, and attachments; and it represents private control over productive property not as a salutary barrier to the pretensions of the state, but as a bedrock of economic dependency and an obstacle to popular sovereignty.

In rejecting the dual liberal partitions—private–public and chooser–learner—and thus departing from the liberal tradition, we are not suggesting that liberal democratic society step outside its historical trajectory to inaugurate a new order. We believe that liberal democratic capitalist society has itself produced the conditions that make our postliberal democratic vision historically relevant. Without minimizing the obstacles to the development of a democratic order, we may cite three factors favorable to the emergence of such a vision of postliberal democracy. First, this vision represents a political development directly in line with the transformation of the discourse of rights discussed in chapter 6 and the expansionary tendency of personal rights charted in chapter 2; hence its realization requires no fundamental shift in social dynamics.

Second, by stressing workplace and community empowerment as opposed to state expansion, the vision of postliberal democracy avoids one of the great dead ends encountered in the expansion of personal rights and simultaneously addresses a key weakness of social democracy. By stressing that the extension of democracy is not synonymous with the extension of state power, postliberal democracy affirms the sentiment that neither the centralized state nor the capitalist corporation will be the vehicle of human liberation.

Third, as we shall see presently, there is an economic logic that may propel elements of the postliberal democratic vision to prominence. Just as the technical and economic environment of the early modern period of European history generally favored the expansion of commerce and the encroachment on feudal hegemony, new technical and organizational demands being made upon economic life today may favor a radical extension of democratic principles to the economy. The continuing growth of output and the shift from the production of goods to the production and processing of information, culture, and other services, the democratic challenge to hierarchical authority, the growing centrality of knowledge as the sine qua non of economic dynamism, and the increasingly costly predation of nature have combined, and will continue to combine, to raise the costs of maintaining the capitalist order. Correspondingly, we will argue, these developments may propel more democratic and egalitarian forms from postscarcity utopias to practical means of addressing the not-soon-to-be-banished problem of scarcity.

But it would be misleading to claim that postliberal democracy represents the only, or even the most likely, resolution of the current dilemmas of liberal capitalism. While unlikely, the possibility of the complete demise of liberal democratic institutions, along lines suggested by George Orwell and Aldous Huxley, can by no means be ruled out. More prosaically, new accommodations may emerge involving the extension of capitalism at the expense of democracy—the reverse of our postliberal democratic solution. Among these, two relatively well-defined alternative models of the relationship among politics, economics, and democratic decision making may be discerned. Each of these possible post-Keynesian accommodations involves a fundamental reordering of the substantive relationships among citizen rights and property rights. The first, which we term *global liberalism*, represents the worldwide expansion of markets and mobility of capital and their heightened encroachment on the sovereignty of democratic states. The second, *neo-Hobbesian liberalism*, would enhance unaccountable but ostensibly necessary hierarchical authority in the family, capitalist firm, and state at the expense of both the market and the democratic accountability of key state functions. Elements of the two, of course, might well be combined.

Despotism, Scarcity, and Freedom

The novelty of the global liberal, neo-Hobbesian, and postliberal models ought not be overstressed. Each is a reasonable extrapolation of present tendencies. Each is also amply prefigured in the history of political and economic philosophy. For each addresses in its own way the relationship among three fundamental terms in the liberal tradition: despotism, scarcity, and freedom. The neo-Hobbesian model is inspired by the representation of the problem of order in Hobbes's *Leviathan*, the global liberal model is a modern elaboration of the concept of the market as a form of order, found in the writings of Bernard Mandeville and Adam Smith, and the postliberal democratic model finds its roots in Rousseau's concept of popular sovereignty. Before turning to the present impasse and its likely issue, it will be instructive to explore the theoretical antecedents of these competing approaches.

How, asked Hobbes, might a society of self-interested people, engaged in a perpetual contest for wealth and power, escape disorder and dissolution? His solution was the renunciation of the liberty of each through a collective contract of obedience to an absolute sovereign. One could not be at once free and ruled, and being ruled was to be preferred in view of the alternatives. Hobbes responded to the objection "that the condition of subjects is very miserable; as being obnoxious to the lusts and other irregular passions of him, or them that have so unlimited a power in their hands" by reference to "that dissolute condition of masterless men, without subjection to laws and a coercive power to tie their hands" and with the observation "that the estate of Man can never be without some incommodity or other."[5]

Harnessing of the passions implied, for Hobbes, the paramount importance of obedience to a single individual—the sovereign. Giambattista Vico, in his *Scienza Nuova*, was quick to note that Hobbes had passed too swiftly from a valid question to an arbitrarily limited answer. Referring to divine providence, Vico wrote,

> through its intelligent laws the passions of men who are entirely occupied by the pursuit of their private utility are transformed into a civil order which permits men to live in human society.[6]

The "laws" regulating the passions, as other writers soon glimpsed, could be secular as well as divine, and economic as well as juridical.

Bernard Mandeville's "solution" to Hobbes's problem is ingenious: let the contest for power take the form of competition for purchasing power regulated by the exchange of claims to private property on competitive markets.[7] In Mandeville's *Fable of the Bees* self-interested individual action was reconciled with a rational order through markets.[8] What later commentators have found attractive about Mandeville's solution to Hobbes's problem was its capacity to circumscribe the scope of hierarchical state authority by invoking the beneficial effects of competitive economic relationships presented as natural (or divine) law.

Rousseau's approach, by contrast, was to concede the importance of collective authority but to render it democratic. Maurice Cranston writes that Rousseau "rejects Hobbes' claim that men must choose between being free and being ruled." Cranston continues, "Rousseau's solution to the problem posed by Hobbes is wonderfully simple. Men can be both ruled and free if they rule themselves."[9] Rousseau shares with other great political thinkers a conviction that a society without authority is unimaginable; his departure is an insistence on popular sovereignty as the ultimate basis of legitimate rule.

We seek to develop this insight in opposition to the current expressions of what we have termed the Hobbesian and the Mandevillian positions. The connection between the three contemporary models—global liberal, neo-Hobbesian, and postliberal democratic—and their antecedents is perhaps more metaphoric than direct. But the most fundamental commitments of each approach—to markets, hierarchy, and popular sovereignty, respectively—suggest a striking continuity in the abiding lines of debate in political and economic philosophy.

However, if we are right, the debate itself—whether carried on within the liberal and Marxian traditions or between them—has run its course. Neither tradition today provides a conceptual framework adequate to the task of making good (or even making clear) Rousseau's promise of a popular sovereignty. Nor can either explain how this objective might be reconciled with the equally central goal of liberty.

By "liberty" we intend the familiar and limited "negative liberty" sense developed by Isaiah Berlin: liberty is freedom from coercive interference by others in one's private affairs. In defining "popular sovereignty" we follow Adam Przeworski in saying that

> individuals acting on the basis of their current preferences are collectively sovereign if the alternatives open to them are constrained only by conditions independent of anyone's will. Specifically, people are sovereign to the extent that they can alter the existing institutions, including the state and property, and if they can allocate available resources to all feasible uses.[10]

We might add that sovereignty entails the ability to alter the conditions under which members of a community come to have the preferences referred to in Przeworski's working definition. Popular sovereignty obtains to the extent that social outcomes are responsive to people's preferences. Unlike the standard definitions of liberal democracy, which equate it to the functioning of a particular system of rules for decision making (universal suffrage, majority rule, civil liberties), this conception of democracy focuses on the results (not the process) of decision making. Its fundamental commitments are hence not to a particular set of institutions but to a political ideal: liberty and the democratic accountability of social power. Our critique of the capitalist economy has been that it systematically frustrates popular sovereignty and perpetuates conditions of economic dependency which are inimical to liberty.

Although the roots of this theme in political theory may be located in Rousseau, our development of the concept would probably have perplexed the Citizen of Geneva. The advocacy of popular sovereignty does not presume the existence of a popular will or the preeminence of universal over individual sentiment and action. It presumes only that we can identify the socially consequential exercise of power, that we can tell when it is accountable, and, when it is not, that we can devise institutions rendering it more accountable. Our concept of popular sovereignty does not privilege some forms of political action—participation—and denigrate others—representation. Rather, it treats forms of political action simply as means toward the ends of accountability and liberty. Further, it does not presume that the impetus for political action comes from "the people"; effective political leadership and unanticipated innovation by individuals or groups other than "the whole" is fully consistent with the ideal of popular sovereignty as long as both leadership and innovation are subject to effective ex post facto deliberation and accountability.

Shorn of the Rousseauian general will and the Marxian expressive theory of action, why cannot the objective of popular sovereignty be readily assimilated within contemporary liberal discourse? There can be no doubt that the liberal vision of an end to despotism and poverty has provided the dominant ideology of an epoch that has seen substantial progress toward the achievement of both. But if the analysis of the previous chapters is correct, the vision is doubly flawed. For it is founded on an insupportable conception of the relationship of human development and interests to politics, and it systematically masks the forms of domination—notably class and patriarchy—which its favored institutions support. As a result, neither liberty nor sovereignty may adequately be grasped within its terms.

For these reasons we argue that an adequate political theory today must be postliberal. It must be a transformation of liberal discourse which preserves its elevation of liberty but which nonetheless alters liberalism's *differentia specifica*, the dual partitions of actors into learners and choosers, and of social space into private and public. A democratic theory today must also be post-Marxian, retaining the acute attention to domination in the Marxian tradition, but encompassing a plurality of forms of domination and terrains of social conflict, and overcoming the Marxian (and Rousseauian) expressive theory of action.

The political lacunae in Marxian theory stem from its overarching focus on class exploitation at the expense of more sustained attention to state despotism and other nonclass forms of domination. These weaknesses of Marxian theory cannot be overcome simply by introducing a more heterogeneous conception of domination, as has been proposed, for example, by various Western Marxian structuralist authors. For any thoroughly structuralist approach—one that conceives of action as simply expressive of the logic of a structure—will fail to address the two most frequently raised objections to the idea of an alternative to capitalism: the problem of liberty and the problem of motivation to work.

William Connolly insightfully criticises the marginalization of choice in structuralist Marxism:

> First, by placing agency at the level of structure and displacing the idea of the subject, it bypasses the issue of securing personal freedom in a socialist polity. If there are no agents capable of acting freely, it is not necessary to appraise an order in terms of its support for the principle of freedom. Secondly, if the behavior of role-bearers is structurally determined in all orders, including the socialist order, the theorist does not have to worry too much about motivating people to bear new roles once the new mode of production is intact. The role-bearers, once the structure is in place, become the "supports" of the structure.[11]

We have attempted in the preceding chapters to develop some of the concepts that might contribute to such a post-Marxian and postliberal theory of democracy. Though our project has been almost entirely theoretical, our intent is eminently practical: to forge tools to help us understand the present trajectory of our societies and thereby to contribute to the possibility of a society of popular sovereignty and liberty. We are not brash enough to attempt in our closing chapter a blueprint of such a social order.[12] Our interest in such blueprints is confined to the light they might shed on the concrete issues concerning the manner in which liberal democratic capitalist societies might evolve toward one or more of these models and how such a democratic model might reproduce itself if attained.

Our approach is neither empirical nor utopian. Rather, we seek to combine a visionary and historical mode of reasoning, "taking men as they are and laws as they might be," to borrow a phrase from the first sentence of Rousseau's *Social Contract*. Our objective is to describe novel historical processes and opportunities, not to spin out democratic utopias and dystopias. For this reason we will address the contrasting historical logics of quite abstract versions of the global liberal, neo-Hobbesian, and postliberal democratic models, asking how these initiatives might promote a dynamic process of democratization (or its antithesis) through the forms of human development, solidarity, and political participation implied by each.

A Democratic Dynamic

Even those who find the idea of a postliberal democracy appealing may wonder how it might come about. The answer, we think, is that the joint project of popular sovereignty and liberty will come to fruition, if at all, not through the substitution of the unprecedented for the familiar, but in the transformation of the present and in the development of structures and meanings already prefigured in today's society and discourse. When asked for his opinion of Western civilization, Mahatma Gandhi said he thought it would be a good idea. He was perhaps overly generous, but his quip points to the radical potential contained in contemporary liberal discourse.

The key to understanding the future of democracy is to find a way to represent the mutual evolution of democratic rules and democratic sentiments and capacities, not as a teleological imperative but as the possible outcome of the constrained projects of collective social actors. Jean Jacques Rousseau expresses this interaction of rules and sentiments as acutely as any recent political theorist:

For a newly formed people to understand wise principles of politics and to follow the basic rules of statecraft, the effect would have to become the cause; the social spirit which must be the product of social institutions would have to preside over the setting up of those institutions; men would have to have already become before the advent of law what they become as a result of law.[13]

Rousseau's perceptive quandary arises because he recognizes the manner in which rules make actors and actors make rules. The problem of building a democratic society is thus one of a dynamic interaction of rules and actors, with the actors rendering the rules more democratic, and the increasingly democratic rules rendering the actors more firmly committed to and skilled at democratic participation and decision making. We term this process a *democratic dynamic*.

We can also imagine a society that lacks this democratic dynamic, one in which the structure of the rules reproduces a body politic with the sentiments, capacities, and forms of organization leading to the reaffirmation of the rules rather than their change. This static society is characterized by what we term an *institutional equilibrium*, in which those with the power to change the rules lack the intent, and those with an interest in changing the rules lack the power to carry through their political projects.

A conception of postliberal democracy that is at once visionary and historical, then, is one which describes a democratic dynamic leading to a reproducible democratic institutional equilibrium. This visionary-historical conception may be contrasted with a utopian model, which displaces historical concerns and simply develops an ideal structure that meets favored normative standards. Utopian conceptions of democratic society are indispensable aids to thinking critically about our own society, and to dispelling the disabling myth that there are no alternatives. But by ignoring questions of social reproduction, and more broadly, of history, the utopian approach sets aside these two critical questions: How does one get there? And if one did get there, would one stay?

We would be foolish to follow this ahistorical course of reasoning. The ill-fated vision that market economies could be coupled with democratic polities of small-holding property owners—the democratic utopias of Thomas Jefferson, James Harrington, and Thomas Paine—is a reminder that it is the historical logic of a system that is crucial to the construction of a democratic society.

This visionary-historical mode of democratic thought may be considerably sharpened by means of a simple dynamic model of the interaction of rules and culture. For simplicity, we represent the complex array of social rules along a single dimension: greater and lesser levels of democracy. By democratic culture we mean the decision-making and participatory capacities of individuals, their commitments to democratic procedures, and their forms of bonding and political organization.

How are rules and culture related? They are simultaneously determined, each at once the cause and effect of the other. Let us suppose, then, that within the range of historically relevant societies, democratic rules give rise to a democratic culture along the lines of the argument developed in chapter 5: both liberty and accountability through democratic participation enhance democratic sentiments and capabilities.[14] Correspondingly, democratic cultures support democratic rules, in part because the costs of enforcing undemocratic rules in a democratic culture are high relative to the costs of maintaining democratic rules. We do not intend to say that the rules governing society respond faithfully to the wishes of the participants or that the rules correspond optimally to the capacities of the populace. Our claim is more modest: the more democratic the culture, the more likely will be the emergence and survival of democratic rules.

Because actors make rules and rules make actors, only some combinations of democratic culture and institutional arrangements are historically stable. A highly democratic culture will not coexist for long with highly undemocratic rules. By contrast, where the rules support a culture that in turn is consistent with the perpetuation of the rules, an institutional equilibrium may be said to exist. Where rules and culture are not mutually reproducing—that is, aside from the positions of institutional equilibrium—the process by which both rules and culture respond to the other is crucial.

Two possibilities present themselves. In one, a democratic dynamic, a democratic set of rules induces a more democratic culture, and this in turn leads actors to render the rules more democratic, further enhancing democratic culture and eventually leading, perhaps, to a highly democratic institutional equilibrium. Equally possible, however, is an antidemocratic dynamic, in which the rules promote a less democratic culture, and this less democratic culture in turn fosters the progressive erosion of democratic rules. The result of this downward spiral may be an undemocratic institutional equilibrium.

We do not consider this possibility of an undemocratic institutional equilibrium or an antidemocratic spiral a mere curiosity; indeed, we believe it is the possible outcome of the successful inauguration of either the neo-Hobbesian or the global liberal model.

The antidemocratic dynamic, like its democratic counterpart, gathers force as it proceeds. If we are correct, many liberal democratic capitalist societies may be represented as being between the one and the other, capable of either enhancing democracy or to eroding it. Talk of capitalism and democracy at the crossroads has been considered overdramatic and alarmist. We consider the possibility quite realistic: either of the two forks in the road, once traveled, may be a one-way street. When actors make rules and rules make actors, time is not reversible, and steps taken may not easily be retraced.

The possibility of an irreversible antidemocratic dynamic gives a special urgency to considering the structure and appeals of the global liberal and neo-Hobbesian models, to which we now turn.

Global Liberalism

We may conceive of a multiplicity of futures for the contemporary liberal democratic capitalist nations. This array of alternatives corresponds to each nation's peculiar institutions, its location in the global environment, and political choices taken within it. Our examination of the successive accommodations of capitalism and the liberal state has alerted us to the impressive malleability and variety of social systems. In retrospect, however, we have been able to identify an underlying logic of these successive accommodations, each allowing the joint reproduction of contrasting systems of economic privilege and increasingly general political rights of representation. Each of these accommodations was established through the collective action of people seeking to further their particular projects; yet none of these underlying logics was the result of a coherent and intentional strategy of reproduction of privilege or extension of democratic rights.

Does our exercise in hindsight contribute to our foresight? The Keynesian accommodation is shattered, probably beyond repair. The imminent demise of either capitalism or liberal democracy appears almost as unlikely as a revival of the Keynesian harmony. What new accommodation might we expect to see arise from the ongoing collision of personal rights and property rights and the forms of solidarity and conflict to which the clash of rights endlessly gives rise?

Global liberalism represents one of two possible avenues by which capitalist social relationships might contain the radical potential of democratic social relations. The logic of the global marketplace and the international mobility of capital can reduce the effective latitude for state action to such a degree that the nation-state—whether democratic or not—is sovereign in name alone. The resulting challenge to democratic sovereignty, it should be clear, does not arise from the existence or scope of global exchange or from the periodic relocation of production. It arises from the economic dependency of each nation-state's citizens that results from the highly concentrated private ownership of productive assets and the effective control that international mobility confers upon this ownership.

The global liberal model is based on the power of what we in chapter 3 called capital strike. Firms will locate and relocate their production on a global scale so as to minimize their expected future costs; the employment prospects in each country will therefore depend on each nation-state's ability to create an attractive business climate; and the ability of any governing group to secure reelection will depend in important measure on the employment situation in the period preceding elections.

The effectiveness of capital strike obviously requires insulating the power of credit creation from democratic accountability, for if democratically elected governments can readily obtain and extend credit irrespective of their economic and social policies, the mobility of capital will impinge only marginally on the sovereignty of states. Indeed, the evolution of international monetary policy since before World War I has witnessed an acute awareness of just this fact on the part of forward-looking business groups and their advocates. The effect of the International Monetary Fund (IMF) in disciplining Third World states on behalf of international and domestic capital is well documented.[15] Advanced nation-states are no less subject to these influences, for the supply of credit within a national economy is now quite beyond the control of any nation-state. The influential *McCracken Report*, written in the late 1970s by leading economists and policy makers in Europe and North America, observes,

> The limits of reserve creation have become ill-defined and fluid, being set now by the private market's judgment of the credit-worthiness of individual countries rather than by official multilateral evaluation of the needs of the system as a

whole . . . the international monetary system has taken on some of the characteristics of a domestic credit system without a central bank.[16]

The power of capital strike is well illustrated by the reaction of the financial community to the 1981 electoral victory of François Mitterand's Socialist party in France. Between 1965 and 1980, real gross fixed capital formation in France grew at an average rate of 4.4 percent, and it never declined in two successive years over this period. With the advent of the socialist government, this growth trend immediately reversed, declining steadily over the next three years (the only period for which we have figures) at an annual rate of −1.21 percent.[17] This reversal occurred far too rapidly to reflect the actual policies of the new government. It rather reflects the displeasure of investors. Direct U.S. investment in France, for instance, which grew at an annual rate of approximately 11 percent between 1965 and 1981, declined in every year since Mitterand's victory, falling at an average annual rate of 6 percent per year.[18]

The result of a successful implementation of the global liberal model is a competition among dozens of nation-states, each seeking to maintain employment and promote economic growth, and each thus constrained to promote a favorable business climate in order to attract international capital. The state is thereby reduced to the equivalent of the perfectly competitive firm in neoclassical economics. Unable to control prices and other aspects of the economic environment, it simply does the best it can within the constraints set by these parameters.

Ironically, it is the more democratic states whose freedom of action is more stringently controlled by this competition; states less responsive to the wishes of the populace are more likely to survive the flight of capital and the economic distress accompanying it. Gary Becker captures the irony of this powerlessness of those in power:

> An ideal political democracy would be perfectly responsive to the "will" of the people. The ultimate aim of each party may be to acquire political power, but in equilibrium no one, including those "in power," has any political power. There is no room for choice by political officials because political decisions are completely determined by electoral preferences.[19]

Just as the neoclassical economist understates the latitude for the exercise of power by the owners of the firm, Becker surely understates the scope of leadership and tutelage in a democratic state. But the point of his argument is undeniable. And if electoral preferences are determined in important measure by the pursuit of one's livelihood, which in turn is made possible by access to a job which will be available only if the terms of international capital are met, the global liberal model is complete.

In this form of accommodation the democratic structure of the state is rendered vacuous, not by markets but by the economic dependence of the voters on conditions not under the control of the state. Unless the economy in question has special advantages that make it more attractive to capital, it must do what it can to match the profit-enhancing strategies enacted by competing states. When economies are so thoroughly integrated in the world economic system that the supply of investment in any given economy is highly responsive to small differences in the expected profit rate, the effective range of choices may be reduced to a single set of policies, a global equivalent to Henry Ford's "you can have any color car you want, as long as it is black."

Citizens in some future global liberal world might lament that although their rights have not been trammeled, their ability to affect the course of events in their country certainly has. With the menu of economically viable policy options limited to perhaps little more than a single program, many voters may be content to regard politics as a form of public administration, and resign themselves to leaving the design of effective capital-attracting strategies to bankers and economists. A vigorous democratic political life might nonetheless survive, nourished by the concerns of the body politic not related to economic matters. Yet it seems probable that many might sense that little was at stake, for the imperatives of profitable production that underlie the limited selection of policy options do not end at the boundaries of the firm, but rather extend to the form and extent of schooling, the degree of invidious distinction among workers, and even what might be thought to be the private sentiments of the population. If, as a result, political participation were to decline, the reasoning presented in chapter 5 would lead one to expect that the hope of a robust democratic culture would dim as well, leading perhaps to less concern among the citizenry about the loss of sovereignty and the democratically enforced reign of capital administered by economists. A low-level nondemocratic institutional equilibrium might well be secured, or an antidemocratic spiral initiated.

But the prospects for so tidy a scenario are clouded by the improbable political assumptions and high enforcement cost implied by the model. The downward pressure on wages and intensification of work in the advanced capitalist countries, resulting from the competition among nation-states to augment the rate of profit, would probably foster a sense of unfairness and a hostility toward the rules of the game. A heightened sense of conflict of interest would be accompanied by a reduced ability to find cooperative solutions to domestic conflicts either in workplace bargaining or in the formation of economywide accords on such matters as income policies. As a result, enforcement costs (of either the carrot or stick kind) would most likely mount. Aside from the more obvious of these—an increase in police costs and workplace surveillance—an upward drift in the level of unemployment necessary to stabilize the power relationship between capital and labor seems quite possible. Under these conditions, the state in the global liberal model might well prove vulnerable to populist nationalist assault, as have so many states in Latin America, Asia, and Africa.

Maintaining the conditions for the unimpeded worldwide movement of capital and repatriation of profits presents additional problems. The rapid—by world historical standards—rates of economic growth in the past 200 years and the continuing counterpoint of uneven development have generated major differences in growth rates among the major economies. The unevenness of economic progress has in turn led to an accelerating process whereby the institutional arrangements aimed at securing a stable world monetary and trading system in one decade are prone to recurrent crises and quickly give way to some other system under the pressure of the rapidly shifting relative power of the contending nation-states. It is perhaps for this reason that *Pax Britannica* lasted a century and *Pax Americana* expired after twenty-five years.

The ability of either a single leading state, or perhaps a coalition of states, to secure the monetary and political conditions for the global model is thus far from assured. At the least, the instability of the world economic and political situation would tend to propel the global liberal solution toward a costly interventionist and militaristic foreign policy stance on the part of the leading capitalist nations. This stance itself might be precarious, for a powerful global military presence requires a strong domestic economy and the ability to mobilize an effective cadre of troops. It might prove difficult to mobilize nationalist sentiment on the part of the victims of the global liberal model in the service of making the world safe for multinational capital flight.

The free trade ideology that would be most apt to provide the ideological justification of unlimited international capital mobility is itself likely to impose a considerable cost. To the extent that the unimpeded play of markets—

both domestic and global—imposes substantial irrationalities associated with environmental spillovers, the destruction of community, and the underdevelopment of the society's not easily marketable resources such as knowledge, invention, and even labor itself, the global liberal model may prove highly wasteful, and vulnerable to supersession by more effective economic systems less averse to collective decision making and allocational procedures. It is partly for these reasons that a less market-based alternative is a serious contender against the global liberal model.

Neo-Hobbesian Liberalism

If the virtues of the market represent the normative appeal of the global liberal model, the beneficial effects of authoritarian tutelage are the attraction of neo-Hobbesian liberalism. According to the prescriptions of this model, hierarchically ordered nonmarket institutions—the bureaucratic state, patriarchal family, and capitalist firm—would encroach upon the market, substituting the logic of command for that of exchange in the interest of either efficiency or the preservation of traditional values. A common strand of this thinking, and the basis for its designation as neo-Hobbesian, is the justification of hierarchy on the grounds that rational and free individuals might voluntarily submit to various forms of domination in the interest of order and economic rationality.[20] Another common element in this reasoning, one that represents its great advance over other versions of liberalism, is that it takes explicit account of both the enforcement costs of social relationships and the formation of values, sentiments, and capacities—what we have earlier called learning—as central features of social organization.*

Neo-Hobbesian arguments for family and state hierarchies abound. As we have seen, the family head in the "new family economics" is an all-powerful altruist who uses his beneficence to discourage "shirking," "malfeasance," and other antisocial forms of activity. This representation com-

---

* We do not intend to suggest that the neo-Hobbesian writers constitute a self-conscious and unified school (though the name we have provided them with may encourage such a development!) but simply that they tend to voice common themes about which there is a noticeable silence among other liberals. Nor is the connection to Thomas Hobbes more than metaphoric: indeed some of the writers we have deemed neo-Hobbesian evoke Edmund Burke more than Hobbes.

bines the two basic elements of the neo-Hobbesian view: the ubiquity of malfeasance as an ineluctable result of self-seeking behavior, and the beneficial effects of hierarchy in limiting its nefarious effects. The new family economics also illustrates the underlying political presumptions of this model. Annie Cot writes, "The connection which Becker makes between despotism and the invisible hand constitutes the new family economics as a microcosm of the more general representation of the liberal social order."[21]

If liberalism has generally stressed choice, regarding the necessary forms of coercion entailed in the management of learning as a philosophical embarrassment and a subject best left to social engineers, neo-Hobbesians are more inclined to address the issue directly and without apology. Writing from a perspective quite different from that of Becker, the Reverend Jerry Falwell states,

> The strength and stability of families determine the vitality and moral life of society. The most important function performed by the family is the rearing and character formation of children, a function it was uniquely designed to perform, and for which no remotely adequate substitute has been found. The family is the best and most efficient "department of health, education, and welfare."[22]

Others are willing to advocate an expansion of state activities designed to further the necessarily social process of human development. In a work pointedly titled *Statecraft as Soulcraft*, George Will returns to the political theory of Saint Augustine or Edmund Burke.

> The United States acutely needs a real conservatism, characterized by a concern to cultivate the best persons and the best in persons. It should express renewed appreciation for the ennobling functions of government. It should challenge the liberal doctrine that regarding one important dimension of life—the "inner life"—there should be less government—less than there is now, less than there recently was, and less than most political philosophers have thought prudent.

Will shares our view of the broad scope of politics:

> Political philosophy is about "the polity," which is much more than government institutions. It includes all the institutions, dispositions, habits and mores on which government depends and on which therefore, government should strive to have a shaping influence. . . . Democratic government must be a tutor as well as a servant to its citizens, because citizenship is a state of mind.[23]

Other neo-Hobbesian contributions to contemporary political analysis advocate a strengthening of the executive branch of the government vis-à-vis both the legislative branches and the press. In major policy areas—economic planning, environmental regulation, and the nuclear power industry are prime examples—expanded governmental intervention and the effective insulation of these interventions from popular accountability are advocated.[24]

In advocating state interventionist family policy to regulate sexuality and marriage, as well as an activist state economic policy to attenuate market failures, the neo-Hobbesian vision may be considered statist. But it equally advocates an expansion of the boundaries of the capitalist firm so that economic interactions would increasingly take the form of command relationships *within* a given ownership unit, rather than market exchanges *between* units.

A key to the development of a neo-Hobbesian economics is the concept of transactions costs, or what we term *enforcement* costs. We have seen that traditional liberal economics has generally assumed that the enforcement of the terms of an exchange is costless to the exchanging parties. C. B. Macpherson comments, "Property is a claim which the individual can count on having enforced in his favour by society or the state, by custom or convention or law."[25] Neo-Hobbesians, by contrast to traditional liberal theorists, treat the problem of enforcing the terms of exchange as a strategic concern of economic actors, making the resulting costs central to their theory.

The major fruit of this theoretical innovation is an extension of the neoclassical theory of the capitalist enterprise, which bears a superficial resemblance to the Marxian view in that it focuses on the authority relations internal to the firm. Unlike the Marxian approach, however, the neo-Hobbesian model presents the authoritarian structure of the firm as a natural and efficient response to the intrinsic disutility of labor and the resulting problem of "shirking."

The firm has always been an anomaly in neoclassical theory, representing a nonmarket system of resource allocation whose ubiquity and survival in a competitive environment is inexplicable to those who regard competitive market exchanges as the most efficient manner of allocating resources. In an early contribution to this approach, "The Nature of the Firm," Ronald Coase asks "why a firm emerges at all in a specialized exchange economy."[26] The resolution of this puzzle, according to the neo-Hobbesian approach, is that hierarchical organization—or what economists candidly term "command" relations—are often more efficient than market exchanges. In Coase's words,

> The main reason why it is profitable to establish a firm would seem to be . . . that the operation of a market costs something and by forming an organization and allowing some authority . . . to direct the resources, certain marketing costs are saved.[27]

In this, the neo-Hobbesian approach has borrowed a page from Max Weber:

> The decisive reason for the advance of bureaucratic organization has always been its purely technical superiority over any other form of organization . . . the very large modern capitalist enterprises are themselves unequaled models of strict bureaucratic organization.[28]

However, whereas Weber favored bureaucracy as a structurally superior alternative to older forms of hierarchy (for example "unremunerated honorific service"), the neo-Hobbesians find its value in its superior ability to limit worker "shirking" and other forms of "malfeasance."

In this view, the hierarchical structure of the firm is not an expression of the power of the owner or the boss but merely a cost-minimizing method of organizing work. Indeed, as the following passages from Armen Alchian and Harold Demsetz make clear, it is a form that would be created by a team of equal workmates in their own interest. Asserting a general propensity to shirk by the "owners of cooperating inputs" (that is, workers), these authors observe,

> One method of reducing shirking is for someone to specialize as a monitor to check the input performance of team members. But who will monitor the monitor? . . . [A] constraint can be imposed . . . give him title to the net earnings of the team, net of payments to other inputs. If owners of cooperating inputs agree with the monitor that he is to receive any residual product above prescribed amounts, the monitor will have an added incentive not to shirk as monitor.[29]

The monitor, it appears, not only must have the status of residual claimant on income but must also exercise the powers of the capitalist employer:

> To discipline team members and reduce shirking, the residual claimant must have power to revise the contract terms and incentives of individual members.

... Hence team members who seek to increase their productivity will assign to the monitor not only the residual claimant right, but also the right to alter individual membership and performance on the team.[30]

The result is not only a theory of the voluntary origins of monitoring—as if from a state of nature—but an explanation of why those higher up in the pyramidal structure of the firm should be paid more, and have the right to hire and fire, in the interest of the team. The monitor, in short, must be a capitalist. A more striking analogue to Hobbes's conception of citizens in the state of nature creating a sovereign state and voluntarily agreeing to place themselves under its authority is difficult to imagine.

Oliver Williamson, a leading contributor to the neo-Hobbesian literature, provides this overview:

Examination of complex organizations of all kinds—corporate and noncorporate, capitalist and noncapitalist, within and between nation states and political systems, and over time—discloses strong common features ... (1) all complex organizations need to come to terms with the attributes of human nature as we know it; ... (3) efficiency is served by hierarchy; (4) system integrity is promoted by separating operating from strategic decisions and controls.[31]

Thus the hierarchical firm, in place of its status as a tainted anomaly in conventional neoclassical economic theory, is reintroduced as a rational collective solution to the problem of scarcity. A rehabilitation of the reputation of the bureaucratic enterprise is then in order. Alchian and Demsetz write:

It is common to see the firm characterized by the power to settle issues by fiat, by authority, or by disciplinary action superior to that available in the conventional market. This is delusion. It has no power of fiat, no authority, no disciplinary action any different in the slightest degree from ordinary market contracting between any two people.... [The firm] can fire or sue, just as I can fire my grocer by stopping purchases from him or sue him for delivering faulty products.[32]

This benevolent view of firm hierarchies, coupled with the acute awareness of transactions costs and resulting market failures, leads neo-Hobbesian economists to minimize the normative distinction between the two.

In contrast to markets and cities, which can be viewed as publicly or nonowned market places, the firm can be considered to be a privately owned market; if so we could consider the firm and the ordinary market as competing types of markets.[33]

When environmental spillover or other externalities are prominent, the firm may represent a superior alternative both to market and to state regulation, provided the ownership units are permitted to grow large enough to internalize what would have been external effects in an economic world made up of the small firms that populate the neoclassical textbook. Demsetz identifies the economic advantages of shopping malls and proprietary towns:

> The owner of a department store or a shopping plaza can provide a general environment that is conducive for shopping, such as pleasant plantings, escalators, and other customer services that merchants who owned their own land might hesitate to pay for, hoping instead that neighboring landowners would incur the necessary expenses from which all would benefit.[34]

The implications for the relationship between property rights and personal rights are inescapable, and to Demsetz, irresistible:

> The closing of the land into a single ownership entity which often undertakes to provide services usually provided by government from tax revenues, such as streets, sidewalks, refuse collection, and even police protection, allows the owner to exclude those who refuse to pay rentals which cover the cost of these services. The competition of various plazas and department stores will provide ample opportunity for merchants to select the services that they wish to buy without fearing or counting on free-loading. . . . The development of these institutional arrangements provides an interesting challenge to political institutions for the provision of many of the services generally presumed to be within the scope of the polling place.[35]

The neo-Hobbesian model thus represents a curious amalgam of the modern and the traditional. Burkean in its acceptance of traditional values, it is more akin to the forward-looking social engineering of Saint-Simon or Frederick Winslow Taylor in its embrace of efficiency rather than choice as its normative anchor. The unity of these two strands is their common commitment to authoritarian social relationships.

The form of accommodation of personal rights and property rights suggested by the neo-Hobbesian model would be based on the institutional ghettoization of personal rights, not through the structured powerlessness of the state, as in the global liberal accommodation, but through the expansion of the terrain over which property rights reign, the contraction of the domain of personal rights, and the construction of unaccountable state institutions for planning and tutelege.

The trajectories of both the global liberal and neo-Hobbesian models are profoundly antidemocratic. The former promises accountability without sovereignty and the latter promises sovereignty without accountability. Both are liberal in respecting the fundamental partitions of liberal thought: private and public and learner and chooser.*

The emergence of the neo-Hobbesian liberal vision as part of conservative corporatist initiatives since World War I, and particularly its contemporary expressions as an expansion of the realm of intrafirm command relationships, has no doubt been favored by a growing hostility to the market and the state alike. The market is increasingly seen as corrosive of society, unfair, and wasteful of resources; the state is seen as an ersatz community given as much to inefficiency as to military adventures and bureaucratic pretensions.

In this view, neo-Hobbesians are not alone. Socialists, populists, feminists, and social democrats alike are rejecting the terms of the old market versus state debate: as means toward egalitarian and democratic ends, market and planning are at once indispensable and insufficient. Radical democrats have put forward a vision of a society supporting a multiplicity of democratically constituted nonstate public spaces—workplaces, neighborhoods, and cultural institutions. This latter vision, which shares with the neo-Hobbesian model an interest in expanding the scope of social arenas beyond state and market but proposes a quite different structure for them, is integral to the concept of postliberal democracy. Part of the underlying logic of the postliberal model is best revealed by an analysis of the contradictions of the neo-Hobbesian solution.

Exchange, Bureaucracy, and Postliberal Democracy

That the neo-Hobbesian model constitutes a threat to democracy may be widely appreciated; that it is as seriously flawed economically and likely to become increasingly so may become increasingly apparent.

* Neo-Hobbesian writers on the state and the family stress the necessary activities of these institutions in promoting socially beneficial learning, whereas neo-Hobbesian economists tend to presume an instrumental mode of action, setting aside the manner in which human subjects are formed.

The costs of enforcing any set of rules, whether they be contractual exchanges, systems of racial domination, town meetings, patriarchal sex-gender systems, or bureaucratic hierarchies, depends intimately on the constitution of the actors—on their skills, sentiments, and understandings. If the rules foster a sense of commitment and legitimacy, the enforcement costs will tend to be low. If on the other hand the rules appear to be unfair, and if they foster solidarity among the ruled, resistance may mount. Then resorts to costly forms of coercion will probably be frequent. The foremost Marxian historian of slavery, Eugene Genovese, comments, "Ruling classes differ, and each must rule differently. But . . . each must confront the problem of coercion in such a way as to minimize the necessity of its use."[36] Moreover, the enforcement costs of a set of rules depend critically on the activities the rules regulate. Some activities are most suitably regulated by market exchange, others by bureaucratic authority, and yet others by collective reciprocal relationships. It is perhaps illustrative of the way the nature of an activity itself favors particular types of social organization that even in the most diverse cultures babies are raised in what we call families. To take quite a different example, throughout the nineteenth century around the world, sugar was raised on plantations and tobacco was grown on small owner-operated farms, even (as in Cuba) where these crops were part of a single economy and social system.

The central economic flaw in the neo-Hobbesian model is this: far from being an efficient solution to the problem of scarcity given the ostensible human disinclination to work, authoritarian social relationships in a liberal social environment are increasingly wasteful, inducing growing levels of resistance and inviting mounting enforcement costs. Human wants and our means of satisfying them continue to develop in ways that make the types of labor necessary to provide our livelihood increasingly unamenable to bureaucratic authority. At the same time, inegalitarian bureaucratic systems are seen as increasingly illegitimate, in part because of the expansionary nature of the logic of personal rights. The result of these technological, economic, political, and cultural developments is a growing mismatch between the nature of labor and of popular discourse on the one hand, and the demands of bureaucratic hierarchy on the other.

Hierarchy replaces market exchange, according to the neo-Hobbesian approach, when the transactions costs of exchange exceed the enforcement costs of hierarchy. Transactions costs of exchanges tend to be high when the good or service being exchanged is costly to measure with precision.

When measurement costs are low—as for example, in the monitoring of the flow of electricity from a seller to a buyer—market exchanges will have low transactions costs even when the exchanging parties have sharply conflicting interests. This will be the case because, given the low cost of measurement, attempts to take advantage of one's exchange partner will be easily detected and rectified, if necessary by recourse to a court of law. This low measurement cost case is paradigmatic for the concept of private property as a claim readily enforceable by resort to external authority.

But what about the reverse case, when the activities being exchanged are difficult to measure? If conflicts of interest between the exchanging parties remain severe, some costly form of organization will result: either litigious markets or the proliferation of surveillance activities within a bureaucratic authority. The neo-Hobbesian model favors the latter.

Two general developments in the liberal democratic capitalist societies are likely to render this solution ever more costly. The first development tending to raise the costs of hierarchical order concerns people's orientation toward the labor process itself and the manner in which it is organized. Recall that the neo-Hobbesian writers' "propensity to shirk" is the result of a natural dislike of work on the part of a self-interested actor. "Opportunism is a key attribute of human agents," observes Oliver Williamson. Harold Demsetz refers to the "people could be different fallacy."[37] Taking a page from sociobiology, neo-Hobbesian economics considers the "disutility of labor" to be a universal human condition.[38]

The neo-Hobbesian approach is surely right to focus on how systems of organization can induce people to do things they would otherwise not do, for it is unlikely that any social order will ever banish unpleasant necessities. But it seems considerably more plausible to posit that people's attitude toward their work depends on how the work is organized, how the rewards are distributed, and how they personally are treated at work, as well as on the more general structure of social relationships including those of the family and the state. More pointedly, a society that elevates self-interested behavior to a privileged form of rational action and at the same time fosters high levels of inequality and conflict of interest might expect to be faced with unusually severe problems of malfeasance and mounting enforcement costs. "The central objection that modern moralists make to Hobbes' doctrine," writes C. B. Macpherson, "is that the rational self interest of Hobbes' appetitive calculating individuals . . . is bound to set up a perennial disposition to neglect or deny obligation to the sovereign."[39] Further, when work is organized by and for another probably unknown and even unseen person, it is quite likely that it will be experienced, as Marx suggested, as something alien and oppressive. Neither capitalist society nor liberal discourse produced the problem of self-interested opportunism, but it seems reasonable to suggest that they have exacerbated it.

The second reason to expect mounting costs of the neo-Hobbesian solution concerns the structure of the economy itself. With economic growth, people are changing the manner in which they seek to meet their needs. Most obviously, services—ranging from education and health to finance, insurance, and psychiatric advice—are replacing goods as the main product of labor, now accounting for well over half of the output of some advanced economies. Services, however, are generally more difficult to measure than are goods simply because they are intangible.

Equally important, the nature of production itself is changing. Technical innovation and information have assumed an ever-more important role in affecting economic performance. Economic systems that falter in the management of technical change and the production of knowledge will be less and less able to take advantage of possibilities readily exploited by more adept social systems. It follows that the raw material of economic activity is also changing. The natural environment which labor transformed three centuries ago could reasonably enough be presented as "land and natural resources." The "man with the hoe" metaphor for labor was indeed apt. But today a substantial part of our labor is devoted to a transformation of ourselves. If land was the critical input in John Locke's day, and capital goods from Karl Marx's day to our own, it may well be that knowledge and the human body itself will share the honors in the next century. The trinity of a political economy of the twenty-first century may not be Land, Labor, and Capital, but rather the Body, Labor, and Knowledge.

The import of this speculation is immediately apparent. While both land and machines can be owned and can be exchanged on markets with relatively low transaction costs, neither knowledge nor the human body can be exchanged as property—at least not easily so. This is because, barring slavery, the human body is inalienable from its owner. The exceptionally high transactional costs and moral dilemmas posed by today's fledgling market in organs, babies, and genetic material is perhaps suggestive of this.

Knowledge is difficult to exchange not because it cannot be separated from its owner but for the converse reason: because it is so easily stolen or shared. The costs of reproducing knowledge are so low compared to the costs of producing it that it is nearly impossible to exclude others from its use, and it is almost always irrational from a societywide standpoint to attempt to do so. Kenneth Arrow, one of the preeminent students of information and technical change, concludes,

> To sum up, we expect that a free enterprise economy to underinvest in invention and research (as compared with an ideal) because it is risky, because the product can be appropriated only to a limited extent, and because of increasing returns in use. This underinvestment will be greater for more basic research. Further, to the extent that a firm succeeds in engrossing the economic value of inventive activity, there will be an under-utilization of that information as compared with an ideal allocation.[40]

The evolution of the work process and the objects of labor itself thus join the expansion of the discourse of personal rights to render the neo-Hobbesian model an anachronistic source of waste and social contestation. Yet these shortcomings of the neo-Hobbesian approach do not point to strengths of the global liberal model; indeed, they are in part arguments for the ubiquity of the market failures that constitute a major drawback of the more traditional liberal approach.

The economic promise of the postliberal democratic model is the converse of the neo-Hobbesian, not the management and containment of conflict through bureaucratic hierarchy, but its attenuation through the proliferation of democratic commitment and egalitarian forms of social reciprocity.

Preface to the Political Economy of a Postliberal Democracy

Although the neo-Hobbesian and global liberal models may provide the outlines for a new—perhaps hybrid—accommodation between capitalism and liberal democracy, each in its own way consolidating capitalism while eroding democracy, postliberal democracy departs so significantly from both capitalism and liberal democracy that one can hardly consider it a new form of accommodation. It is more accurately described as a process leading to a new social order.

The analysis in the preceding chapters has committed us to a particular vision of how the economic structure of a postliberal democratic social order might look, and to a conception of the historical process by which such a society might come about and survive.

Our vision of a postliberal democracy is based on the following propositions, each derived from the reasoning of earlier chapters. First, the capitalist economy—and indeed virtually any feasible alternative—is a public arena whose structure regulates the distributional, appropriative, political, cultural, and other projects of various social actors. No coherent conception of democracy can escape the conclusion that the powers thus conferred on individual and collective actors in the economy ought to be subject to democratic accountability.

Second, lack of secure access to one's livelihood is a form of dependency, one that confers power on those who control the means of life. Economic dependency—whether in the form of the financial dependence of women on men, unemployment induced deliberately by macroeconomic policy to discipline the labor force, or the instrumental use of the threat of capital flight—arbitrarily limits individual choices and erodes democratic accountability even where it is formally secured. Economic dependency is thus antithetical to both liberty and popular sovereignty.

Third, the economy, the state, and the family produce people. The lifelong development of the capacities, preferences, sentiments, and identities of individuals results from an interaction between genetic potential and structured social practices. The impact of social structure on human development ranges from the relationship between the sexual division of labor and what Nancy Chodorow calls "feminine personality,"[41] to the connection between the hierarchical structure of work and the value that parents place on obedience in their children, and to the effect of the decline of residential neighborhoods on civic orientations. Because the growth and effectiveness of democratic institutions depend on the strength of democratic capacities, a commitment to democracy entails the advocacy of institutions that promote rather than impede the development of a democratic culture. Further, because learning, or more broadly, human development, is a central and lifelong social activity of people, there is no coherent reason for exempting the structures that regulate learning—whether they be schools, families, neighborhoods, or workplaces—from the criteria of democratic accountability and liberty.

Fourth, the power of unaccountable authority and the limitations of personal choice in liberal democratic capitalist societies derive in part from the manner in which our personal identities are intimately bound up with un-accountable collectivities, whether they be the nation-state, the patriarchal family, or the modern corporation. The near-monopoly exercised by these institutions on our sense of social identity is rivaled only by equally anti-democratic invidious distinctions of class, race, and gender. But the modern ideal of universalist values, by leaving the autonomous individual face-to-face with the abstract state, is more likely to exacerbate than to solve the problem. Both liberty and popular sovereignty would be served by the vitality of democratic communities standing between the individual and the state, and by the related possibility of a proliferation of noninvidious distinctions among people.

One cannot derive specific institutional prescriptions from these four quite general propositions. But they do point unmistakably toward the de-mocratization of the economy, the attenuation of economic inequality, the democratization of the learning process, and the promotion of what Hannah Arendt calls "new public spaces for freedom."[42] On balance, these objectives are complementary, yet none is without its dilemmas and contradictions.

The main imperatives of the democratization of the economy are clear—workplace democracy, democratic economic planning, and community ac-cess to capital—but as we shall see, the relationships among them are com-plex at best and possibly contradictory. The logic of the democratic workplace is that democratic decision making in production units will replace unac-countable hierarchy with democratic participation and commitment. One might hope thereby to contribute to a more effective system of production through the reduction in enforcement costs, as well as to support a participa-tory learning environment and an autonomous democratic community.*

By democratic economic planning we mean the socially accountable de-termination of the broad outlines of the pattern of economic structure and its evolution. Accountability entails the collective deliberation and control over investment decisions, for as we have seen, it is the concentrated control over the accumulation process that places the present and future techno-logical, spatial, environmental, sectoral, and other aspects of economic evo-lution beyond the realm of popular sovereignty.

Although the central position of democratic control of investment is clear,

---

* Although we believe these expectations—and those discussed later—are supported by much available evidence and are well within the realm of possibility, it seems pointless to review the relevant empirical studies, for the applicability of current experience to social experimentation under quite different social circumstances is somewhat problematic.

the instruments by which the overall accountability of the economy might be achieved most effectively cannot be prejudged in advance or in general. The debate on the merits of centralized planning and direct allocation of resources relative to the use of markets is a practical matter to be decided by study of the associated costs in particular cases. Our analysis does not favor one over the other, but rather poses new criteria for the evaluation of each: the evaluation of apparently specialized economic institutions such as markets or systems of economic planning must balance the claims of democratic and other valued forms of human development against the more traditional claims based on the alleviation of scarcity, the enhancement of liberty, and the like. Similarly, the question of public or private ownership of the means of production may be variously answered under differing particular conditions, according to the norms of liberty and democratic accountability.

A generation ago R. H. Tawney observed that a society in which some have more than they need while many do not have enough to get by may possibly claim many virtues, but liberty cannot be among them.[43] Nor, we might add, will popular sovereignty flourish under these circumstances. Our concern with democracy has lead us, like Tawney, to a political critique of economic inequality. We propose that democrats ought to regard the access to a socially acceptable standard of living as a right; depriving people of their livelihood would thus be as contrary to social norms and legality as depriving people of their liberty or violating their physical person. The reasoning of the preceding pages provides ample support for such a notion. We will touch on a perhaps overlooked argument in favor of this egalitarian commitment—what Michael Walzer calls "provision for the sake of community"—and then turn to a problem raised by this argument.

A society that regularly, and as a necessary part of its ordinary functioning, allows a significant fraction of its members to live in conditions of financial insecurity and material distress expresses a degree of indifference or callousness toward its members which both exhibits and fortifies social division and invidious comparison rather than community. If, as Marshall Sahlins says, gifts make friends, it may also be said that ignoring the plight of one's fellow people makes strangers if not enemies. Michael Walzer observes,

The idea of distributive justice presupposes a bounded world within which distributions take place: a group of people committed to dividing, exchanging, and sharing social goods, first of all among themselves. That world . . . is the political community.

Walzer continues,

> Membership is important because of those things the members of a political community owe to one another and to no one else, or to no one in the same degree. And the first thing they owe is the communal provision of security and welfare. This claim might be reversed: communal provision is important because it teaches us the value of membership. If we did not provide for one another, if we recognized no distinctions between members and strangers, we would have no reason to form and maintain political communities.[44]

A mutual commitment to securing each person's conditions of life builds the respect and communal identification upon which a democratic culture must rest, but it also raises economic problems. We have emphasized the problem of inducing people to work and stressed the manner in which capitalist societies rely heavily on economic insecurity as a major if often implicit disciplinary and motivational device. Although capitalist society and the hierarchical workplace in particular probably exacerbate the underlying problem, we doubt that any society will dispense with the need to motivate work. If the postliberal social order is to guarantee economic security it must simultaneously alter the meaning of work so that it no longer appears to so many as an alien imposition.

Our commitment to the right to a livelihood does not mean, of course, that good work cannot be rewarded, only that the stakes should not be so high and that the penalties ought not to include deprivation of an acceptable living standard. More important, democratic work groups in an environment of economic security will be pressed to develop means of eliciting good work from their members; participation in decision making and the equitable sharing of the net revenues of the production unit would undoubtedly be augmented by a wide range of recognitions and sanctions, drawing more heavily on work-team members' capacity for pride and shame than on their economic insecurity.

The attenuation of economic inequality and the democratization of the economy would represent a major step toward a more democratic society. They would also contribute significantly to the democratization of the process of human development, or more concretely, to the systematic application of the norms of both democratic accountability and liberty to the manifold institutions of learning and personal transformation. Economic necessity is today one of the most binding constraints on educational choices over the course of one's life; the guarantee of an acceptable livelihood would open up a more ample array of educational choices by eliminating the threat of personal economic calamity as a possible consequence of a wrong choice. More obviously, the democratization of the economy would itself constitute a major step toward accountability and liberty in a major learning environment.

As with the other economic structural characteristics of a postliberal democratic society, the democratization of learning is not without its problems. Any philosophically self-conscious viewpoint must grapple with the difficult issues of choice, authority, and social ends that are necessarily bound up in the analysis of learning. But the apparent intractability of these issues within the liberal framework may stem more from the characteristics of liberal thought than from the peculiar difficulties to which the educational encounter gives rise. Amy Gutmann identifies the key contradiction of both major strands of modern liberalism as educational philosophies in this way:

> Utilitarians and . . . rights theorists . . . agree on one point about the education of children: at least in principle they both are committed to providing an education that is neutral among substantive conceptions of the good life.[45]

We do not share this liberal neutrality concerning the good life. Nor, we suspect, do many liberals in their daily activities as parents, teachers, friends, and citizens.

Our commitment to democracy is both to a means and to an end, although in both cases the commitment is an admittedly minimal and insufficient basis for a fully articulated philosophy of education. Our commitment implies that people ought to learn what they choose to learn when they make choices in a general environment of liberty and popular sovereignty. We do not know what people would choose to become under these conditions: our moral and political commitment is to try it and see. Many, indeed most, educational choices are not now made under these conditions. But to the extent that some are made under conditions approximating liberty and accountability we see the possibility of a democratic learning dynamic, one that would inhabit the imperfect realms of democracy and choice in our society and progressively transform ever-wider circles of social life toward democratic ends.

The economic institutions and commitments required to make good the promise of postliberal democracy—the displacement of profit-driven capital markets by the democratically accountable planning of investment and resource allocation, the organization of workplaces and other communities by means of representative and participatory institutions, and the attenuation of economic inequality—are all familiar objectives of democratic socialist movements over the past century. We have chosen to term our visionary-historical alternative postliberal democracy rather than socialism simply because we regard those time-honored commitments of socialists not as ends in themselves but as means toward securing an expanded conception of liberty and popular sovereignty. Our treatment of socialism—and the elimination of class exploitation—as means toward the achievement of democracy in no way diminishes our commitment to these objectives, though it does express our rejection of the not uncommon tendency of socialists to relegate democracy to the status of a means, however indispensable, for the achievement of classlessness.

Our insistence on the priority of the terms "democracy" and its constituent elements—"popular sovereignty" and "liberty"—over more traditional economic phrases of the socialist lexicon, such as the "abolition of exploitation" and "public ownership of the means of production," thus expresses our conception of the political nature of economic concerns, not their unimportance. For example, we have addressed the central issue of economic inequality not primarily from the standpoint of distributive justice but rather as a form of dependency that limits personal freedom. And we have advocated social control over investment not primarily to achieve a more efficient allocation of resources but as a necessary means toward securing popular sovereignty in the face of the threat of capital strike.

Our choice of terms reflects a recognition of both the hegemony of liberal democratic discourse as the virtually exclusive medium of political communication in the advanced capitalist nations and the profoundly contradictory, malleable, and potentially radical nature of this discourse. No less important, the privileged status of democracy in our discourse reflects our central moral commitment and political project: to the creation of a new social order in which people—individuals and communities—are more nearly the authors of their own individual and collective histories.

209

Democracy, Agency, and History

Among the consolations of modern life is the widespread faith that history is on the side of freedom. Whether rooted in the indomitable human spirit, the growth of Reason, or the civilizing character of science and technology, the idea that time is on the side of liberty and equality is deeply ingrained in modern culture. It appears in the liberal notion of modernization as a passage toward affluence, tolerance, and the pluralist commonwealth, and in the Marxian vision of communism as the first society in which the freedom of each is the prerequisite for the freedom of all. It appears as well in our calm belief in the inevitability of Hitler's failure, in the irreparable economic backwardness of authoritarian state socialism, and in the impossibility that relocation camps, napalm, wholesale torture, murder, and the rest of the U.S. coercive state repertoire could be turned against capitalism's "internal enemies."

It will not come as a surprise to the reader that no such faith comforts us. The indomitable human spirit can be broken. Reason is a cruel master. And modern science ever refines the tools for dominating not just nature, but people as well. Not the inevitability of freedom, but rather its existence against great odds, is the true monument to the human spirit.

History, Leon Trotsky wrote, is the natural selection of accidents. Democracy may be, quite simply, an accident of history—an exotic social variety heady with possibilities but with questionable survival capacity. The question the democrat must face is simply this: what conditions contribute to democracy's survival power, and how may our understanding of these conditions allow us to extend and deepen democratic culture and institutions?

Our answer is that the historical viability of a commitment to democracy flows from the dominance of the discourse of rights in the context of a set of rules of the game promoting representative government and individual liberty. At first glance this answer appears to condone a defensive strategy of opposing social innovation in the interest of preserving liberal democratic institutions. However, we have also seen that these very rules of the game involve the joint expansionary logic of personal and property rights, and hence a continuing clash of rights. The further expansion of capitalist property relations seems likely to come at the expense of democratic institutions. And because it is currently capitalism that puts people to work and places food on their tables, it is democracy that will be forced to cede in any confrontation in which democrats shrink from offering alternative economic policies. But the lesson of capital strike in the global economy is that minimal and timid democratic initiatives will probably be either ineffective or quickly defeated by capital's freedom to move. A defensive strategy for the protection of democracy is consequently untenable in the long run. Democracy can only survive by expanding to cover areas of social life now dominated by prerogatives of capitalist property.

But why should economic democracy provide a viable alternative to traditional capitalist institutions? The answer was long ago given by Tocqueville, who noted,

> Democracy . . . spreads through the body social a restless activity, superabundant force, and energy never found elsewhere, which, however little favored by circumstance, can do wonders. Those are its true advantages.[46]

There is a huge logical gap in the economic theory that defends the capitalist economy. This theory can justify the importance of markets in reducing information costs associated with the allocation of resources; it can point to the value of competition in promoting innovation and cost reduction. But it cannot solve or even address the problem of agency.

For the capitalist economy to work well workers must somehow be induced to work hard enough at low enough wages so that a surplus flows into the hands of their employers. And their employers, in turn, must somehow be persuaded to invest this surplus in a manner that maintains or improves the functioning of the economy. Yet the defenders of capitalism cannot logically explain why workers would be committed to the success of the enterprises for whom they work, or why those who control the surplus would invest in ways productive of higher living standards in the country in question. These issues loom especially large in an increasingly global economy, and in one marked by the emergence of needs that will be met by goods and services whose measurement and supervision are increasingly costly.

It is here that the economic benefits of democracy come in: economic democracy, by providing an alternative to unaccountable hierarchical authority in investment and production, can promote loyalty, commitment, and accountability on the part of workers and those who control investable resources.

Democracy's first successes were precisely of this nature. People think the lamb is cute, but they are really impressed by the lion. Liberty, equality, and fraternity meant little to the despots of Europe until the rallying cries of the French Revolution were turned into the impressive power of Napoleon's army of untrained but loyal peasants. The American democratic temper that so impressed Tocqueville fired the energies of European democrats in part because it vanquished an imperial enemy and fashioned a viable economic system from the doctrines of free men, free trade, and free soil. The perhaps temporary extension of the welfare state in recent decades was consolidated not so much by a higher level of egalitarian social consciousness, but rather by the evident capacity of the Keynesian accommodation to deliver the goods.

Capitalism could, of course, turn the economic advantages of workplace democracy to its own ends, with owners exercising the power of the purse but no longer directing production. Indeed a hybrid accommodation of globally mobile finance capital and democratically organized workplaces might appear to be a possible outcome of the present period of institutional innovation. Were the power of the purse to remain secure, of course, these arrangements would not achieve the accountability of the power of capital. On the contrary, they would contribute to its invisibility by eliminating its most obvious face-to-face aspect: the relation of boss to worker.

But why should not the workers who have won control of their workplaces also want to make good the promise of democracy writ large? Would the capacities and sentiments fostered in the democratic workplace not seek to range more widely and more effectively over the terrains of finance and investment? Our reading of the history of the expansion of personal rights suggests that a global finance capital/workplace democracy accommodation might be quite unstable.

The position of capital would be considerably weakened by its increasingly obvious rentier status. The lesson of the demise of feudal power is instructive in this respect. In the late medieval period, feudal lords began their long march toward extinction by withdrawing from production and taking their sustenance from rents and taxes. Marc Bloch described this situation by saying that

> the lord had abdicated from his position as head of a large agrarian and semi-industrial undertaking. . . . Politically speaking, the lord was still a leader to his men, he remained their military commander, their judge, their born protector. But his economic leadership had gone—and all the rest could easily follow. He had become a "stockholder" in the soil.[47]

Like the feudal lords before them, capitalists might be superannuated. They would then be readily transformed in political discourse from their representation today as a bearer of a particular conception of the common interest to just another claimant on income, and not a particularly deserving or productive one at that. Writing in the 1940s, Joseph Schumpeter did not share our confidence that a democracy would revolutionize the capitalist economy. But he understood well the political implications of the reduction of the capitalist class to mere income claimants:

> The capitalist process, by substituting a mere parcel of shares for the walls of . . . a factory, takes the life out of the idea of property. . . . It loosens the grip that was once so strong . . . the holder of the title loses the will to fight, economically, physically, politically, for "his" factory and his control over it, to die if necessary on its steps. And this evaporation of what we may term the material substance of property . . . affects not only the attitude of holders but also that of the workmen and of the public in general. . . . Eventually there will be *nobody* left who really cares to stand for it—nobody within and nobody without the precincts of the big concerns.[48]

Whether the optimistic scenario of a no doubt tumultuous encroachment by economic democracy on the economic prerogatives and ideological hegemony of capital will come to pass will depend in large measure on the ability of democrats first to understand, and then to effectively pursue, the historic project of the expansion and deepening of democratic personal rights in the face of the tenacious and no less expansionary claims of property.

NOTES

Chapter 1

1. Ronald Dworkin, *Taking Rights Seriously* (Cambridge, Mass.: Harvard University Press, 1978), xi.

2. This argument is made more fully in Samuel Bowles, "The Post-Keynesian Capital Labor Stalemate," *Socialist Review* 65 (1982): 45–74; and Thomas E. Weisskopf, Samuel Bowles, and David M. Gordon, "Two Views of Capitalist Stagnation: Underconsumption and Challenges to Capitalist Control," *Science and Society* 49 (Nov. 1985).

3. We could not agree more with Sheldon Wolin's wide-ranging critiques of economic models as the basis of democratic thought. He writes:

> I want to suggest that in the American political tradition, the people has two "bodies," with each standing for a different conception of identity, of power, and of the terms of power. . . . The one collectivity was political and democratic and can be called a body politic; the other was primarily economic and intentionally antidemocratic and it can be called a political economy. (Sheldon Wolin, "The People's Two Bodies," *Democracy* 1 [1981]: 11.)

4. Gareth Stedman Jones, *Language of Class: Studies in English Working Class History, 1832–1982* (Cambridge: Cambridge University Press, 1983), 105.

5. Ibid., 106.

6. Alfred Plummer, *Bronterre: A Political Biography of Bronterre O'Brien, 1804–1864* (London: George Allen & Unwin, 1971), 177.

7. Jones, *Languages of Class*, 112.

8. Ibid., 106.

9. Harold Lasswell, *The Political Writings of Harold D. Lasswell* (Glencoe, Ill.: Free Press, 1951).

10. Friedrich von Hayek, interview in *El Mercurio* (Chile), 12 April 1981. Quoted in Philip O'Brien, "Monetarism in Chile," *Socialist Review* 14 (1984): 77–78.

11. Even considering a more limited case—liberalism in America—the once-secure notion that its diverse strands could be comfortably housed under the Lockean rubric has been questioned by the importance not only of Florentine republicanism, but of Hobbesian thought as well. J. G. A. Pocock, whose work has done much to displace the putative hegemony of Lockean thought in favor of a more heterogeneous conception, observes, "The problem with the concept of a Lockean consensus . . . is that it carries the idea of a prolonged ideological serenity" (J. G. A. Pocock, "Virtue and Commerce in the Eighteenth Century," *Journal of Interdisciplinary History* 3 [1972]: 132). On Hobbes's influence see Frank Coleman, *Hobbes and America: Exploring the Constitutional Foundations* (Toronto: University of Toronto Press, 1977).

12. This heterogeneity of liberalism is recognized by virtually every historian who has dealt with the relevant periods. See, for instance, Harold J. Schultz, *History of England* (New York: Barnes & Noble, 1971), 295; and Peter Gay and R. K. Webb, *Modern Europe* (New York: Harper & Row, 1973), 538–39. Yet this diversity has generally been considered of marginal importance in social theory. As we shall see in chapter 2, it is central to understanding social change in liberal capitalist society.

13. Our conception of liberalism may be distinguished from other common definitions in the literature. Liberalism is perhaps most widely defined by its particular political principles. In L. T. Hobhouse's strategy in *Liberalism* (London: Oxford University Press, 1964), for instance, the elements of liberalism are taken to consist in constitutionalism and in principles of civic, fiscal, personal, and economic liberty. But recognizing that liberal principles expand and contract from period to period, others have sought to define liberalism as a specific set of general paradigmatic beliefs. Thus in Ludwig von Mises's *Nation, State, and Economy* (New York: New York University Press, 1983) and in Guido de Ruggiero's *The History of European Liberalism* (Boston: Beacon Press, 1959), 350, liberalism is specified as a method of understanding society and justifying social institutions on the basis of methodological individualism. For others, such as Andrew Levine, *Liberal Democracy: A Critique of its Theory* (New York: Columbia University Press, 1981), liberalism is characterized by a particular set of values—the belief in protecting individual privacy and limiting political authority. We reject these approaches because we can find no method or set of values that all, or even most, who have acted as liberals and in the name of liberalism

Citations are given in full on first reference; subsequent references to works are in abbreviated form.

would willingly accept. The same applies to any synthesis of liberal political principles. Perhaps the most rigorous treatments of liberalism consider its unity as a political philosophy. For Michael Sandel (*Liberalism and the Limits of Justice* [Cambridge: Cambridge University Press, 1982]), for instance, liberalism is a political philosophy based on the priority of the right over the good, and of justice over other socially desirable ends; for Dworkin (*Taking Rights Seriously*), liberalism is a unified theory of rights. We believe, by contrast, that the attempt to see liberalism as a unified intellectual construct fails to understand its most fundamental commitments. Indeed, we argue that liberalism's theoretical tasks have been historically varied and have been defined by its existence as a political discourse central to the process of stability and change in a conflictual and highly dynamic social order.

14. We are using a strong—or what Michael Sandel calls "constitutive"—conception of community (see *Liberalism and the Limits of Justice*, 150), a notion we develop in more detail in chapters 5 and 6.

15. Michael Walzer, "Liberalism and the Art of Separation," *Political Theory* 12 (1984): 315. Similarly, Gerald Frug writes: "Liberalism is not a single formula for interpreting the world; it is instead a view based on seeing the world as a series of complex dualities" (Gerald Frug, "The City as a Legal Concept," *Harvard Law Review* 93 [1980]: 1075).

16. Jean Elshtain, in *Public Man, Private Woman* (Chicago: University of Chicago Press, 1981), uses a similar private–public distinction as the basis for her feminist reading of the history of political theory. See also Joan Landes, "Women and the Public Sphere: A Modern Perspective," *Social Analysis* 15 (1984).

17. Walzer, "Liberalism," 317.

18. Karl Marx, *Capital* (New York: Vintage, 1977), 1: 92.

19. Eric Hobsbawm, *Workers* (New York: Pantheon, 1984), 304–5, 310.

20. Ernesto Laclau and Chantal Mouffe are notable for having addressed this issue, not as a practical problem of politics, but as a theoretical challenge. See Ernesto Laclau and Chantal Mouffe, *Hegemony and Socialist Strategy: Towards a Radical Democratic Politics* (London: Verso, 1985); Rosa Luxemburg, "Social Reform or Revolution," in Dick Howard, ed., *Selected Political Writings of Rosa Luxemburg* (New York: Monthly Review Press, 1971); and Nicos Poulantzas, *State, Power, Socialism* (London: New Left Books, 1978).

21. The reader may wonder why we have referred only to relatively traditional versions of Marxism in depicting the theory's shortcomings. Why have we not considered such innovations as the structuralist Marxism of Louis Althusser, the critical theories of Herbert Marcuse and Jurgen Habermas, the humanism of Bertell Ollman and Leszek Kolakowski, or the singular contributions of such thinkers as Jean Paul Sartre, Andre Gorz, and Antonio Gramsci? We answer first by directing interested reader to chapter 6, and second by pleading lack of space. But without wishing to denigrate its often brilliant and decisive contributions to social theory, we may summarize our distance from these strands of neo-Marxism as follows. First, in the face of the failure of Marx's economic theory, contemporary Marxists have downgraded the importance of economic theory in general, and have turned to philosophy, psychology, hermaneutics, and other elegant critical pursuits that fail to confront the key position of the economy in social life. Second, neo-Marxist theories have failed in the critical task of developing a heterogeneous conception of power, and have never even approached the depth of the liberal understanding of state despotism, the feminist understanding of sexism, or comparable analyses of racial, religious, and ethnic oppression. Finally, neo-Marxist theories generally have not incorporated the logic of individual choice into their conceptual apparatus, have not understood the critical importance of the micro social aspects of macrosocial activity, and have not embraced the emancipatory status of individual liberty. Even in the tradition of critical theory, which is most sensitive to social oppression, the negation of "domination" is not "liberty," but rather "truth," "reason," "undistorted communication," or even "in conformity with real human needs"—all quite distinct from the "choice" orientation of our approach, and one we take as central to building a democratic society.

22. Adam Przeworski has developed this point with great insight in "Proletariat Into Class: The Process of Class Formation," *Capitalism and Social Democracy* (Cambridge: Cambridge University Press, 1985), 47–97.

23. That the improbable combination of these two logics is widely misunderstood is suggested by the argument of T. H. Marshall's justly admired *Citizenship and Social Class* (Cambridge: Cambridge University Press, 1950). Marshall divided the growth of rights into three phases: civil, political, and social. Civil rights include liberty of the person, freedom of speech and thought, and due process. These were achieved, Marshall argued, roughly by the end of the eighteenth century. Political rights are precisely the right to participate in the exercise of political power, and were achieved roughly by the end of the nineteenth century. Social rights include education, health and medical care, and in general

the ministrations of the welfare state. These began to be installed in the twentieth century and, as Marshall stresses, are still in the process of being achieved. Marshall incisively charts the expansionary logic of personal rights. But his commitment to an evolutionary ideology led him systematically to downplay the conflictual basis of this logic and to neglect the analysis of this dynamic as a contradictory logic posing repeated threats to dominant distributions of power. Reinhard Bendix's *Nation-Building and Citizenship* (New York: Wiley, 1964) is another contribution in this tradition, but is considerably more careful in its historical treatment and is circumspect in its conclusions. Both works remain invaluable sources for the student of the development of rights.

Chapter 2

1. Milton Friedman, *Capitalism and Freedom* (Chicago: University of Chicago Press, 1962), 21.

2. See C. B. Macpherson, *The Political Theory of Possessive Individualism: Hobbes to Locke* (London: Oxford University Press, 1962), chap. 3.

3. These quotes are taken from the collection by G. E. Aylmer, ed., *The Levellers in the English Revolution* (Ithaca, N.Y.: Cornell University Press, 1975), 100–108.

4. Friedman, *Capitalism and Freedom*, 8.

5. Louis Hartz, *The Liberal Tradition in America* (New York: Harcourt, Brace & World, 1955). Hartz's work was extended in the landmark works of Seymour Martin Lipset, *Political Man: The Social Bases of Politics* (Garden City, N.Y.: Doubleday Anchor, 1963), and Bendix, *Nation-Building and Citizenship*, and it was a major reference point for Barrington Moore, Jr.'s, classic analysis of the roots of twentieth-century totalitarianism, *The Social Origins of Dictatorship and Democracy: Lord and Peasant in the Making of the Modern World* (Boston: Beacon Press, 1967).

6. Hartz, *The Liberal Tradition in America*, 89.

7. Ibid., 5–6.

8. Ibid., 94, 101.

9. Karl Marx, "The Eighteenth of Brumaire of Louis Bonaparte," in David Fernbach, ed., *Karl Marx: Political Writings*, vol. II (New York: Vintage, 1974), 190.

10. Alexis de Tocqueville, *Democracy in America* (Garden City, N.Y.: Doubleday, 1969), 238.

11. Eric Hobsbawm, "Mass-Producing Traditions: Europe, 1870–1914," in Eric Hobsbawm and Terence Ranger, eds., *The Invention of Tradition* (Cambridge: Cambridge University Press, 1983), 267–69.

12. Samuel Finer, "State and Nation Building in Europe: The Role of the Military," in Charles Tilly, ed., *The Formation of Nation States in Western Europe* (Princeton, N.J.: Princeton University Press, 1975), 155.

13. Stanislav Andreski, *Military Organization and Society* (Berkeley: University of California Press, 1971), 68–69.

14. Finer, "State and Nation Building," 153.

15. Bendix, *Nation-Building and Citizenship*, 94.

16. Joyce Appleby, *Capitalism and a New Social Order: The Republican Vision of the 1790s* (New York: New York University Press, 1984), 14.

17. R. R. Palmer, *The Age of Democratic Revolution* (Princeton, N.J.: Princeton University Press, 1959), 4–5.

18. Tocqueville, *Democracy*, 575–79.

19. Like the Keynesian accommodation, which was already well under way in Sweden, the United States, and elsewhere prior to the publication in 1936 of John Maynard Keynes's *The General Theory of Employment, Interest, and Money* (New York: Harcourt, Brace, & World, 1964) the Lockean accord owes little to the writings of the great thinker himself.

20. In England, for instance, when Liberals divided over the question of suffrage after the death of Lord Palmerston in 1865, Disraeli managed to push a drastic franchise measure through the House of Commons. The suffrage reform of 1884 owed even more to political calculation of this sort. See D. G. Wright, *Democracy and Reform, 1815–1885* (London: Longman Group, 1970), 13.

21. See Stein Rokkan, "Electoral Mobilization, Party Competition, and National Integration," in Joseph LaPalombara and Myron Weiner, eds., *Political Parties and Political Development* (Princeton, N.J.: Princeton University Press, 1966), 262; and C. Vann Woodward, *The Strange Career of Jim Crow* (Oxford: Oxford University Press, 1955).

22. The statistics concerning the extent of British suffrage are taken from D. G. Wright, *Democracy and Reform*.

23. Witness the following exhortation of Thomas Macaulay in parliamentary debate:
The danger is terrible. The time is short. If this bill be rejected, I pray to God that none of those who concur in rejecting it may ever remember their votes with unavailing remorse, amidst the wreck of laws, the confusion of ranks, the spoilation of property and the dissolution of the social order. (Quoted in D. G. Wright, *Democracy and Reform*, 33.)

24. For a treatment of the English Philosophical Radicals see, for instance, J. Salwyn Schapiro, *Liberalism and the Challenge of Fascism* (New York: McGraw-Hill, 1949).

25. William Henry Maehl, Jr., ed., *The Reform Bill of 1832* (New York: Holt, Rinehart and Winston, 1967), 10.

26. William Langer, *Political and Social Upheaval, 1832–1852* (New York: Harper & Row, 1969), 2. In Britain, the cabinets of the period 1832–1866 included sixty-four ministers who were aristocrats, but only twelve who were lawyers and as few as five who were businessmen. In southern, central, and eastern Europe, the landed classes were even more secure.

27. Ibid., 54.

28. In eastern, central, and southern Europe, commercial interests were sufficiently weak and liberalism sufficiently persecuted that a radical liberalism, with a genuine democratic commitment, tended to emerge among intellectuals, professionals, and artisans in the years after the July Revolution. In Italy, following the lead of Filipo Buonarrotti and Giuseppe Mazzini, liberal goals included nationalistic visions of constitutional, democratic republics. While the dominant strand of liberalism continued to reject political democracy and the Rights of Man, these radical liberal movements displayed a deep commitment to democracy. In Germany, for instance, the widely popular Heinrich Heine and Ludwig Borne exemplified the increasing admiration for Enlightenment anticlericism and rejection of bourgeois morality. They advocated universal suffrage and a powerful parliament, and articulated the modern cosmopolitan demands for sexual equality and easier divorce. See Langer, *Political and Social Upheaval*.

29. Volker Rittberger, "Revolution and Pseudo-Democratization: The Formation of the Weimar Republic," in Gabriel A. Almond, Scott C. Flannigan, and Robert J. Mundt, eds., *Crisis, Choice, and Change: Historical Studies of Political Development* (Boston: Little, Brown, 1973), 291.

30. F. H. Hinsley, "Introduction," *New Cambridge Modern History* (Cambridge: Cambridge University Press, 1962), 11: 26–34.

31. Theodor Scheider, "Political and Social Developments in Europe," *New Cambridge Modern History*, 11: 245.

32. Goran Therborn, in "The Rule of Capital and the Rise of Democracy," *New Left Review* 103 (1977): 3–42, provides a careful comparative analysis of the development of suffrage and parliamentary institutions in liberal nations. The following is a country-by-country summary of his findings.
Australia: Universal and equal white suffrage was instituted by a liberal–labor coalition in 1903. Exclusion of nonwhites continued until 1962.
Austria: Universal and equal male suffrage was instituted in 1907 after massive working-class demonstrations. Parliamentary government and female suffrage were established in 1918 after the fall of the Hapsburgs. Democracy was overturned in 1934 by farmer-based Christian Social party, which in turn was swallowed up by German fascism in 1938.
Belgium: Working-class strikes for universal suffrage were repressed in 1886, 1888, 1891, 1893, 1902, and 1913. After World War I, universal suffrage was instituted in principle and became complete in 1948.
Canada: The struggle for military conscription led a Conservative government to considerably extend the franchise in 1917 and in 1920. Racist restrictions continued through the 1930s.
Denmark: An alliance of big landowners and the urban bourgeoisie to limit universal suffrage to the lower house in a bicameral system continued until World War I.
Finland: The general strike and mass worker demonstrations of 1905 led to universal suffrage and a unicameral legislature, but Finnish independence awaited the conclusion of World War I. A liberal republic was proclaimed in 1919.
France: The democratic constitutions following the French revolutions of 1789 and 1848 were never implemented. Full male suffrage dates from 1884, and universal suffrage from 1946.
Germany: Universal suffrage, the result of the popular movements of 1848–1849, was quickly overturned in a procapitalist royal reaction. A weak parliamentary regime followed the military defeat of Wilhelmine Germany, to be swallowed up in the fascist period. Liberal democracy was restored by Allied forces after World War II.
Italy: Universal male suffrage was instituted by Giovanni Giolitti before World War I, to secure

popular support for his Libyan war. Democracy was weak, short-lived, and restricted to male suffrage until destroyed by Mussolini. Democracy was restored after World War II.

Netherlands: The Dutch had a narrow property-based franchise until the twentieth century. Universal male suffrage was instituted in 1917 as payment for working-class support of a new coalition of national unity. Female suffrage came in 1919.

Norway: Universal male suffrage was achieved in 1898 as a result of labor-movement agitation. Female suffrage was added fifteen years later.

Sweden: Universal suffrage was instituted in response to the working-class turmoil of 1918.

Switzerland: Male suffrage dates from 1874, and female suffrage was achieved ninety-seven years later.

33. Bendix, *Nation-Building and Citizenship*, 64.

34. Lipset, *Political Man*, 73.

35. Here we draw upon the work of Barrington Moore, Jr. (*Social Origins*). Moore was concerned to find the roots of the twentieth-century partition of advanced industrial societies into totalitarian and liberal democratic societies. He developed a sophisticated variant of Louis Hartz's thesis that the key to the political character of contemporary industrial societies lies in their emergence from a feudal past. He does not, however, address the dynamics of the resulting liberal democratic capitalist societies. Our analysis of the emergence of liberal democracy differs from Moore's, attributing more importance to the potentially independent power of the state. Where the state was both strong and heavily beholden to the landed elites (as in Russia, Prussia, Japan), these elites were likely to draw the bourgeoisie into an alliance prevailing over liberalizing forces. Where the state was weak, even if it was greatly beholden to the landed classes (as in England), the factions of the latter vied for the support of the "lower orders," the long-term result being liberal reform. Where the state was strong yet unalterably at odds with the aristocracy (as in France), the bourgeoisie stood to gain little from an alliance with the landed elites, and the liberal outcome was virtually assured. Finally, when the needs of war in periods of highly labor-intense military technology (as was the case in Europe throughout the nineteenth century) required mass armies, the balance of power shifted perceptibly toward popular constituencies, rendering likely a liberal accommodation. When, on the contrary, the state modernizers had full control over military resources (as in many developing countries today), the thrust for democratic reform was severely compromised.

36. Merrill Jensen, *The Articles of Confederation* (Madison: University of Wisconsin Press, 1963). Whether property qualifications were central to assuring social stability may nonetheless be doubted. Appleby, *Capitalism*; Pauline Maier, *From Resistance to Revolution* (New York: Vintage, 1974); Eric Foner, *Tom Paine and Revolutionary America* (Oxford: Oxford University Press, 1976); and others have placed considerably more stress on deference and ideology. It is difficult to evaluate all the competing claims in this complex area. The extent of property restrictions is, however, well documented. In the Colony of New York of 1700, for instance, freeholders could vote in several counties if they owned land in each. Elections were held on different days in each county to make multiple voting convenient for the propertied. The New York legislature in 1737 affirmed the right of nonresidents who owned land to vote where their land lay. Both policies continued up to 1775. Albert Edward McKinley, *The Suffrage Franchise in the Thirteen English Colonies in America* (Philadelphia: University of Pennsylvania Press, 1905). Throughout much of the eighteenth century, Pennsylvania was controlled by an oligarchy of Quaker merchants. With a property qualification of 50 pounds, only 335 out of 3,452 taxable males qualified to vote in Philadelphia in 1775 (see Jensen, *Articles*). Over all, at the time of the Revolution, twelve of the thirteen colonies had property qualifications for voting, and the remaining colony, Pennsylvania, had a taxpaying qualification. Four of these colonies had shifted to taxpaying qualification by 1792, and four more did so in the period between 1810 and 1821. The final four changed over between 1842 and 1846, two to taxpaying qualification, and the others to simple residency. A simple residency requirement had been instituted in three of the colonies by 1810, and seven by 1850. On the eve of the Civil War, six of the original colonies still had a taxpaying qualification. See Kirk H. Porter, *A History of Suffrage in the United States* (New York: AMS Press, 1971), 110. The effect of property restrictions on actual participation remains a matter of disagreement. According to Louis Hacker, before the Revolution, the proportion of potential voters varied from one-sixth to one-fiftieth of the male population in the different colonies. Louis M. Hacker, *The Triumph of American Capitalism* (New York: Columbia University Press, 1940), 167. But such judgments, based on the distribution of land ownership, are subject to considerable error. For instance, as Chilton Williamson, *American Suffrage from Property to Democracy: 1760–1860* (Princeton, N.J.: Princeton University Press, 1960), has stressed, the freehold criterion was at times stretched to include owners of church pews, taxpayers, and possessors of indefinite leases. However, the vote was often denied to free blacks, Catholics, Jews, and

women, whether or not they were property owners or taxpayers. On the other hand, the freehold qualification often may have been simply ignored. Williamson, *American Suffrage*, 49.

37. Williamson, *American Suffrage*, 80, 82; see also Foner, *Tom Paine*, on the Philadelphia militia and political radicalism in Pennsylvania.

38. See Harry L. Watson, *Jacksonian Politics and Community Conflict: The Emergence of the Second American Party System in Cumberland County, North Carolina* (Baton Rouge: Louisiana State University, 1981). We take this assessment as accurate, although the evidence of heightened popular political participation in this period is largely impressionistic. Quantitative support for this impression is difficult to find in the statistics on suffrage. One student of the period has remarked that "it is doubtful if the right to vote in Massachusetts just before the Civil War was any more widely shared than it had been before the American Revolution, despite the 'democratization' of the suffrage" (Williamson, *American Suffrage*, 195). The extent of voter participation, however, presents a different picture. Walter Dean Burnham estimates that the proportion of adult white males who cast presidential ballots rose from 27 percent in 1824 to 80 percent in 1840. Burnham's estimates and notes appear in U.S. Department of Commerce, Bureau of the Census, *Historical Statistics of the United States* (Washington, D.C.: U.S. Government Printing Office, 1975), 1067–69, and 1072.

39. Carl Becker, *The Declaration of Independence* (New York: Knopf, 1922), provides the classic analysis of Jefferson's roots in Locke's political philosophy. Garry Wills, *Inventing America* (Garden City, N.Y.: Doubleday, 1978), and Morton White, *The Philosophy of the American Revolution* (New York: Oxford University Press, 1978), have relocated Jeffersonian ideas in the contemporary Scottish school of moral philosophy. This does not seriously affect our understanding of his theory of property, however. To the end of his life, for instance, Jefferson opposed redistributive taxation and the taxation of inheritance on traditional Lockean grounds. See Daniel Walker Howe, "European Sources of Political Ideas in Jeffersonian America," *Reviews in American History* 10 (1982): 28–44.

40. Since Cecelia M. Kenyon wrote her critique of the Progressive historian's notion of Federalism as aristocratic and Antifederalism as its populist-democratic response ("Men of Little Faith: The Anti-Federalists on the Nature of Representative Government," *William and Mary Quarterly* 12 [1955]: 5–43), it has been more common to argue that *all* political camps in early America were firmly republican in commitment—but republican in the conservative Renaissance sense of the theorists of "civic virtue." This view is developed in Caroline Robbins, "Algernon Sydney's *Discourses Concerning Government*: Textbook of Revolution," *William and Mary Quarterly* 4 (1947): 267–96; Stanley Elkins and Eric McKitrick, "The Founding Fathers: Young Men of the Revolution," *Political Science Quarterly* 76 (1961): 181–216; Jackson Turner Main, *The Anti-Federalists: Critics of the Constitution* (Chapel Hill: University of North Carolina Press, 1961); J. G. A. Pocock, *The Machiavellian Moment: Florentine Political Thought and the Atlantic Republican Tradition* (Princeton, N.J.: Princeton University Press, 1975); and John M. Murrin, "The Great Inversion, or Court versus Country: A Comparison of the Revolution Settlements in England," in J. G. A. Pocock, ed., *Three British Revolutions: 1641, 1688, 1776* (Princeton, N.J.: Princeton University Press, 1980). For a review of the early literature on the "new republican synthesis," see Robert E. Shalhope, "Toward a Republican Synthesis: The Emergence of an Understanding of Republicanism in American Historiography," *William and Mary Quarterly* 39 (1972): 49–80. Joyce Appleby, "What Is Still American in the Political Philosophy of Thomas Jefferson?" *William and Mary Quarterly* 29 (1982): 287–309, has shown that this is not true of John Adams, who believed in a mixed government on the British model. Gerald Stourzh, *Alexander Hamilton and the Idea of Republican Government* (Stanford, Calif.: Stanford University Press, 1970), has shown Hamilton to be no friend of republican virtue. Joyce Appleby also convincingly demonstrates that Jefferson's republicanism was a far cry from the Machiavellian republicanism popular in elite circles of revolutionary America:

> As challengers to those in power in the 1790s, the Republicans took advantage of the shortfall between radical revolutionary rhetoric and conservative political practices. An earlier vague and high-flown allusion to equality became for them a literal insistence upon exact numerical voting shares. Equally literal was their interpretation of the venerable doctrine of popular sovereignty. (Appleby, *Capitalism*, 85.)

Jefferson's democratic commitment is illuminated by his zeal in translating and disseminating Destutt de Tracy's bitter critique of Baron de Montesquieu's *Spirit of the Laws*, which was used in France and America to justify "mixed" aristocratic, monarchical, and republican government. See Antoine Louis Destutt de Tracy, *Commentaire sur l'Esprit des Lois de Montesquieu* (Paris: Nizet, 1974).

41. Quoted in Appleby, "What Is Still American?" 299.

42. Julian P. Boyd, ed., *The Papers of Thomas Jefferson, Volume I: 1760–1776* (Princeton, N.J.: Princeton University Press, 1950), 349.

43. Ibid., 358.

44. Appleby, "What Is Still American?" 297. Jefferson's reputation as a great democrat was impugned by the Progressive historians because of his support for extensive governmental checks and balances. Indeed, his drafts of the Virginia Constitution, like Adams's *Thoughts on Government*, show a deep concern for the careful separation of powers (legislative, judicial, and executive), as well as a bicameral legislature with the lower house electing the upper, either for long or for life tenure (see John Adams, "Thoughts on Government" [pp. 50–56] and "A Defence of the Constitution of the United States of America" [pp. 77–113], in Adrienne Koch and William Peden, eds., *The Selected Writings of John Adams* [New York: Knopf, 1946]). Whereas the radical democrats had faith in the people, or were willing to live with their relatively harmless mistakes, Jefferson was considerably more circumspect:

> I have ever observed that a choice by the people themselves is not generally distinguished for its wisdom. The first secretion from them is usually crude and heterogeneous. But give to those so chosen by the people a second choice themselves, and they will generally choose wise men. (Boyd, *Papers*, 503.)

These statements may not cast aspersions on Jefferson's democratic leanings, however, unless one is imbued with a romantic conception of direct democracy. One need not share Jefferson's misgivings in order to take them for what they were—careful efforts to forge representative democratic institutions. Elisha P. Douglass, *Rebels and Democrats* (Chapel Hill: University of North Carolina Press, 1955), and Jesse Lemisch, "The American Revolution from the Bottom Up," in Barton Bernstein, ed., *Towards a New Past: Dissenting Essays in American History* (New York: Vintage, 1967), show clearly that Jefferson's racial views and antiurban prejudices are not compatible with his reputation as a cosmopolitan humanist, but this is quite another matter.

45. For the first of these reasons Jefferson supported the addition of a bill of rights to the Constitution, and held out for the mandatory rotation of office. See D. Lewis, ed., *Anti-Federalists versus Federalists: Selected Documents* (San Francisco: Chandler, 1967), 119–20.

46. Appleby, "What Is Still American?" 308, argues cogently that supporters of the Constitution, such as Jefferson, were mainly opting for the promotion of commercial over anticommercial visions of the future.

47. Property ownership among freeborn male household heads is surveyed in Main, *The Anti-Federalists*, and Gary Nash, *Class and Society in Early America* (New York: Prentice-Hall, 1970). The size of the slave labor force is estimated from data in U.S. Dept. of Commerce, *Historical Statistics*, 1975, 14.

48. Terrance Powderly, *Thirty Years of Labor: 1859–1889* (New York: Sentry Press, 1889), 20–21.

49. Joseph Schumpeter, *Capitalism, Socialism, and Democracy* (New York: Harper & Row, 1942), 140.

50. Lawrence Goodwyn, *The Populist Moment* (London: Oxford University Press, 1979).

51. Aristotle, *Politics*, trans. Benjamin Jowett (New York: Random House, 1943), lines 1279b40–1280b5.

52. Karl Marx, *Class Struggles in France—1848–50* (New York: International Publishers, 1937), 69–70.

53. Quoted in Charles Beard, *An Economic Interpretation of the Constitution* (New York: Macmillan, 1935), 25.

54. Alexander Hamilton, John Jay, and James Madison, *The Federalist* (New York: Doubleday, 1961). The quotes used in the text are found on page 20.

55. Howe, "European Sources of Political Ideas in Jeffersonian America," 37.

56. Robert A. Dahl, *Preface to Democratic Theory* (Chicago: University of Chicago Press, 1956), 142.

57. See Steven Koblik, *Sweden's Development from Poverty to Affluence* (Minneapolis: University of Minnesota Press, 1975), especially the contributions of Sven Lundkvist, Berndt Schiller, and Carl-Goran Andrae.

58. Alexander Gerschenkron, *Bread and Democracy in Germany* (Berkeley: University of California Press, 1943), 127.

59. Ibid., 28.

60. David M. Gordon, Richard Edwards, and Michael Reich, in *Segmented Work, Divided Workers: The Historical Transformation of Labor in the United States* (Cambridge: Cambridge University Press, 1982), describe part of this process in the United States:

> In the homogenization period, from the 1870s to the onset of World War II, the organization of work and the structure of labor markets were profoundly transformed. More and more jobs in the capitalist sector of the economy were reduced to a common, semiskilled operative denominator,

and control over the labor process became concentrated among employers and their foremen, who used direct supervision or machine pacing to "drive" their workers. (P. 3.)
There was nothing automatic in the accumulation process assuring this homogenization, however. According to the same authors, the ensuing period was marked by increased segmentation of workers.

61. Per capita product fell considerably in France and the United States from 1929 to 1938; it grew slowly in the United Kingdom and Italy; and expanded at an average rate of over 4 percent annually in Germany and Japan. The Swedish economy, already committed to nascent social democracy, grew at an average rate considerably above its historical average during the depression years. Growth rates calculated from President's Council of Economic Advisors, *Economic Report of the President* (1979) (Washington, D.C.: U.S. Government Printing Office, 1983); and B. R. Mitchell, *European Historical Statistics: 1750–1975* (London: Macmillan, 1980).

62. Calculated from U.S. Bureau of Labor Statistics, "Comparative Real Gross Domestic Product, Real GDP Per Capita, and Real Gross Domestic Product per Employed Person, 1950–1981," mimeo (Washington, D.C.: 1982); and U.S. Department of Commerce, *Long Term Economic Growth, 1860–1970* (Washington, D.C.: U.S. Government Printing Office, 1973).

63. The decline in profitability was considerably sharper in manufacturing, falling from 25 percent to 9 percent. Philip Armstrong and Andrew Glyn, "Accumulation, Profits, State Spending: Data for Advanced Capitalist Countries, 1952–1981," *Oxford Institute of Economics and Statistics*, Oxford University (1984). See also Philip Armstrong, Andrew Glyn, and John Harrison, *Capitalism Since World War II: The Making and Breakup of the Great Boom* (London: Fontana, 1984), for an insightful comparative account of the capitalist economies in the post–World War II era.

64. The material touched on in this section is dealt with in detail in Armstrong, Glyn, and Harrison, *Capitalism,* passim; Samuel Bowles and Herbert Gintis, "The Crisis of Liberal Democratic Capitalism," *Politics and Society* 11 (1982): 51–93; and Samuel Bowles, David Gordon, and Thomas Weisskopf, *Beyond the Waste Land: A Democratic Alternative to Economic Decline* (Garden City, N.Y.: Doubleday, 1983), passim; and Bowles, "Post-Keynesian Capital Labor Stalemate," 45–74. See also Bowles, Gordon, and Weisskopf, "Power and Profits: The Social Structure of Accumulation and the Profitability of the U.S. Economy," *Review of Radical Political Economics* (1986); and Juliet Schor, "Changes in the Cyclical Pattern of Real Wages: Evidence from Nine Countries, 1955–1980," *Economic Journal* 95 (1985): 452–68.

65. In the late 1970s, averaging over fifteen advanced capitalist nations, about a third of the typical worker's living standard took the form of the social wage. Bowles, "Post-Keynesian Capital Labor Stalemate."

66. In the United States an empirical estimate of the cost to the typical worker of job termination fell to half its late 1950s level by the late 1960s. Juliet Schor and Samuel Bowles, "The Cost of Job Loss and the Incidence of Strikes," Harvard Institute of Economic Research Discussion Paper, October 1985. This measure of the bargaining power between capital and labor appears to contribute significantly to the explanation of both the growth of real wages and the productivity slowdown.

67. See Schor, "Changes"; Bowles, "Post-Keynesian Capital Labor Stalemate"; and Bowles, Gordon, and Weisskopf, *Beyond the Waste Land* for economic and political background. The latter article demonstrates that the failure of the labor market effectively to discipline labor has historically been uniquely associated with economic crisis periods in U.S. history: the 1970s, 1930s, and 1890s.

68. V. I. Lenin, "Preface to the Russian Translation of Letters by Johannes Becker," in *Collected Works,* 45 vols. (Moscow: Foreign Languages Publishing House, 1960–1970), 12: 364.

69. Harvey Klehr, "Leninism, Lewis Corey, and the Failure of American Socialism," *Labor History* 18 (1977): 255.

70. Karl Marx and Friedrich Engels, *Letters to Americans, 1848–1895* (New York: International Publishers, 1963).

71. Lewis Corey, "Recreating Socialism," *Workers Age* 9 (1940): 4.

72. Peter Bachrach, "Class Struggle and Democracy," *Democracy* 2 (1982): 29.

Chapter 3

1. Robert A. Dahl, "On Removing Certain Impediments to Democracy in the United States," *Dissent* 25 (1978): 310–24.

2. Abram Chayes, "The Modern Corporation and the Rule of Law," in E. Mason, ed., *The Corporation in Modern Society* (Cambridge, Mass.: Harvard University Press, 1959), 28.

3. Abba Lerner, "The Economics and Politics of Consumer Sovereignty," *American Economic Review* 62 (1972): 259.

4. Joseph Schumpeter, *The Theory of Economic Development: An Inquiry into Profits, Capital, Credit, Interest and the Business Cycle* (Oxford: Oxford University Press, 1934), 21 (the essay was written in 1911).

5. Robert Nozick, *Anarchy, State, and Utopia* (New York: Basic Books, 1974), 248.

6. Nozick, *Anarchy*, 151.

7. John Rawls, *A Theory of Justice* (Cambridge, Mass.: Harvard University Press, 1971); for an elaboration of this critique, see Barry Clark and Herbert Gintis, "Rawlsian Justice and Economic Systems," *Philosophy and Public Affairs* 7 (1978): 302–25.

8. Thomas Hobbes, *Leviathan*, ed. C. B. MacPherson (New York: Penguin, 1968), 150.

9. *Holden* v. *Hardy*, 169 U.S. 366 (1898), cited in Michael Reich, *Racial Inequality and Class Conflict* (Princeton, N.J.: Princeton University Press, 1980).

10. D. H. Robertson, *Control of Industry* (New York: Harcourt and Brace, 1923): 85.

11. R. H. Coase, "The Nature of the Firm," *Economica* 4 (1937): 400.

12. The content of the exchange may establish, or help establish, the unequal power relations among the exchangers, but not the involuntary character of the exchange. Nozick (*Anarchy*, 263) shows the peculiarities of considering the worker's contract with the capitalist as "nonvoluntary." The very notion of "voluntary" is brought into question, and with it the justification of liberty of action, if an action is considered "involuntary" solely on the basis of its being constrained by social institutions or by the choices of others.

13. Paul Samuelson, "Wages and Interests: A Modern Dissection of Marxian Economics," *American Economic Review* 47 (1957): 894.

14. Here is Marx's precise argument:

> The exchange between capital and labour . . . splits into two processes which are not only formally but also qualitatively different, and even contradictory: (1) The worker sells his commodity [labor power] . . . which has a use-value, and, as commodity, also a *price*. . . . (2) The capitalist obtains labour itself . . . he obtains the productive force which maintains and multiplies capital. . . . *In the exchange between capital and labour, the first act is an exchange, falls entirely within ordinary circulation; the second is a process qualitatively different from exchange, and only by misuse* could it have been called *any sort of exchange at all*. (Karl Marx, *Grundrisse: Introduction to the Critique of Political Economy* [Baltimore: Penguin Books, 1973], 274–75.)

15. The case of piece rates is somewhat more complex. Piece-rate payment is a combination of a wage-labor payment with the purchase of a labor service coupled with free rental of productive equipment. Our argument can be shown to apply to piece-rate payment as well as the more common wage system. But this refinement is not essential to our argument. See Samuel Bowles, "The Production Process in a Competitive Economy: Walrasian, Neo-Hobbesian, and Marxian Models," *American Economic Review* 75(1): 16–36.

16. See Herbert Gintis, "The Nature of the Labor Exchange and the Theory of Capitalist Production," *Review of Radical Political Economics* 8 (1976): 36–54; Samuel Bowles and Herbert Gintis, "Structure and Practice in the Labor Theory of Value," *Review of Radical Political Economics* 12 (1981): 12–26; William Lazonick, "The Subjugation of Labor to Capital: The Rise of the Capitalist System," *Review of Radical Political Economics* 10 (1978): 1–59; and Stephen Marglin, "What Do Bosses Do?" *Review of Radical Political Economics* 6 (1974): 60–112.

17. See A. A. Alchian and H. Demsetz, "Production, Information Costs, and Economic Organization," *American Economic Review* 52 (1972): 777–95; E. G. Furubotn and S. Pejovich, eds., *The Economics of Property Rights* (Cambridge, Mass.: Ballinger, 1974); H. G. Manne, ed., *The Economics of Legal Relationships: Readings in the Theory of Property Rights* (St. Paul: West, 1975); and Oliver Williamson, *Markets and Hierarchies: Analysis and Antitrust Implications* (New York: Free Press, 1975).

18. George A. Akerlof, "A Theory of Social Custom, of Which Unemployment May Be One Consequence," *Quarterly Journal of Economics* 94 (1980): 749–75.

19. The reader may wonder why, having praised Marx as providing the first critique of the labor commodity proposition, we do not follow his analysis of the problem. Marx's formulation of the problem was tied to the labor theory of value which, for reasons that will not detain us in this book, we find less than enlightening. See Bowles and Gintis, "Structure and Practice," and "The Labor Theory of Value and the Specificity of Marxian Economics," in Stephen Resnick and Richard Wolff, eds., *Rethinking Marxism: Struggles in Marxist Theory* (Brooklyn, N.Y.: Autonomedia, 1985).

20. Bowles, "Production Process"; and Herbert Gintis and Tsuneo Ishikawa, "Wages, Work Discipline, and Macroeconomic Equilibrium," mimeo, Department of Economics, University of Massachusetts, July 1985.

21. See Gintis, "Nature"; Carl Riskin, "Incentive Systems and Work Motivation," *Working Papers* 1 (1974): 27–92; William F. Whyte, *Money and Motivation* (New York: Harper & Row, 1955).

22. See Gintis, "Nature"; John Roemer, "Divide and Conquer: Microfoundations of a Marxian Theory of Wage Discrimination," *Bell Journal of Economics* 10 (1979): 695–705; Reich, *Racial Inequality*; and Bowles, "Production Process."

23. See Derek C. Jones and Jan Svejnar, eds., *Participatory and Self-Managed Firms* (Lexington, Mass.: Lexington Books, 1982); Juan Espinosa and Andrew Zimbalist, *Economic Democracy: Workers' Participation in Chilean Industry, 1970–1973*; Raymond Katzell, Daniel Yankelovich, et al., *Worker Productivity Experiments in the United States* (New York: New York University Press, 1977), and the references cited therein.

24. Schumpeter, *Theory of Economic Development* (Cambridge, Mass.: Harvard University Press, 1934), 21.

25. These three empirical propositions are hardly open to question among economists and political scientists. The importance of the profit rate as a determinant of the rate of accumulation is demonstrated in a number of econometric studies. See Bowles, Gordon, and Weisskopf, *Beyond the Waste Land*.

26. This argument has been expounded insightfully by Charles E. Lindblom, *Politics and Markets: The World's Political-Economic Systems* (New York: Basic Books, 1977); Joshua Cohen and Joel Rogers, *On Democracy: Towards a Transformation of American Society* (New York: Penguin Books, 1983); and Fred Block, "The Ruling Class Does Not Rule: Notes on the Marxist Theory of the State," *Socialist Revolution* 7 (1977): 6–28.

27. John Maynard Keynes, "National Self-Sufficiency," *Yale Review* 22 (1932–33): 761–63. Students of the history of economic thought will recognize Keynes's critique of free trade as a generalization of the now widely accepted "infant industry" argument first put forward by Friedrich List but applied by Keynes to the process of learning and experimentation in society as a whole rather than in a particular industrial process. See Friedrich List, *The National System of Political Economy* (London: Longmans, Green, 1909).

28. Sandel, *Liberalism and the Limits of Justice*, 183. Sandel here attributes liberalism's compromise of agency to the fact that it has "put . . . the self beyond the reach of politics," a problem we discuss in chapter 5.

Chapter 4

1. We have also applied this framework to the social structures and historical dynamics of late feudal and early modern Europe in Samuel Bowles and Herbert Gintis, "State and Class in European Feudalism," in Charles Bright and Susan Harding, eds., *Statemaking and Social Movements: Essays in History and Theory* (Ann Arbor: University of Michigan Press, 1984).

2. Michel Foucault, *The History of Sexuality* (New York: Vintage, 1980), 1: 92–93.

3. Thomas Wartenberg, "Foucault's Archaeological Method," *Philosophical Forum* 15 (1984): 362.

4. Karl Marx, "Theses on Feuerbach," in Robert C. Tucker, ed., *The Marx–Engels Reader* (New York: Norton, 1978), 143.

5. Pierre Clastres, in his seminal work *Society Against the State* (New York: Urizen, 1974), 14–15, writes, "There are no societies without power. . . . Political power as coercion (or as the relation command-obedience) is not *the* model of true power, but simply a *particular case*. . . . [T]he political can be conceived apart from violence."

6. In "Class, Status and Party" Max Weber writes, "we understand by 'power' the chance of a man or a number of men to realize their own will in a communal action even against the resistance of others who are participating in the action." H. H. Gerth and C. Wright Mills, eds., *From Max Weber: Essays in Sociology* (Oxford: Oxford University Press, 1946), 180. For an interest-centered interpretation of power, see the lucid discussion in Steven Lukes's *Power* (London: Macmillan, 1974), which contrasts what he terms "one-dimensional," "two-dimensional," and "three-dimensional" conceptions of power. These correspond respectively to the ability to affect the *behavior* of others, the capacity to set the *decision-making agenda*, and the ability to affect the *preferences* of others. Lukes's critique of one- and two-dimensional views of power is valuable, but we find little merit in his overall conception of power, namely, that "A exercises power over B when A affects B in a manner contrary to B's interests" (p. 34). The concept of "interest" implied by his approach cannot serve as the lens through which power is analyzed, because it is incompatible with the conception of practices as constitutive of interests, and hence of interests in significant measure as the *effect* of a particular distribution of power.

7. Weber apparently borrowed this conception of the state from Leon Trotsky. Our treatment follows

Max Weber's not only in this respect, but also in his conscious strategy of extending Marxian concepts of domination, as the following passage indicates:

> The state is a relation of men dominating men. . . . All states may be classified according to whether they rest on the principle that the staff of men themselves *own* the administrative means, or whether the staff is "separated" from these means of administration. This distinction holds in the same sense in which today we say that the salaried employee and the proletarian in the capitalistic enterprise are "separated" from the material means of production. (Gerth and Mills, eds., *From Max Weber*, 78, 81.)

Weber, however, rejected a property-based notion of class and favored a notion of politics considerably narrower than our own: "We wish to understand by politics only the leadership or the influencing of the leadership of a *political* association, hence today of a *state*" [emphasis in the original] (Gerth and Mills, eds., *From Max Weber*, 77). Weber, moreover, based a theory of collective action on the concept of charismatic leadership, whereas ours is grounded in the manner in which the heterogeneous forms of domination give rise to distinct forms of bonding and social organization of both dominant groups and the oppressed.

8. This is clearly a procedural rather than a substantive definition of liberal democracy: it refers to a system of rules and rule making rather than a relationship between, say, what the voters want, and what the state does. In this it follows the practice of most liberal political scientists. See, for example, Robert Dahl, *Political Opposition in Western Democracies* (New Haven, Conn.: Yale University Press, 1966). This concept may be distinguished from our use of the word *democracy* to refer both to liberty (which is encompassed in the definition of liberal democracy) and popular sovereignty (which is not).

9. Unlike most writers, we do not identify labor, sexuality, biological reproduction, or any other practice as the prime activity organized by the family. Ann Ferguson, for example, sees the family as the organizer of "sex-affective production" in "On Conceiving Motherhood and Sexuality: A Feminist Materialist Approach," in Joyce Tribilcot, ed., *Mothering: Essays in Feminist Theory* (Totowa, N.J.: Roman and Allenheld, 1982), 153–82. See also Joan Kelly-Gadol, "The Social Relation of the Sexes: Methodological Implications of Women's History," *Signs* 1 (1976): 809–24. Gayle Rubin defines the "sex-gender system" as "the set of arrangements by which a society transforms biological sexuality into products of human activity, and in which these transformed sexual needs are satisfied," in "The Traffic in Women: Notes on the 'Political Economy' of Sex," in Rayna Reiter, ed., *Towards an Anthropology of Women* (New York: Monthly Review Press, 1975), 157–210, 159. See also Kate Young, Carol Wolkowitz, and Roslyn McCullagh, *Of Marriage and the Market: Women's Subordination in International Perspective* (London: CSE Books, 1981). By contrast, Isaac Balbus defines patriarchy as "a male-dominated sexual division of labor," in *Marxism and Domination* (Princeton, N.J.: Princeton University Press, 1982), 66. Nancy Folbre defines patriarchy as a mode of production,

> a distinctive set of social relations, including but by no means limited to control over the means of production, that structures the exploitation of women and or children by men within a social formation that may include other modes of production, none of which is necessarily dominant. (Nancy Folbre, "A Patriarchal Mode of Production," in *Alternatives to Economic Orthodoxy: A Reader in Political Economy*, ed. Randy Albelda, Christopher Gunn, and William Waller, Jr. [New York: M. E. Sharpe, 1986].)

Our conception of patriarchy is closest to that of Heidi Hartman who represents patriarchy simply as a relationship among adult men whereby they wield disproportional power over women and children. Heidi Hartmann, "Capitalism, Patriarchy, and Job Segregation by Sex," in Zillah R. Eisenstein, ed., *Capitalist Patriarchy and the Case for Socialist Feminism* (New York: Monthly Review Press, 1979), 206–47.

10. Maurice Godelier, "Infrastructure, Societies, and History," *New Left Review* 112 (1978): 86.

11. The isomorphism of sites and practices, though by no means unique to structuralist Marxism, is clearly revealed in the following comments by Louis Althusser and Etienne Balibar, in *Reading Capital* (New York: Pantheon, 1970), 240: "The social formation is presented as constituted out of different levels (we shall also speak of them as instances and practices). Marx lists *three:* the economic base, the legal and political superstructures, and the forms of social consciousness." See also Louis Althusser, *For Marx* (New York: Vintage, 1970).

12. We develop this point at length in Bowles and Gintis, "Structure and Practice in the Labor Theory of Value." Marx is clearly on the shakiest of grounds in claiming, "If production has a capitalist form, so too will reproduction." Marx, *Capital* (New York: Vintage, 1977), 1: 711. By contrast, Claude Meillassoux notes:

> labor-power . . . cannot be sold by those who produce it. . . . Thus, to reproduce itself, the capitalist mode of production depends upon an institution which is alien to it, but which has until now

maintained as that most adapted to this function . . . by exploiting the emotional attachment which still dominates parent-child relations. (Claude Meillassoux, *Maidens, Meal, and Money* [Cambridge: Cambridge University Press, 1981], 142.)

Bruno Lautier and Ramon Tortajada (Ecole, Force de Travail, et Salariat: Materiaux Pour Une Critique de l'Economie de l'Education [Grenoble: Presses Universitaires de Grenoble, 1978]) likewise refer to the "exteriority of the reproduction of the producers" with respect to capitalist production proper (p. 110).

13. We see no more reason to presume that the rules will be reproductive than that they will be efficient. When Douglass C. North, *Structure and Change in Economic History* (New York: Norton, 1981, 205) writes, "The constitutional rules are the most fundamental organizational constraints of a [political-economic] system. Their objective is to maximize the utility of the rulers," one wonders by what fortuitous mechanism this synergy of rules and ruling-class interests is secured. One might defend this position by attributing uncontested control over rule changing to a single dominant group in society. But this would locate political power in a single source in two senses: denying the heterogeneous nature of power, and then, having reduced power to a single binary relationship, identifying one pole as all-powerful.

14. Max Weber writes:

Organized domination, which calls for continuous administration, requires that human conduct be conditioned to obedience towards those masters who claim to be the bearers of legitimate power. On the other hand, by virtue of this obedience, organized domination requires the control of those material goods which in a given case are necessary for the use of physical violence. Thus organized domination requires the control of the personal executive staff and the material implements of administration. (Gerth and Mills, eds., *From Max Weber*, 80.)

15. In this respect we agree entirely with Douglass North's *Structure* departure from the neoclassical presumption that selection of social structures according to the Darwinian principle of the survival of the fittest will produce technically efficient rules. See chapter 6, "Structure and Change in Economic History," 59–68.

16. Nancy Folbre, "The Black Four of Hearts: Towards a New Paradigm of Household Economics," in Judith Bruce and Daisy Dwyer, eds., *Women and Income in the Third World*, 1986.

17. See especially Rubin, "Traffic in Women"; and Hartmann, "Capitalism, Patriarchy, and Job Segregation by Sex"; "The Family as the Locus of Gender, Class and Political Struggle: The Example of Housework," *Signs: Journal of Women in Culture and Society* 6 (1981): 366–94; and "The Unhappy Marriage of Marxism and Feminism: Towards a More Progressive Union," *Capital and Class* 8 (1979): 1–33.

18. Friedman, *Capitalism and Freedom*, 12.

19. Folbre, "Black Four of Hearts," 9; Gary Becker, *A Treatise on the Family* (Cambridge, Mass.: Harvard University Press, 1981).

20. Folbre, "Black Four of Hearts," 8. Annie Cot, in similar vein, observes (translation ours):

In avoiding anything which could become the basis for a . . . representation of power within the family, Becker assigns to the family head the traditional functions of the enlightened despot of the eighteenth century: to ensure the natural economic order through a "personal and legal despotism" and to minimize the transaction costs associated with the social contract. (Annie Cot, "Nouvelle Economie, Utopie et Crise," in Wladimir Andreff et al., *L'Economie-fiction: Contre Les Nouveaux Economistes* [Paris: Maspero, 1982], 146.)

21. Hartmann, "The Family as the Locus." Contemporary feminist scholars have acknowledged the need for such a strategy, recognizing the power of Marx's terms but wishing he had focused his attention more broadly. Nancy Hartsock states:

An adequate theory of power would provide answers for women akin to those Marx's account provided for workers. It would give an account of how social institutions have come to be controlled by only one gender; it would locate the points at which conflicts between men and women are generated and make clear specific relations between individual intentional actions and structural constraints. (Nancy Hartsock, *Money, Sex, and Power: Toward a Feminist Historical Materialism* [New York: Longmans, 1983], 254–55.)

Hartsock may be unduly generous in suggesting that Marx actually accomplished all of this (and unduly limited to say that he did it "for workers"). But Hartsock's agenda is certainly that of a feminist historical materialism.

22. Rubin, "Traffic in Women," 160, 177.

23. Hartmann, "Capitalism, Patriarchy, and Job Segregation by Sex," as we have seen, defines patriarchy as a relationship among men. See also Kathleen Stewart, "Meanings of Gender and Rank

in American Culture," *Michigan Discussions in Anthropology*, Department of Anthropology, University of Michigan, 1981.

24. Rubin opposes the use of the term *patriarchy* for just this reason. The general use of the word "is analogous to using capitalism to refer to all modes of production, whereas the usefulness of the term capitalism lies precisely in that it distinguishes between the different systems by which societies are provisioned and organized" (Rubin, "Traffic in Women," 167).

25. Ferguson, "Motherhood and Sexuality." Jean Pyle's concept of a social structure of patriarchy and particularly the patriarchal state, along with her application of these concepts to the distinct forms of patriarchal domination in contemporary Ireland is an important contribution along these lines. See Jean Pyle, "Women and Development in an Open Economy," Ph.D. dissertation, University of Massachusetts, 1985.

26. It may be regarded as overly demanding to expect Marxian theory to have addressed these contemporary questions. But the same questions were contemporary among socialists and utopians in Marx's day as well. Marx was not, as some would generously concede, "inadequate to today, but ahead of his time in his day" in the conceptualization of gender issues. We find Harold Benenson's argument persuasive:

> In breaking with the earlier utopian socialist mode of analysis, Marx simultaneously revised the utopians' conception of women's involvement in social emancipation. Two developments directly influenced this dimension of Marx's analysis: the emergence of a conservative Victorian ideal of female domesticity in the early 19th century and the rise of working men's movements which appealed to the new Victorian norm to buttress their demands. In this context Marx abandoned the utopians' recognition of women's interest in social transformation and emphasis on changing family arrangements. (Harold Benenson, "Victorian Sexual Ideology and Marx's Theory of the Working Class," *International Labor and Working Class History* 25 [1984]: 1.)

27. See Hartmann, "Unhappy Marriage." Isaac Balbus writes:

> Marx himself could shed little light on the problem of patriarchy. Indeed, he assumed that this problem was rapidly being solved by capitalism itself, i.e. that the development of the capitalist mode of production would undermine the material basis of a male-dominated sexual division of labor both within the family and throughout the society at large. Marx never anticipated the problem that preoccupies contemporary feminists—the problem of how to make an anticapitalist revolution that is also antipatriarchal—because he assumed that the inner logic of capitalism is antipatriarchal. (Balbus, *Marxism and Domination*, 63.)

28. Nancy Chodorow, *The Reproduction of Mothering* (Berkeley: University of California Press, 1978), 10. Dorothy Dinnerstein, *The Mermaid and the Minotaur: Sexual Arrangements and the Human Malaise* (New York: Harper & Row, 1976) has developed similar arguments. For a nonpsychoanalytic analysis stressing the division of labor in biological reproduction, see Lorenne M. G. Clark and Lynda Lange, eds., *The Sexism of Social and Political Theory* (Toronto: University of Toronto Press, 1979).

29. Chodorow, *Reproduction*, 173.

30. Ibid., 7.

31. Ibid., 174.

32. Indeed, Chodorow sees strong links between economy and family:

> The sex-gender system is analytically separable from and is never entirely explainable in terms of the organization of production, though in any particular society, the two are empirically and structurally intertwined. Developments in the sex-gender system can affect and in different societies have affected changes in the mode of production. In the modern period, however, the development of capitalism and contemporary developments in socialist societies have changed the sex-gender system more than the reverse. (Ibid., 8–9.)

33. States do not always insist on this monopoly, as the widespread acceptance of lynching in the post-Reconstruction U.S. South suggests. The French state under Cardinal Richelieu, Louis XIII, and Louis XIV fought a century-long war against the noble usurpation of this state monopoly in the form of the duel. Although the duel was fought among social equals, and violence against women is almost always one-sided, there may be other parallels. The duel, writes one of its more insightful historians, was "not an isolated practice but a code of conduct central to the self-image of the nobility: thus to challenge the nobility on these grounds was to challenge the ideology of the class upon which the power of the monarch ultimately depended." See Robert Schneider, "Swordplay and Statemaking: Aspects of the Campaign against the Duel in Early Modern France," in Charles Bright and Susan Harding, eds., *Statemaking and Social Movements: Essays in History and Theory* (Ann Arbor: University of Michigan Press, 1984), 277–78. Robert Harding writes, "The extraordinary receptivity of the French lesser nobility to the code of the duel after 1560 was directly related to the crisis of the old system of clientage

that hitherto had given them a means of advancing themselves," in his *Anatomy of a Power Elite* (New Haven: Yale University Press, 1978), 77. Schneider continues, "An extreme response to be sure, the duel was one way in which noblemen 'adjusted' to a social situation characterized by an increasingly crowded field of elites in which the grounds for advancement, the criteria of rank, indeed, the very nature of the hierarchy were open to question" (p. 271). Surprisingly, Jean Bodin, the political theorist most closely associated with the emergence of the idea of unitary sovereignty, defended the duel as a relatively harmless outlet for social tension that might otherwise take the form of rebellion.

34. It is generally thought that in most advanced capitalist societies such a transfer takes place within couples, the woman working more hours relative to the labor time embodied in her consumption of goods and services than the man. Although there is convincing evidence that such a transfer takes place in some noncapitalist societies (see Jeanne Koopman Henn, *Peasants, Workers, and Capital: The Political Economy of Labor and Incomes in Cameroon*, Ph.D. dissertation, Harvard University, 1978; and "Feeding the Cities and Feeding the Peasants: What Role for Africa's Women Farmers?" *World Development* 11:1043–55), such a transfer in the advanced capitalist countries may be difficult to document. Numerous studies of the uses of time at wage work and in the home (including child care) allow an estimate of the amount of time spent working by married men and women. See Joseph Pleck, "Husbands' and Wives' Family Work, Paid Work, and Adjustment," *Center for Research on Women*, Wellesley College, Working Paper no. 95, 1982; F. T. Juster et al., *Time Use in Economic and Social Accounts—Codebook* (Ann Arbor, Mich.: Inter-University Consortium for Political and Social Research, 1978); Victor Fuchs, "His and Hers: Gender Differences in Work and Income, 1959–1979," mimeo, National Bureau of Economic Research, Cambridge, Mass., 1984, working paper no. 1501; R. Quinn and G. Staines, *The 1977 Quality of Employment Survey* (Ann Arbor, Mich.: Institute for Social Research, 1978); Frank Stafford and Greg J. Duncan, *The Use of Time and Technology by Households in the United States* (Ann Arbor, Mich.: Institute for Social Research, 1979). When women work outside the home (about half of all adult women in the United States) the total number of work hours of women exceeds that of men; the reverse is true for couples in which women do not work outside the home. On balance the transfer of surplus labor time within the household appears to represent a very small proportion of the total time worked. These data alone do not allow us adequately to address the question, of course; to do this we would need information on the levels of consumption, and perhaps on the intensity of labor. Moreover, the transfer of surplus labor time between men as a group and women as a group cannot be understood simply by studying women and men in couples. The low incomes and long working hours of single women family heads would, for example, weigh heavily in any such collective average. Nonetheless we doubt that the nature of the sex-gender system is illuminated adequately by a focus on the balance of hours worked in one direction or another.

35. Elaine McCrate, "The Growth of Non-Marriage among U.S. Women, 1954–1983," Ph.D. dissertation, University of Massachusetts, 1985, 32. The underlying ideas concerning economic dependence may be traced to early feminists such as Elizabeth Cady Stanton, Charlotte Perkins Gilman, and others.

36. Ibid., 33.

37. The implicit strategies of the Chodorow and McCrate approaches—shared parenting and equal pay—are generally thought to be complementary. But the intuitively appealing inference that more equal treatment of women in labor markets will induce more job sharing and male parenting of children may be unfounded. The increase in women's wages will result in an increase in women's bargaining power within a couple. If men do not adjust to the new situation by offering women a better deal within the couple—reallocating the housework, for example, the result may be the decline in marriage and an increase in exclusive female parenting.

38. McCrate, "Growth of Non-Marriage," has estimated an index of economic dependence encompassing many of the criteria given here and she has used it quite effectively to statistically explain changing family structure in the United States.

39. Nancy Folbre, "The Pauperization of Motherhood: Patriarchy and Public Policy in the U.S.," *Review of Radical Political Economics* 16(4):75, 85.

40. Indeed, although conservative opposition to the welfare state is generally interpreted to represent an expression of the economic interest of the well-to-do, it may as well reflect gender interests. See Folbre's account of conservative social policies in this regard (Folbre, "Pauperization"). As patriarchy goes public it appears less as an interpersonal relationship between man and woman (one easily attributed to the personality or other aspects of the two individuals) and more as a structure of domination affecting all women. What Marx thought the accumulation process would do for workers—create the conditions for the transparency of capitalist exploitation and thus promote a common working-class identity and consciousness—"public patriarchy" may well do for women.

41. Friedman, *Capitalism*, 13.

42. Our approach may be considered as putting theoretical flesh on Marx's evocative assertion:

> Men make their own history, but they do not make it just as they please; they do not make it under circumstances chosen by themselves, but under circumstances directly encountered, given and transmitted from the past. ("The Eighteenth Brumaire of Louis Bonaparte," in Fernbach, ed., *Political Writings*, 146.)

Our approach is therefore similar to the efforts of those who have made power central to their analysis and also have attempted, according to Anthony Giddens, to

> transcend the opposition between "action" theories and "institutional" theories. . . . This move is accomplished by the concept of what I call the *duality of structure*. By the duality of structure I mean that the structured properties of social systems are simultaneously the *medium and outcome of social acts* [emphasis in original]. (Anthony Giddens, *A Contemporary Critique of Historical Materialism* [Berkeley: University of California Press, 1981], 19.)

43. Robert Dahl, *Who Governs* (New Haven, Conn.: Yale University Press, 1961), 316–17.

44. Arthur Bentley, *The Process of Government* (Cambridge, Mass.: Harvard University Press, 1908), 210.

Chapter 5

1. Jeremy Bentham cited in Robin Evans, "Bentham's Panopticon: An Incident in the Social History of Architecture," *Architectural Association Quarterly* (1971): 21–37. Evans includes extensive illustrations of Bentham's design, and those influenced by it.

2. Ibid., 31.

3. Thomas Hobbes, *The Citizen* (1651), quoted in Christine Di Stefano, "Masculinity as Ideology in Political Theory: Hobbesian Man Considered," *Women's Studies International Forum* 6 (1983): 637; Di Stephano's comment is on p. 638.

4. Hartsock, *Money, Sex, and Power*; Elshtain, *Public Man, Private Woman*; Landes, "Women and the Public Sphere," passim.

5. Amy Gutmann, "What's the Use of Going to School?" in Amartya Sen and Bernard Williams, eds., *Utilitarianism and Beyond* (New York: Cambridge University Press, 1982), 261.

6. Marshall Cohen, ed., *The Philosophy of John Stuart Mill* (New York: Modern Library, 1961), 197–98.

7. The reader may be surprised that we limit our critique of the liberal model of action to this one point. We are of course aware that the traditional criticisms leveled against the liberal model of the individual lie elsewhere—in its purported attribution of such traits as rationality, egotism, hedonism, subjectivism, instrumentalism, and atomism to the individual actor. We contend, however, that such critiques are either invalid, or can be more pointedly argued in terms of the liberal presumption of the *a priori* character of wants. For an exploration of the liberal model of choice complementary to that presented in this chapter, see Jan Elster, *Ulysses and the Sirens* (Cambridge: Cambridge University Press, 1979), and *Sour Grapes* (Cambridge: Cambridge University Press, 1983).

8. Mill, in Cohen, ed., *Philosophy of John Stuart Mill*, 198.

9. Karl Marx, *Capital* (New York: Vintage, 1977), 283.

10. Albert Hirschman, *Exit, Voice, and Loyalty* (Cambridge, Mass.: Harvard University Press, 1970). Liberal theory typically does not even address the remaining term of Hirschman's trilogy: loyalty.

11. This idea is extensively developed by Ferruccio Rossi-Landi, "Linguistics and Economics," in Thomas A. Sebeok, ed., *Current Trends in Linguistics*, Volume 12: *Linguistics and Adjacent Arts and Sciences* (The Hague: Mouton, 1974), 1788–2017, though in directions we do not find entirely persuasive. Our own approach will be developed in the following chapter.

12. Marshall Sahlins, *Stone Age Economics* (Chicago: Aldine Press, 1972), 186. Sahlins, however, attributes this aspect of exchange to the decentralization of force and the absence of the state in primitive society. Thus he asserts that "exchange in primitive communities has not the same role as the economic flow in modern industrial communities" (p. 187). We believe that the constitutive nature of exchange is quite general, though its centrality in the constitution of social actors may be particularly great in nonstate societies.

13. Rubin, "The Traffic in Women," 174.

14. Sahlins, *Stone Age Economics*, 187.

15. Karl Polanyi, "Aristotle Discovers the Economy," in George Dalton, ed., *Primitive, Archaic and Modern Economies: Essays of Karl Polanyi* (New York: Doubleday, 1968), 82. The last sentence is from Karl Polanyi, *The Great Transformation* (New York: Farrar and Rinehart, 1944), 3–4.

16. Charles Schultze, *The Public Use of Private Interest* (Washington, D.C.: Brookings Institution, 1977), 18.

17. James Buchanan, *The Limits of Liberty* (Chicago: University of Chicago Press, 1975), 17.

18. It may be argued with some justice that Marx's theory of alienation is just such a theory, asserting as it does that we become who we are—both as individuals and as communities—in large measure through the way in which we work. But although Marx's writings (from his *1844 Manuscripts* through *Capital*) are highly suggestive in this respect, and their development in the hands of contemporary Marxist humanists and others is a major contribution to the reorientation of economic thinking, the productivist ontology in Marx's own writing and in the dominant tradition since Marx is clearly indicated by the central part played by the labor theory of value in both. Whatever the merits of this theory, its contribution to our understanding of the production and reproduction of people cannot be included among them. See Karl Marx, *Economic and Philosophical Manuscripts of 1844* (Moscow: Foreign Language Publishing House, 1959); and Bowles and Gintis, "Structure and Practice."

19. Lionel Robbins, *An Essay on the Nature and Significance of Economic Science* (London: Macmillan, 1932), 15.

20. Carole Pateman's *Participation and Democratic Theory* (Cambridge: Cambridge University Press, 1970) is a classic statement of this position. That the structure of work is a major determinant—direct or indirect—of human development is suggested in works as diverse as Melvin Kohn, *Class and Conformity: A Study in Values* (Homewood, Ill.: Dorsey Press, 1969); Samuel Bowles and Herbert Gintis, *Schooling in Capitalist America: Educational Reform and the Contradictions of Economic Life* (New York: Basic Books, 1976); and Gabriel Almond and Sidney Verba, *The Civic Culture: Political Attitudes and Democracy in Five Nations* (Princeton, N.J.: Princeton University Press, 1963). The latter authors comment:

> The structure of authority at the workplace is probably the most significant—and salient—structure of the kind with which the average man finds himself in daily contact. . . . In each nation [of those studied by these authors and their collaborators] those who report that they are consulted about decisions on their job are more likely than others to score high on the scale of subjective political competence. (Pp. 363, 365.)

21. Concerning the division of labor, which he saw as one of the most economically progressive aspects of capitalism, Adam Smith wrote that

> the employment of the great body of the people comes to be confined to a few simple operations; frequently to one or two. But the understandings . . . of men are necessarily formed by their ordinary employments. The man whose whole life is spent in performing a few simple operations of which the effects too are perhaps always the same . . . has no occasion to exert his understanding or to exercise his invention in finding out expedients for removing difficulties which never occur. He naturally loses, therefore, the habit of such exertion and generally becomes as stupid and ignorant as it is possible for a human creature to become. . . . [he is incapable] of forming any just judgement concerning many even of the ordinary duties of private life. Of the great and extensive interests of his country, he is altogether incapable of judging. (Adam Smith, *The Wealth of Nations* [New York: Modern Library, 1937], 2: 365–66.)

22. See Samuel Bowles, "The Production Process"; and Gintis and Ishikawa, "Wages, Work Discipline, and Macroeconomic Equilibrium," draft, July 1985.

23. Albert Hirschman, *The Passions and the Interests* (Princeton, N.J.: Princeton University Press, 1977).

24. Quentin Skinner, *The Foundations of Modern Political Thought* (Princeton, N.J.: Princeton University Press, 1978), 48.

25. Mancur Olson, *The Logic of Collective Action* (Cambridge, Mass.: Harvard University Press, 1965), 1, 2.

26. Though quite foreign to the structure of liberal theory per se, this commonsense idea is hardly novel. It has been taken in interesting directions by Brian Fay, "How People Change Themselves: The Relationship Between Critical Theory and its Audience," in T. Hall, ed., *Political Theory and Praxis* (Minneapolis: University of Minnesota Press, 1977), among others. Adam Przeworski, "Proletariat into Class: The Process of Class Formation," in idem, *Capitalism and Social Democracy* (Cambridge, England: Cambridge University Press, 1985), addressed the issue of class interests along these lines.

27. Jefferson to John Cartwright, 5 June 1824, and Jefferson to John Tyler, 26 May 1810, both cited

in Hannah Arendt, *On Revolution* (New York: Viking Press, 1963), 257.

28. Arendt, *On Revolution*, 258.

29. Communities are groups of people who come together for instrumental reasons (the Hobbesian community), for reasons of common concern (what Sandel terms the sentimental community), or for reasons of identity. We intend the term *community* in all three senses. Of the members of the third type, Sandel, in *Liberalism and the Limits of Justice*, writes:

> For them community describes not just what they *have* as fellow citizens but also what they *are*, not a relationship they choose (as in a voluntary association) but an attachment they discover, not merely an attribute but a constituent of their identity. In contrast to the instrumental and sentimental conceptions of community, we might describe this strong view as the constitutive conception. (P. 150.)

30. Charles Taylor, *Hegel* (Cambridge: Cambridge University Press, 1975), 416.

31. Hannah Arendt, *The Human Condition* (Chicago: University of Chicago Press, 1958), 52–53.

32. Charles Tilly, "Charivaris, Repertoires and Urban Politics," in John M. Merriman, ed., *French Cities in the Nineteenth Century* (New York: Holmes and Meier, 1981), 76.

33. Ibid., 76.

34. Frug, "The City as a Legal Concept," 1080.

35. Ibid., 1081. Here and in the following paragraphs we follow Frug's account.

36. Ibid., 1121.

37. Marx, "Manifesto of the Communist Party," in Tucker, *The Marx-Engels Reader*, 475.

38. Bernard Mandeville, *The Fable of the Bees, or Private Vices, Public Benefits* (Oxford: Oxford University Press, 1924), originally published in 1714.

39. Denis Patrick O'Brien, *The Classical Economists* (Oxford: Oxford University Press, 1975), 272.

40. Otto Gierke, *Political Theories of the Middle Ages*, trans. F. W. Maitland (Cambridge: Cambridge University Press, 1958), 87.

41. Karl Marx and Friedrich Engels, *Collected Works*, vol. 4: *The Holy Family* (New York: International Publishers, 1975), 37.

42. N. Okishio, "Technical Change and the Profit Rate," *Kobe University Economic Review* 7 (1961): 86–99; Samuel Bowles, "Technical Change and the Profit Rate: A Simple Proof of the Okishio Theorem," *Cambridge Journal of Economics* 5 (1981): 183–86.

43. Karl Marx, *Grundrisse: Introduction to the Critique of Political Economy* (Baltimore: Penguin, 1973), 80–82.

44. Friedrich Engels, *The Origin of the Family, Private Property, and the State* (New York: International Publishers, 1971), 158.

45. Friedrich Engels, "Introduction," in Karl Marx and V. I. Lenin, *Civil War in France and the Paris Commune* (New York: International Publishers, 1940), 22.

46. V. I. Lenin, Speech of September 1917, in "Preface to the Russian Translation of Letters by Johannes Becker," in *Collected Works*, 127–28.

47. Dahl, "On Removing Certain Impediments to Democracy," develops a cogent and quite different critique of arguments for direct democracy.

48. Jean Jacques Rousseau, *The Social Contract*, Maurice Cranston, ed. (Harmondsworth, England: Penguin, 1968), 141.

49. Lucio Colleti, *From Rousseau to Lenin* (New York: Monthly Review, 1972), 147, 151.

50. Leszek Kolakowski, *Main Currents of Marxism* (Oxford: Oxford University Press, 1981), 127, 131.

51. See Carmen Siriani, "Participation, Opportunity, and Equality: Toward a Pluralist Organizational Model," in Carmen Siriani and Frank Fischer, eds., *Critical Studies in Organization and Bureaucracy* (Philadelphia: Temple University Press, 1984), 482–503. This is no less true of the contemporary feminist strand of participatory politics as it is of the Marxian. See Jane Mansbridge, "Feminism and the Forms of Freedom," in Siriani and Fischer, *Critical Studies*, 272–81.

52. For a different but extremely provocative approach, see Jean Paul Sartre, *Critique of Dialectical Reason* (London: New Left Books, 1976).

53. This aspect of social interaction has been emphasized by the classical Chicago school of sociologists; see in particular Charles Horton Cooley, *Social Organization* (New York: Charles Scribner's Sons, 1909); and George H. Mead, *Mind, Self, and Society* (Chicago: University of Chicago Press, 1934). Their promising work was eclipsed in the 1950s by the Parsonian school, and has been a source of inspiration only among phenomenologists, whose theoretical project is quite different from our own.

54. Michael Walzer, "Liberalism and the Art of Separation," *Political Theory* 12 (1984): 317.

Chapter 6

1. Hobsbawm, *Workers*, 313.

2. Foucault, *The History of Sexuality*, is quite correct to insist that "discourses are not once and for all subservient to power or raised up against it . . . there is not, on the one side, a discourse of power, and opposite to it, another that runs counter to it" (p. 101).

3. Quoted in Tucker, *The Marx-Engels Reader*, 43. We have corrected a grammatical error in the translation.

4. Marx expected working-class consciousness to be the direct outcome of the workers' struggle to meet daily needs in an increasingly crisis-prone and transparently exploitative social order. In the face of the dashing of Marx's millennial hopes, more searching treatments have been offered. Althusser, *For Marx*, for example, has maintained that Marxists have been insufficiently aware of the "relative autonomy" of politics and ideology. Colletti, *From Rousseau to Lenin*, and V. N. Volosinov, *Marxism and the Philosophy of Language* (New York: Seminar Press, 1973), on the other hand, have held that Marxists have placed consciousness in the superstructure, although its proper position lies in the base of social relations. Such approaches, however, merely displace the problem: *wherever* politics and culture are located with respect to base and superstructure, the expressive theory of action cannot explain the concrete forms of social bonding which transform heterogeneous individuals into collective initiators of social change. Perhaps realizing this, many twentieth-century Marxists have followed a different route. Rather than abandoning consciousness as an explanatory variable, they have attempted to account for the theory's descriptive weaknesses in terms of the purported *false* consciousness of competing classes. This strategy, we shall contend, is critically flawed. Accounting for working-class reformism in terms of false consciousness appears in such diverse guises as Antonio Gramsci's "ideological hegemony," Herbert Marcuse's "one-dimensional thought," Henri Lefebvre's "reproduction of consciousness in everyday life," and Jurgen Habermas's "systematically distorted communication." See Antonio Gramsci, *Prison Notebooks* (New York: International Publishers, 1971); Herbert Marcuse, *One-Dimensional Man* (Boston: Beacon Press, 1964); Henri Lefebvre, *The Sociology of Marx* (New York: Vintage, 1969). Our approach, by contrast, treats consciousness as an aspect of the forms of discourse appropriated in social practice.

5. Sean Wilentz, *Chants Democratic: New York City and the Rise of the American Working Class, 1788–1850* (New York: Oxford University Press, 1984), 14. Gareth Stedman Jones similarly proposes to "study the production of interest, identification, grievance and aspiration within the political languages themselves," in his *Languages of Class*, 22.

6. Ludwig Wittgenstein, *The Blue and Brown Books* (Oxford: Blackwells, 1969), 191.

7. See William P. Alston, *Philosophy of Language* (Englewood Cliffs, N.J.: Prentice-Hall, 1964).

8. Thomas Hobbes, in *Leviathan*, ed. C. B. MacPherson (Harmondsworth, England: Penguin, 1968), 101.

9. John Locke, *An Essay concerning Human Understanding*, ed. A. Pringle-Pattison (Oxford: Clarendon Press, 1924), book 3, chap. 2.

10. See Gottlob Frege, *The Foundations of Arithmetic* (Oxford: Blackwell, 1950). See also Peter Winch, *The Idea of a Social Science* (New York: Humanities Press, 1965), and Hannah Fenichel Pitkin, *Wittgenstein and Justice* (Berkeley: University of California Press, 1972), for applications of these ideas quite at variance with our own. Jurgen Habermas, *Communication and the Evolution of Society* (Boston: Beacon Press, 1976), also has attempted to assess the relevance of modern notions of language to social science, although we have not followed his research agenda and differ considerably from his conclusions. For a more promising treatment of the importance of Wittgenstein for social theory, see David Bloor, *Wittgenstein: A Social Theory of Knowledge* (New York: Columbia University Press, 1983).

11. Ludwig Wittgenstein, *Philosophical Investigations* (New York: Macmillan, 1958), 6e, 20e.

12. Austin is not saying merely that speech acts have consequences, which is true of all action. An assertion may "dazzle someone," a promise may mislead, a warning may sadden, and so on. But these are results of discourse, rather than social facts constituted by discourse. J. L. Austin, *How to Do Things with Words* (Cambridge, Mass.: Harvard University Press, 1962).

13. Treatments of what might be called feminist and utilitarian liberal architectural discourse are found in Dolores Hayden, *The Grand Domestic Revolution* (Cambridge, Mass.: MIT Press, 1981), and Evans, "Bentham's Panopticon," 21–37, respectively.

14. See the discussion in Foner, *Tom Paine*, 66.

15. Clifford Geertz, *Negara: The Theatre State in Nineteenth-Century Bali* (Princeton, N.J.: Princeton University Press, 1980), 103.

16. Eric Hobsbawm, "Introduction: Inventing Traditions," in Hobsbawm and Ranger, eds., *The Invention of Tradition*, 7.

17. Little novelty may be claimed for the notion that words are tools. T. D. Weldon, writing more than three decades ago, observed:

> If words and especially nouns always have meanings, we should, if we are pertinacious and fairly clever, usually be able to unearth those meanings. . . . The application of this to political inquiries is almost painfully evident. It is that we must begin by asking for the meanings of "justice," "freedom," "authority," and similar words, and then, when we have discovered what these meanings are, we shall be qualified to pronounce on whether Communism is to be praised or condemned. The inquiry, however, is doomed to sterility because words do not have meanings in the required sense at all; they simply have uses. (T. D. Weldon, *The Vocabulary of Politics* [London: Penguin, 1953], 18–19.)

18. J. G. A. Pocock, *Politics, Language and Time* (New York: Atheneum, 1973), 15.

19. Geertz, *Negara*, 120, 104.

20. This observation is the basis of our rejection of the notion of collective (class, group, national) consciousness as an explanation of group practices. In the expressive theory of action, group consciousness is a (true or false) reflection of group interests, and individual consciousness is an expression of group consciousness. Because in this view individual behavior reflects individual consciousness, action thus comes to express group interests. In our approach, collective consciousness is without meaning, and individual consciousness, rather than being a repository of ideas or desires, is simply a realm of human experience and sensation. As Wittgenstein put it, "the mental experiences which accompany the use of a sign undoubtedly are caused by our usage of the sign in a particular system of language." Wittgenstein, *The Blue and Brown Books*, 78.

21. Foner, *Tom Paine*, xv, xvii.

22. Marx, "The Eighteenth of Brumaire of Louis Bonaparte" in Fernbach, ed., *Political Writings*, 146. Indeed, in the same paragraph Marx compares revolution to learning a new language.

23. Mark Blaug, *Ricardian Economics* (New Haven, Conn.: Yale University Press, 1958).

24. William Sewell, *Work and Revolution in France: The Language of Labor from the Old Regime to 1848* (Cambridge, Mass.: Cambridge University Press, 1980), ix, 162.

25. Ibid., 194. Jones, *Languages of Class*. The previously cited work of Eric Foner and Sean Wilentz have also contributed greatly to our understanding of the relationship of class conflict to discourse.

26. Sewell, *Work and Revolution*, 204.

27. Carl J. Friedrich, *Constitutional Government and Democracy* (Boston: Ginn, 1950), 17.

28. Ibid.

29. Taylor Cole, *European Political Systems* (New York: Knopf, 1953), passim.

30. Friedrich, *Constitutional Government*, 29, 31.

31. The French philosophes in general supported a movement from heredity to property as the basis of political participation. Many tended to reject the Physiocratic model of property ownership in favor of a more egalitarian distribution of landed estate. Holbach, Helvetius, and Diderot explicitly discussed the redistribution of property toward the creation of a broad class of small peasant proprietors. But democratic rule was quite beside the point. Voltaire expressed a common prejudice in asserting:

> I understand by "people" the populace which has only its hands to live by. I doubt that this order of citizens will ever have the time or capacity to educate itself. . . . It is not the day laborer who must be educated, but the good bourgeois, it is the city dweller; this enterprise is formidable and great enough. (Voltaire to Damilaville, 1 April 1766, *Correspondences* [12358], quoted in Harry C. Payne, *The Philosophes and the People* [New Haven, Conn.: Yale University Press, 1976].)

32. John Plamenatz, *Man and Society* (New York: McGraw-Hill, 1963), 1: 52.

33. For an eloquent statement of this situation, see Cornelius Castoriadis, "On the History of the Workers' Movement." *Telos* 30 (1976–1977): 3–42.

34. Hobsbawm, *Workers*, 305–9.

35. Wittgenstein, *Philosophical Investigations*, 8e.

36. In *Allgeyer* v. *Louisiana*, 165 U.S. 578, 1897, the Supreme Court held that liberty included not only the right of the citizen to be free from the mere physical constraint of his person, as by incarceration; but the term is deemed to embrace the right of the citizen to be free in the enjoyment of all his faculties . . . to earn his livelihood by any lawful calling; . . . and for that purpose to enter into all contracts which may be proper, necessary, and essential to his carrying out to a successful conclusion the purposes above mentioned.

37. We have stressed throughout this book that capitalist interests influence state policy significantly through the threat of capital strike; that is, the slackening of investment demand and the flight of capital. But this influence is surely heightened by the fiction that corporations, as "persons," ought to enjoy access to government policy through such "private" actions as lobbying, forming advisory commissions, financing political campaigns, and funding policy research institutes. Indeed, the legalities according to which such influence is exercised are justified precisely by the analogy of corporations with persons. For instance, Senator Augustine O. Bacon, confronted with a scandal in the early days of lobbying prior to World War I, set the tone for many a future defense of this privileged access:

> I do not think that a man who comes here [to Congress] to represent an interest . . . is a lobbyist. . . . I think a man has an absolute right to be heard on any matter which is going to affect his interests. It is an unthinkable thing that he should be denied that right. (Quoted in Grant McConnell, *Private Power and American Democracy* [New York: Random House, 1966], 15.)

38. Morton J. Horwitz, *The Transformation of American Law, 1780–1860* (Cambridge, Mass.: Harvard University Press, 1977), 1–2.

39. Ibid., 34, 37.

40. Ibid., 24–26.

41. Ibid., 28.

42. Robert Green McCloskey, *American Conservatism in the Age of Enterprise, 1865–1910* (New York: Harper & Row, 1951), vi, 2–3.

43. Ibid., 5–6.

Chapter 7

1. Tocqueville, *Democracy*, 240.

2. The centrality of the rights to bear arms and the broad ownership of property is a hallmark of what Pocock in *The Machiavellian Moment* terms the Atlantic republican tradition.

3. This quote is found on the page facing the title page of Mill's "On Liberty," in Cohen, *The Philosophy of John Stuart Mill*, 185–320.

4. C. B. Macpherson expresses this notion as follows:

> As soon as democracy is seen as a kind of society, not merely a mechanism of choosing and authorizing governments, the egalitarian principle inherent in democracy requires not only "one man, one vote" but also "one man, one equal effective right to live as fully humanly as he may wish." (C. B. Macpherson, *Democratic Theory: Essays in Retrieval* [Oxford: Clarendon Press, 1973], 51.)

Our debt to Macpherson is sufficiently great in this respect that the reader may imagine that our views are more similar to his than they are. Where he has treated liberalism as an ideology justifying capitalist exploitation, we see it as a contradictory discourse providing effective tools for radical anticapitalist political movements. Further, unlike Macpherson, we emphasize the "rights" components of liberal discourse—derived from the partitions of social space and agency that characterize it—rather than its utilitarian aspect. Utilitarian reasoning is important only in liberal economic theory, we believe, and even there it cannot justify capitalist property relations. Finally, we do not share Macpherson's conviction that "market principles" and scarcity itself bar the development of "a fully democratic society." Macpherson, *Democratic Theory*, 55, 77.

5. Thomas Hobbes, *Leviathan*, ed. C. B. Macpherson (New York: Penguin, 1968), 238.

6. Cited in Hirschman, *Exit, Voice, and Loyalty*, 17.

7. Macpherson, in *The Political Theory of Possessive Individualism* and *Democratic Theory*, holds that Hobbes recognized or implied a market model in his own writings. He can undoubtedly be read in this manner, as, for example, when he writes that "the value or worth of a man is, as of all other things, his price; that is to say, so much as would be given for the use of his power" (Hobbes, *Leviathan*, 151). But we find it more insightful to let Hobbes remain the theorist of power, and to leave it to the writers of the next century to develop the theory of markets. We detect a neo-Hobbesian revival based not on the defense of markets but of authority; we do not share Macpherson's sense that "It is ironic that we are just beginning to appreciate Hobbes' science of politics when its applicability is becoming more and more limited" (Hobbes, *Leviathan*, 12).

8. Mandeville's *Fable of the Bees* advocated an active state intervention in the economy and did not develop an argument for general market allocations, though his work is best remembered as a first step in this direction. Moreover, it is somewhat generous to Mandeville to attribute to him the entire body

of thought later developed by Adam Smith, Leon Walras, and modern-day welfare economists; but the basic themes of this approach, if not the formal economic logic, may be traced to Mandeville and earlier.

9. Jean Jacques Rousseau, *The Social Contract*, 28–29. Editor Maurice Cranston provides some textual evidence that Rousseau was considerably influenced by Hobbes.

10. Isaiah Berlin, *Four Essays on Liberty* (London: Oxford University Press, 1968); Adam Przeworski, "Popular Sovereignty, State Autonomy, and Private Property" (Department of Political Science, University of Chicago, 1984. Mimeo), 1.

11. William Connolly, *Appearance and Reality in Politics* (Cambridge, Mass.: Cambridge University Press, 1981), 175. Connolly's second critique is directed at the problem of legitimacy, but it could as well be addressed to the question of why people would work diligently and reliably in the absence of economic insecurity.

12. Admirable treatments of economic democracy and the extension of democratic accountability in the state have recently appeared. See, for example, Martin Carnoy and Derek Shearer, *Economic Democracy* (White Plains, N.Y.: M. E. Sharpe, 1980); Alec Nove, *The Economics of Feasible Socialism* (London: George Allen and Unwin, 1983); Carmen Siriani and Frank Fischer, eds., *Critical Studies in Organization and Power* (Philadelphia: Temple University Press, 1984); Joshua Cohen and Joel Rogers, *On Democracy: Towards a Transformation of American Society* (New York: Penguin, 1983); Philip Green, *Retrieving Democracy: In Search of Civic Equality* (Totowa, N.J.: Rowman & Allenheld, 1985).

13. Rousseau, *Social Contract*, 86. Rousseau's solution to the problem he poses—to endow the lawgiver with "sublime reason" and divine sanction—strikes the modern reader as a deus ex machina, but this is beside the point.

14. This need not be, and indeed in some instances, may not be, the case. In some countries the extension of the vote, for example, may have been critically involved in the displacement of political activity from community-based grass-roots activism to a relatively less participatory form of political activity—voting. The result may not have been an augmentation of democratic culture or capabilities, reasonably interpreted. The presuffrage generations who expressed their political sentiments through charivaris, tarring and featherings, and other pageants may have exhibited important characteristics of democratic culture unavailable to the political actors of ostensibly more democratic times. See Tilly, "Charivaris, Repertoires and Urban Politics," in Merriman, *French Cities in the Nineteenth Century*.

15. On the evolution of the world monetary system see Fred Block, "The Ruling Class Does Not Rule: Notes on the Marxist Theory of the State," *Socialist Review* 33 (1977): 6–28. Pastor's econometric study shows that IMF interventions consistently have little or negative effects on the ostensible targets of their policies—controlling inflation, accelerating economic growth, and improving trade balances, but that they consistently shift the distribution of income in favor of capital. See Maurice Pastor, "The Effects of IMF Programs in the Third World: Debate and Evidence for Latin America," mimeo, Occidental College, 1985.

16. Paul McCracken et al., *Towards Full Employment and Price Stability* (Paris: Organization for Economic Cooperation and Development, 1977, 130.

17. *National Product Accounts*, Organization for Economic Cooperation and Development, various years.

18. U.S. Department of Commerce, "U.S. Direct Investment Abroad" (Washington, D.C.: Government Printing Office, 1984), supplemented by unpublished Department of Commerce data.

19. Gary Becker, "Competition and Democracy," *Journal of Law and Economics* 1 (1958): 107.

20. Leading contemporary neo-Hobbesian works include Alchian and Demsetz on hierarchy in the capitalist firm, "Production, Information Costs, and Economic Organization"; Harold Demsetz on property rights, "The Exchange and Enforcement of Property Rights," *Journal of Law and Economics* 7 (1964): 11–26; Gary Becker on the family, *A Treatise on the Family* (Cambridge: Harvard University Press, 1981); and contributors to the Trilateral Commission's work on democracy, Michael J. Crozier, Samuel P. Huntington, and Joji Watanuki, *The Crisis of Democracy* (New York: New York University Press, 1975). Our thinking about the issues raised by the neo-Hobbesian model has also benefited from William Ouchi's insightful "Markets, Bureaucracies, and Clans," *Administrative Science Quarterly* 25 (1980): 129–41.

21. Cot, "Nouvelle Economie, Utopie et Crise," in Andreff et al., *L'Economie-fiction*, 146–47 (translation ours).

22. Jerry Falwell, *The Fundamentalist Phenomenon: The Resurgence of Conservative Christianity* (Garden City, N.Y.: Doubleday, 1981), 206.

23. George Will, *Statecraft as Soulcraft* (New York: Simon and Schuster, 1983), 24.

24. Leading examples are Crozier, Huntington, and Watanuki, *The Crisis of Democracy*, and recent

proposals of the United States for an industrial policy and the political views of its leading advocates; see Felix G. Rohaytn, *The Twenty Year Century: Essays on Economics and Public Finance* (New York: Random House, 1984).

25. C. B. Macpherson, *Democratic Theory* (Oxford: Clarendon Press, 1973), 124.

26. Coase, "The Nature of the Firm," 335.

27. Ibid., 336.

28. Weber, "Class, Status, and Party," 214.

29. Alchian and Demsetz, "Production," 781–83.

30. Ibid.

31. Oliver Williamson, "Organizational Form, Residual Claimants, and Corporate Control," *Journal of Law and Economics* 26 (1983): 365.

32. Alchian and Demsetz, "Production," 777.

33. Ibid., 795.

34. Demsetz, "Exchange," 24.

35. Ibid.

36. Eugene Genovese, *Roll, Jordan, Roll: The World the Slaves Made* (New York: Vintage, 1972), 26.

37. Williamson, "Organizational Form," 355; Harold Demsetz, "Information and Efficiency: Another Viewpoint," *Journal of Law and Economics* 12 (1969): 2.

38. One recent contribution even estimates a mathematical equation to demonstrate that pigeons would rather not work: "This paper presents results of experiments that nonhuman workers (pigeons) are willing to trade off income for leisure if the price is right." (Raymond C. Batallio, Leonard Green, and John H. Kagel, "Income-Leisure Trade-Offs of Animal Workers," *American Economic Review* 71 [1981], 621–32 passim.)

39. Hobbes, *Leviathan*, ed. Macpherson, 62–63.

40. Kenneth Arrow, "Economic Welfare and the Allocation of Resources for Invention," in *The Rate and Direction of Inventive Activity* (New York: National Bureau of Economic Research, 1962), 609–25, 619.

41. Chodorow, *Reproduction of Mothering*.

42. Quoted in Sandel, *Liberalism and the Limits of Justice*, 240.

43. R. H. Tawney, *Equality* (London: Allen, 1931).

44. Michael Walzer, *Spheres of Justice: A Defense of Pluralism and Equality* (New York: Basic Books, 1983), 31, 64–65; Sahlins, *Stone Age Economics*, 186.

45. Amy Gutmann, "What's the Use of Going to School?" in Amartya Sen and Bernard Williams, eds., *Utilitarianism and Beyond* (New York: Cambridge University Press, 1982), 261.

46. Tocqueville, *Democracy*, 244.

47. Marc Bloch, *French Rural History* (Berkeley: University of California Press, 1973), 100–101.

48. Schumpeter, *Capitalism, Socialism, and Democracy*, 142.

INDEX

Index

Gunn, Christopher, 224n9
Gutman, Amy, 123, 208, 228n5, 235n45

Habermas, Jurgen, 215n21, 231n4, 231n10
Hacker, Louis M., 218n36
Hall, T., 229n26
Hamilton, Alexander, 49, 219n40, 220n54
Harding, Robert, 226n33
Harding, Susan, 223n1, 226n33
Harrington, James, 132, 177, 186
Harrison, John, 221n63
Hartmann, Heidi, 12, 107, 108, 224n9, 225n17
Hartsock, Nancy, 225n21
Hartz, Louis, 30–31, 216n5, 218n36; critique of, 32, 40, 45, 56, 63
Hayden, Dolores, 231n13
Hayek, Friedrich von, 11–12, 214n10
Heine, Heinrich, 217n28
Henn, Jeanne Koopman, 227n34
Hinsley, F. H., 217n30
Hirschman, Albert, 127, 134, 228n10, 229n23
Hitler, Adolf, 39, 210
Hobbes, Thomas, 72, 121–23, 136, 155, 181–82, 222n8, 228n3, 233n7; Macpherson on, 201; and neo-Hobbesian writers, 193n
Hobhouse, L. T., 214n13
Hobsbawm, Eric, 19, 38–39, 152, 159, 169, 215n19, 216n11
Horwitz, Morton, 172, 233n38
Howard, Dick, 215n20
Howe, Daniel Walker, 53, 219n39
Human development, 126–27; and action, 22, 128; and domination, 126; and democracy, 17; and economic reasoning, 7; in liberal theory, 20–21, 22, 123, 125–26; in Marxian theory, 22; and market exchange, 127–30, 131–35, 228n12; and patriarchy, 107; in postliberal democracy, 178–79, 204, 207–8; and production, 132–33; see also Learning
Humboldt, Wilhelm von, 178
Huntington, Samuel P., 234n20
Huxley, Aldous, 180

Identity: and class, 21; and politics, 8; state as repository of, 16; see also Individual; Human development; Learning
Individual: and action, 138; and interests, 150; see Choice; Rights
Instrumental conception of action, 127, 136–39, 228n7
International Monetary Fund, 189
Ireton, Henry, 28
Ishikawa, Tsunio, 222n20

Italy: development of suffrage in, 217n32; liberalism in, 217n28; per capita product in, 221n61; student and worker uprisings in, 11

Japan, 221n61
Jay, John, 220n54
Jefferson, Thomas, 49, 53, 132, 139, 177, 186, 219n39, 220n45, 220n46; letters of, 229n27; and philosophy, 47–48; and republicanism, 219n40; and separation of powers, 220n44; see also Jeffersonian accommodation
Jeffersonian accommodation, 33, 47, 54; and American exceptionalism, 47–51; crisis of, 49–50; and postliberal democracy, 177–78
Jensen, Merrill, 218n36
Jones, Derek C., 223n23
Jones, Gareth Stedman, 8–9, 163, 214n4, 231n5
Jowett, Benjamin, 220n51
Juster, F. T., 227n34

Katzell, Raymond, 223n23
Kagel, John H., 235n38
Kelly-Godal, Joan, 224n9
Kenyon, Cecilia M., 219n40
Keynes, John Maynard, 57, 65, 83, 89–90, 216n19, 223n27
Keynesian accommodation, 33, 55–62; compared with other accommodations, 57, 61; Concessions in, 57; conflict of rights in, 58; distinctiveness of, 58; economic growth during, 58–59; erosion of, 60–61, 64, 175; extension of personal rights in, 58; see also Keynesian economic policy
Keynesian economic policy, 5, 60–61, 104; contradictory nature of, 33; effect on profits, 104; and full employment, 6
Klehr, Harvey, 63, 221n69
Koblik, Steven, 220n57
Koch, Adrienne, 220n44
Kohn, Melvin, 229n20
Kolakowski, Leszek, 148, 215n21, 230n50

Labor: deradicalization of, 59; and discipline, 60; and Great Depression, 6; impact of, on worker as viewed by Marx, 126; and power, 7; specificity of, 75–79; see also Contract enforcement; Labor-commodity proposition; Labor contract; Working class
Labor-commodity proposition, 68–70, 75, 79; and discrimination, 80; implications of, 81–82; and voluntary unemployment, 80
Labor contract, 81; enforcement costs of, 75–77; Marx on, 222n14; see also Enforcement costs

239

Index

Rousseau, Jean Jacques, 147–48, 181–86, 230n48, 234n9, 234n13

Rubin, Gayle, 107, 109, 224n9, 226n24

Ruggiero, Guido de, 214n13

Rules, 4; and action, 97, 98; and culture, 186–88; as defining sites, 98, 102; enforcement of, 104; and enforcement costs, 200ff; interaction of actor and, 186, 187; of liberal state, 100; North on, 225n13, 225n15; and patriarchy, 105, 106, 110; power as structure of, 94; as producing outcomes, 117; reproduction of, 103–4, 119; Rousseau on interaction of sentiments and, 185–86; stability of democratic, 119; as structuring practices, 104; and structural contradictions, 105; as systems of communication, 15

Sahlins, Marshall, 128, 206, 228n12

Saint Augustine, 194

Saint-Simon, 198

Samuelson, Paul, 60, 222n13

Sandel, Michael, 90, 223n28, 215n13, 215n14, 230n29

Sans culottes, 8, 162

Sartre, Jean Paul, 215n21, 230n52

Schapiro, J. Salwyn, 217n24

Scheider, Theodor, 44, 217n31

Schiller, Berndt, 220n57

Schools, 135; and education in postliberal democracy, 208; and institutional innovation in capitalist society, 142–43; in liberal learning-choosing partition, 125–26, 131

Schor, Juliet, 221n64, 221n66

Schneider, Robert, 226n33

Schultz, Harold J., 214n12

Schultze, Charles, 129, 229n16

Schumpeter, Joseph, 50, 84, 213, 220n49, 222n4, 223n24

Sebeck, Thomas A., 228n11

Sen, Amartya, 228n5, 235n45

Sewell, William, 163–64, 232n24

Sexual equality, 10; and new politics, 11; see also Feminism

Shalhope, Robert E., 219n40

Shearer, Derek, 234n12

Siriani, Carmen, 230n51, 234n12

Sites, 98; and conception of economy as political, 100; and enforcement costs, 104; in modern social theory, 100–101; and practices, 99–100, 105, 224n11; reproduction of, 102–3; and socially consequential power, 101; and structural contradiction, 105

Skinner, Quentin, 136, 229n24

Slavery, 74

Smith, Adam, ix, 128, 132, 143, 181, 229n21

Social change: conflict as engine of, 32; discourse of rights as instrument for, 25, 152–54; and language as synthesizing force, 155, 160; Marx on

language and, 162; visionary-historical approach, 25–26

Socialism: and denial of political rights, 45; and political history of capitalist societies, 62–63; postliberal democracy and Marxian view of, 177–78, 209

Society: as game, 118; as game without core, 149, 161n

Solidarity: as constituted by action, 160–62; and discourse of rights, 170; and political activity, 8; see also Action; Bonding

Stafford, Frank, 227n34

Staines, G., 227n34

Stalin, Josef, 20, 39

Stanton, Elizabeth Cady, 227n35

State, 99; and chartist view of political arena, 8–9; and exit, 127; as hostage in global liberalism, 189–93; in liberalism, 23; in liberal lexicon, 16; in neo-Hobbesian liberalism, 193–95; in postliberal democracy, 179; power of, in Marxism, 23; as public realm, 17, 73–74; and reproduction of patriarchy, 112, 116; rules of action embodied in, 99; as a site of social practice, 98; as viewed by Weber, 224n7; as viewed in liberal political theory, 73; and violence against women, 114

State policy: power of capital over, 67, 87–90, 189–93; and threat of capital flight, 58

State socialism, 12

State and Revolution (Lenin), 12

Stewart, Kathleen, 225n23

Stourzh, Gerald, 219n40

Structure: and action, 118; and rules of the game, 98

Structural contradiction, 105

Suffrage, 56; and clash of rights, 63; development of, in Australia and Canada, 217n32; in Europe, 43, 217n32; extension of, 234n14; extension of, in nineteenth century, middle class view of, 43–45; in United States, 218n36, 219n38

Svejnar, Jan, 223n23

Sweden: per capita product in, 221n61

Tawney, R. H., 235n43

Taylor, Charles, 140, 230n30

Taylor, Frederick Winslow, 198

Therborn, Goran, 216n32

Third World: disciplined by International Monetary Fund, 189; and post-World War II optimism, 56–57

Tilly, Charles, 141, 216n12, 230n32, 234n14

Tocqueville, Alexis de, 30, 38, 42, 46, 132, 134, 176, 211, 212, 216n10

Tortajada, Ramon, 225n12

Tourraine, Alain, 12

Transactions costs, *see* Enforcement costs

Tribilcot, Joyce, 224n9

Trotsky, Leon, 210, 223n7

243